Depression Folk

Depression Folk

Grassroots Music and Left-Wing Politics in 1930s America

Ronald D. Cohen

The University of North Carolina Press
CHAPEL HILL

This book was published with the assistance of the Anniversary Fund of the University of North Carolina Press.

© 2016 The University of North Carolina Press
All rights reserved
Set in Miller and Clarendon types
by Westchester Publishing Services
Manufactured in the United States of America

The University of North Carolina Press has been a member of the Green Press Initiative since 2003.

Cover illustration: From the cover of *Red Song Book: Prepared in Collaboration with the Workers Music League* (New York: Workers Library Publishers, 1932).

Library of Congress Cataloging-in-Publication Data
Names: Cohen, Ronald D., 1940– author.
Title: Depression folk : grassroots music and left-wing politics in 1930s America / Ronald D. Cohen.
Description: Chapel Hill : University of North Carolina Press, [2016] | Includes bibliographical references and index.
Identifiers: LCCN 2015039988| ISBN 9781469630465
  (hardback: alk. paper) | ISBN 9781469628813 (pbk : alk. paper) |
  ISBN 9781469628820 (ebook)
Subjects: LCSH: Folk music—Political aspects—United States. |
  Folk music—United States—History and criticism. | Popular
  music—United States—1931–1940 x History and criticism. |
  Politics and culture—United States—History—20th century.
Classification: LCC ML3917.U6 C63 2916 | DDC 781.62/
  13009043—dc23 LC record available at
  http://lccn.loc.gov/2015039988

Contents

    Introduction, 1

1   On the Trail of Folk Songs, 7

2   Depression's Beginnings and Labor Songs, 22

3   The Early Roosevelt Years, 39

4   Heart of the Depression, 56

5   Woody Guthrie Emerges, 75

6   The New Deal Survives, 96

7   Decade Ends, 118

    Epilogue, 152

    Notes, 159

    Index, 185

A Gallery of Illustrations Follows p. 74

Depression Folk

Introduction

My agenda will be the role of folk music, broadly defined, during the trying years of the Great Depression in the United States, 1929–40. I will particularly focus on the role of left-wing political groups and individuals. "Folk music" is a slippery term including older rural, vernacular songs and styles, mostly derived from British and African roots, as well as more modern personal, topical, and event songs played on acoustic instruments. Commercial compositions from the nineteenth century, such as the songs of Stephen Foster, could even be considered folk songs within a few decades.[1]

Historians have interpreted the vibrant and complex Depression years in various and conflicting ways. Michael Denning's influential book *The Cultural Front: The Laboring of American Culture in the Twentieth Century* begins with the question, "Why did the left have a powerful, indeed an unprecedented, impact on US culture in the 1930s?" In response, he asserts, "The broad cultural social movement known as the Popular Front was the ground on which the workers theaters, proletarian literary magazines, and film unions stood; it was . . . a radical social-democratic movement forged around anti-fascism, anti-lynching, and the industrial unionism of the CIO."[2]

This radical political and cultural shift has been explored by numerous scholars, such as Morris Dickstein in *Dancing in the Dark: A Cultural History of the Great Depression*: "Surprisingly, the Depression was also the scene of a great cultural spectacle against the unlikely backdrop of economic misery. The crisis kindled America's social imagination, firing enormous interest in how ordinary people lived, how they suffered, interacted, took pleasure in one another, and endured." Ira Katznelson's comprehensive study of the New Deal, *Fear Itself*, titled one chapter "Radical Moment," in which he characterized the 1930s as the "dramatic reorganization of American capitalism." Indeed, the era witnessed the expansion of the government's economic, cultural, and social programs, which vastly transformed the country for many years.[3]

In particular, the government promoted a labor and cultural renaissance through the "alphabet stew" of federal programs beginning in 1935, such as the National Labor Relations Act (NLRA, known as the Wagner Act); the Farm Security Administration (FSA), featuring the Photography Unit; and the Works Progress Administration (WPA), which included Federal Project One: the Index of Design, the Federal Writers' Project, the Federal Music Project, and the Federal Theater Project. These governmental programs included not just a paycheck but also a supportive creative environment that coincided with the emergence of radical political movements, in particular the Communist Party, whose membership and influence drastically increased. Denning's cultural front seemed a dominant theme during the decade, although assuredly not the only one.[4]

At the same time, there were popular forces working in opposition to the Roosevelt administration's initiatives and belief in an activist government. Much of the New Deal's domestic legislation passed with strong support from the solid block of southern Democrats in Congress, but only with the guarantee that no laws would disturb the South's rigid segregationist policies and practices, particularly the disenfranchisement of African American voters. The Fair Labor Standards Act in 1938 established a minimum wage and limited working hours, but only after excluding agricultural and domestic workers, the two main jobs for southern blacks, and even then a sizable number of southern Democrats voted against it. Moreover, Congress was unable to pass any antilynching bills, despite strong northern agitation and support. President Roosevelt depended on the solid Democratic South to pass the bulk of his legislation, but he often had to make compromises to bolster that section's rigid racial lines and policies, reinforced by both legislation and violence.

Besides maintaining segregation and discrimination, even in the more tolerant North, where African Americans could vote, the era was marked by strongly conservative, even reactionary, forces. For example, Hollywood film studios adopted the Motion Picture Production Code, known as the Hays Code after its author, Will H. Hays, in 1930, although it was not rigidly enforced until 1934, when the antisemite, Catholic Joseph Breen took over the Production Code Administration (PCA). The code, in upholding a conservative interpretation of Christian morality, banned sexuality, profanity, criticizing religion, men and women in bed together, the illegal drug trade, and sympathy to criminals. Hollywood films became extremely popular throughout the decade, with many outstanding productions, but they had become highly sanitized thanks to the clout of the Catholic Church and its studio allies. On another front, while the radical left gained support, many of its members and organizations became victims of persecution. Violent incidents targeting labor organizers in the North have been well documented, such as the auto workers' struggles in Michigan and the Republic Steel massacre in South Chicago in 1937, but they were also not uncommon in the South. Erik Gellman and Jarod Roll explain in their joint biography of the southern labor organizers and ministers Claude Williams and Owen Whitfield that they "fought a culture of working-class exploitation and racial degradation that was so habitual to their fellow Americans that it seemed as normal and unchangeable as waking up each morning."[5]

The US Congress first got into the hunt for subversives during World War I, and then in 1930, the House of Representatives established a rather tame temporary committee to investigate communists as well as the American Civil Liberties Union. This was followed in 1934 by the Special Committee on Un-American Activities, which concentrated on Nazis, and its successor in 1938 chaired by the antilabor Rep. Martin Dies of Texas. While designed to root out both fascists and communists, the Dies committee, backed by the FBI and bolstered by southern Democrats and northern Republicans, quickly became fixated on the latter, particularly after the Nazi-Soviet nonaggression pact in 1939. Various states established their own Red-hunting agendas, as anticommunism bubbled along through the decade, fueled by the country's conservative political streak, big business, and various right-wing groups. The Rapp-Coudert committee in New York, for example, began hearings in 1940 that led to the firing of numerous faculty members from the City College of New York for their alleged subversive thoughts. At the same time, a witch hunt for political radicals in Oklahoma, backed by the American Legion, led to the ransacking of the Communist Party's bookstore in Oklahoma City, the arrest of customers, and then the trial of party leaders Bob and Ina Wood, Alan Shaw, and Eli Jaffe. The purge led party members Sis Cunningham, a musician and labor organizer, and her husband, Gordon Friesen, a journalist, to flee the state in late 1941 for the safer environs of New York City, where they became involved with Pete Seeger, Woody Guthrie, and the Almanac Singers.[6]

Throughout the political, cultural, economic, and social maelstrom of the Depression years, folk music played a vital role in the musical patchwork of the time—classical, Tin Pan Alley pop, cowboy, country, blues, spirituals and gospel, Broadway show tunes, jazz (swing, New Orleans, sweet), ethnic, and so on. Music was ubiquitous on the radio and in Hollywood films, in jukeboxes, through records, in clubs and juke joints, touring bands, as well as street-corner and home performances. Through the Federal Music Project (1935–39) and its successor the Music Program (1939–43), which transferred control to the states, the government supported professional musicians, the majority of whom were jobless. "The Federal Music Project employed more people than any other WPA cultural venture (nearly sixteen thousand at its peak in 1936) and could also claim to have reached directly the most Americans," Charles Alexander has written. "To a greater extent than the other projects, moreover, [the Federal Music Project] brought to a head the conceptual conflict over professionalism versus service," since it focused on classical musicians with performances in large cities as well as small towns.

A few ethnic groups were included, however, particularly in the Southwest. The musicologist Charles Seeger served as deputy director from 1937 to 1941 in charge of promoting folk music, with a focus on the South. Seeger, along with Benjamin Botkin, the national folklore editor of the Federal Writers' Project, and John Lomax, the "National Advisor of Folklore and Folkways" for the Writers' Project, were also involved with the WPA's Joint Committee on Folk Arts, which coordinated work among all the federal relief arts projects. Still, most musicians, including folk performers, were essentially left to fend for themselves in the private marketplace. Moreover, financial and political pressures devastated the WPA after 1939, as the country began to prepare for war.[7]

Woody Guthrie's songs have become the soundtrack for the troubles of the dust bowl refugees and the Depression's downtrodden, but the balladeer wrote about much more, while the broader vernacular music movement touched on countless other aspects of the times. My story is rooted in a broad definition of folk music, including hillbilly (country) songs, rural blues, spirituals, cowboy songs, western swing, ethnic music and performers, singer-songwriters, labor songsters, and various others. The government supported and collected folk music through the Archive of American Folk Song of the Library of Congress. Numerous folklorists scoured the country for vernacular songs, while commercial companies continued to issue hillbilly and blues records, generally from southern recording sessions, although on a much smaller scale than in the previous decade. Some of the songs had political overtones, particularly if accompanying labor union organizing. There were a few significant individuals, such as Charles and Pete Seeger and John and Alan Lomax, perhaps with connections to the Communist Party (CP) or its affiliates, but the large number of folklorists and musicians mostly had no overt political agenda. The CP took no official position on what music should be performed, although the party's Popular Front agenda after middecade did emphasize vernacular cultural movements. All of those who were interested in folk music were eager to promote a nationalistic agenda, linking past and present. I highlight the complex role that folk music and musicians, collectors and promoters, record companies and others, played during the decade.

I focus on the role that folk music played in the clash between capitalism and the emerging grassroots proletarian movements. Alan Lomax, who played a central role in collecting and promoting folksongs, along with his radical political agenda, appears as a central link throughout the story, while his politically conservative father, John, was also very involved and influential. Numerous performers are also mentioned and discussed, such as Jimmie Rodgers, Woody Guthrie, Aunt Molly Jackson, Big Bill Broonzy, Sonny Terry and Brownie McGhee, and Pete Seeger, to name only a few. I have chosen to structure the chapters roughly in a chronological order because history unfolds year by year—and I am a historian—but I connect the information through various themes: the emergence of left-wing politics and its connection to vernacular music, folk music compared to classical and Tin Pan Alley tunes, the increasing relationship between urban and rural musicians, the connection between folklorists and vernacular musical styles, various regional differences but with a focus on New York City, and the role of the federal government. I have paid little attention to music that was not in English, although ethnic music was alive and well at the time (as Alan Lomax discovered), and not just in New York and other melting-pot cities. Fortunately, much of this music is available today on CDs and through the Internet. My conclusion points the way toward connecting the Depression years with the following decades, when folk music became more commercial and popular.[8]

I have strongly depended on the editorial assistance of Jim Lane, Will Kaufman, Bob Riesman, an anonymous reviewer for the press, and particularly Ron Pen for his thorough, detailed, and most astute comments and suggestions, which I have diligently tried to incorporate. I particularly want to thank Mark Simpson-Vos for his support and enthusiasm for this project. Last, but certainly not least, my longtime companion, Nancy, has always been supportive, keeping me in line as I have pursued my folk music career.

CHAPTER ONE

On the Trail of Folk Songs

By the 1920s, folk music—rural and urban, North and South, black and white, foreign and domestic—from a variety of sources had numerous outlets in the United States, including books and articles by folk music collectors, commercial phonograph records and field recordings, radio programs, public shows and concerts, fiddle contests, folk festivals, and plenty of home entertainments. It posed some commercial competition for Tin Pan Alley tunes and popular band music, while occupying an important musical, social, and cultural niche. The groundwork had been laid for folk music's subsequent role in promoting a nationalist agenda, particularly on the left of the political spectrum.[1]

Carl Sandburg's highly influential songbook *The American Songbag* appeared in 1927 and quickly captured a welcoming audience while documenting the current state of folk music scholarship. He parted company from the established experts, however, in significantly broadening the concept of folk music, following on the heels of John Lomax and the other cowboy collectors since the century's beginning. In contrast, and five years before *The American Songbag*, Louise Pound, an English professor at the University of Nebraska, had issued *American Ballads and Songs* with scores of selections. "The pieces in the following collection depend for their vitality upon oral, not upon written transmission," she explained in the introduction. "They have a subliterate existence, as apart from verse preserved in a form fixed by the printed page. . . . Other characteristics of genuine folk-songs are that they have retained their vitality through a fair period of time and that all sense of their authorship and provenience has been lost by their singers." Pound adhered to the academic definition of a ballad or folk song as having been passed down orally for centuries with no known author.[2]

Sandburg rejected such a narrow approach. Born in Galesburg, Illinois, in 1878, he had dropped out of school after the eighth grade, hit the road during the hard times of the late 1890s, served in the army during the Spanish-American War, and then entered college. He next resumed his travels, began writing poetry, and became a Socialist Party organizer and a journalist. In 1912, he moved with his family to Chicago, which he was to be closely identified with. Within a decade, he became a famed poet and writer, having picked up a love of folk songs along the way. With a rudimentary voice and guitar style, he nonetheless began to sing in public in 1925, starting with "The Buffalo Skinners," which he had learned from John Lomax's collection *Cowboy Songs and Other Frontier Ballads* (1910). While busy with his famed Lincoln biography and extensive public speaking schedule, Sandburg continued to pick up songs and ballads throughout the country; he managed through much hard work to finish *The American Songbag* by late 1927. "There is presented herein a collection of 280 songs, ballads, ditties, brought together from all regions of America," he explained. "The music includes not merely airs and melodies, but complete harmonizations or piano accompaniments. It is an All-American affair, marshaling the genius of thousands of original singing Americans." While "100 pieces, strictly folk songs, have never been published; they have been gathered by the compiler and his friends from coast to coast and from the Gulf to Canada," he nonetheless included a long list of published collections. He divided the songs into numerous sections, illustrating his eclectic approach: dramas and portraits, minstrel songs, pioneer memories, Great Lakes and Erie Canal songs, hobo songs, prison and jail songs, "The Big Brutal City," "Blues, Mellows, Ballets," Mexican border tunes, railroad songs, as well as lumberjack and sailor songs. Sandburg furnished each selection with a prefatory note. His focus was on songs and ballads in English, except for a few in Spanish. An immediate popular and critical success, the songbook remained in print into the next century and served to open the door to a less academic, more comprehensive and straightforward, as well as nationwide, understanding of folk music.[3]

Among the large number of grassroots music collectors besides Sandburg, Robert Gordon explored a variety of musical sources, expanding the field but with little initial impact. Born in 1888 in Bangor, Maine, as an undergraduate and then a graduate student at Harvard, he studied with the ballad scholars George Lyman Kittredge and F. B. Gummere. He next taught in the English Department at the University of California, Berkeley, 1918–24. His interest in folk songs led to his editing the "Old Songs That Men Have Sung" column in *Adventure* magazine, beginning in 1923 for over four years, which reached 2 million mostly male readers. This was similar to the music features in *Railroad Man's Magazine* and *Sea Stories*. Gordon's column reached a national audience, and he received a wide range of song texts from his readers, amateur collectors who were guided by Gordon's advice. He particularly liked collecting songs along the San Francisco waterfront, working with Frank Kester, who ran the sea songs and stories column "The Dogwatch" in the *Oakland Tribune*. Gordon used a cylinder record player to record over 200 local songs, mostly shanties and other sea songs, from sailors and hoboes, but also some Child ballads, blues, and bawdy songs.[4]

Gordon returned to the East in 1924 and the next year began an odyssey that took him to the South, resulting in many hundreds of recordings. In Asheville, North Carolina, he recorded Bascom Lamar Lunsford, a noted banjo player and collector who was also recorded by OKeh Records, since the commercial companies were now hot on the trail of rural black and white musicians in the South for commercial release. One of the pioneering field collectors in the South, along with Lawrence Gellert, Gordon preferred dance tunes and American ballads. From 1926 to 1928, he relocated to Darien, Georgia, where he focused on documenting African American musicians; he even entertained Carl Sandburg in 1927, on the trail for his own folk music research.

For a year (1927–28), Gordon published a series of articles on folk songs in the *New York Times Magazine*, on the basis of his fieldwork. "Of folk-song alone, America has a body perhaps greater in extent than that possessed by any other nation," he wrote in the first issue, "and certainly unsurpassed in interest and in variety of types." Gordon had done much work with African American musicians but had little feeling for their culture or history: "The negro of the South is perhaps our best folk-singer. He possesses not one but a dozen distinct types of folk-song ranging from the tragic and the sentimental to sheer bubbling humor. Some of his types—perhaps most of them—he derived in the beginning from the whites, for he is a marvelous assimilator. But in nearly every case he has so thoroughly made over the material that it would be unfair to say that is not now his own." Subsequent articles dealt with mountain songs, African American sea shanties from coastal Georgia, spirituals, outlaw ballads and jailhouse songs, lumberjack songs, old ballads, banjo tunes, nursery ballads, and cowboy songs—an eclectic mix rich with song lyrics. For those who missed the *Times* articles, the federal government reprinted all of them in 1938, although the publication's circulation was limited.[5]

In early 1927, Gordon offered a complete set of his "Old Songs" columns to Carl Engel, chief of the Music Division of the Library of Congress. Impressed with Gordon's folklore credentials, and with the backing of Herbert Putnam, the librarian of Congress, Engel appointed Gordon to head the newly created Archive of American Folk Song (AAFS) in July 1928 at the Library of Congress. While Gordon continued his research and donated some of his field recordings to the AAFS, he spent little time in Washington; and because of the government's mounting financial problems, his job ended in 1932. He died in 1961 and unfortunately never published a book on folk songs that would have summarized his life's work.

Lawrence Gellert, born Laslo Grunbaum in Hungary in 1898, grew up in New York. He moved to the South in the early 1920s, perhaps due to a nervous breakdown, and was soon living in Tryon, North Carolina, where he became interested in African

American folk songs and folklore. Using a crude machine, he began recording informants in North and South Carolina, as well as parts of Georgia, including in chain gangs. His brother Hugo Gellert, then becoming a noted radical artist, became involved with the Communist Party's publication *New Masses*, first appearing in 1926, with Michael Gold and Joseph Freeman as executive editors. Under Gold's direction, the May 1930 issue included Philip Schatz's article "Songs of the Negro Worker," using some of the songs that Gellert had been sending to Hugo. The article gave a political twist to known African American work songs, but some of Gellert's finds were variants of those that had already appeared in Howard Odum and Guy Johnson's *Negro Workaday Songs* (1926). By the mid-1930s, Gellert's self-styled African American "songs of protest" had become influential within Communist Party circles.[6]

Robert Gordon and Lawrence Gellert were not alone in focusing on the unique range of folk music to be found in the country, soon going beyond the traditional interest in ballads from the British Isles. Francis James Child, a professor of medieval studies and English literature at Harvard, published five volumes of *The English and Scottish Popular Ballads* (1882–96), which quickly dominated the ballad-collecting field. In the United States, William Wells Newell authored two articles on "early American ballads" in the *Journal of American Folklore* (*JAF*) (1899–1900). While Child ballads long continued to fascinate folklorists, a source of native songs was quickly discovered that deftly altered the field. In 1910, John A. Lomax issued *Cowboy Songs and Other Frontier Ballads*, which brought increased attention to these unique tunes. N. Howard "Jack" Thorp's *Songs of the Cowboys* had appeared in 1908, which included "Old Paint," "The Cowboy's Lament (Streets of Laredo)," and "The Old Chisholm Trail," but this limited edition received little notice. Lomax's book, however, made a major impact. Charles Finger followed with *Sailor Chanteys and Cowboy Songs* in 1923; then four years later, he issued the expanded *Frontier Ballads*, now with more from the West but missing the sea songs. Also, in 1927, the writer Frank Shay published *My Pious Friends and*

Drunken Companions, with illustrations by the Jazz Age artist John Held Jr. He included "Casey Jones," "Sam Bass," "The Dying Hobo," and "Clementine." "The music-lover who frequents the symphony concerts and delves deep into the works of Wagner and De Bussy [*sic*] will dismiss them as trivial," Shay explained. "The folk-lorist will dismiss them with the phrases profane and vulgar. To him they are but the product of low resorts, gutter songs, the communal musical expression of an artistically destitute society." For Shay, however, they truly represented the music of the folk.[7]

By 1910, Olive Dame Campbell had assembled a collection of native white songs from Kentucky, Georgia, and Tennessee, but she could find no publisher. She was not the only woman in the South with an interest in local song lore. Katherine Pettit and May Stone, the founders of the Hindman Settlement School in Knott County, Kentucky, in 1902, had been collecting songs from the children at their school; George Lyman Kittredge at Harvard published some of their collection as "Ballads and Rhymes from Kentucky" in the *JAF* in 1907. From 1912 to 1915, E. C. Perrow's "Songs and Rhymes from the South" appeared in the *JAF*, including 270 texts from the Appalachian region. In 1916, Loraine Wyman and Howard Brockway issued *Lonesome Tunes: Folk Songs from the Kentucky Mountains*, quickly followed by Josephine McGill's *Folk-Songs of the Kentucky Mountains* (1917). Wyman's *Twenty Kentucky Mountain Songs* appeared in 1920.[8]

Child, an American, had set the standard for future collectors of British ballads before war had broken out in Europe in late 1914. On the other hand, Cecil Sharp, a British traditional song and dance scholar, first traveled to the United States with his colleague Maude Karpeles in 1914. Returning in 1916, and with the collaboration of Olive Dame Campbell, the wife of a missionary schoolteacher and social reformer in Appalachia—the namesake for the John C. Campbell Folk School in Brasstown, North Carolina, founded in 1925 by his wife following his death—they collected 400 songs from sixty-seven informants in North Carolina, Tennessee, and Virginia. They published much of their collection in *English Folk-Songs of the Southern Appa-*

lachians (1917). The following year, while the Great War raged, Sharp and Karpeles gathered another 600 songs and in 1918 an additional 625 tunes before returning to England. Sharp died in 1924, and in 1932 Karpeles produced *English Folk Songs from the Southern Appalachians*, the final two volumes of their collection, with another 274 songs. Along with the bulk of American collectors at the time, Sharp had the romantic, and highly fanciful, notion that the backwoods southerners were cut off from modern society, living in a cultural cocoon. Many had already migrated to industrial centers, however, while radio programs and phonograph records were soon plentiful, further connecting rural with urban, and modern, influences. There were few isolated settlements by the 1920s.[9]

While Sharp and others were gathering songs and ballads from southern white musicians, a separate group of collectors began focusing on African American singers and songsters. Howard W. Odum, born in Georgia and a graduate of Emory College in 1904, entered the University of Mississippi as a graduate student and soon discovered a wealth of African American songs. While a fellow in Psychology at Clark University in Massachusetts, he published his highly detailed "Religious Folk Songs of the Southern Negroes" in the *American Journal of Religious Psychology and Education* in 1909. Next, armed with a cylinder record player, he collected and published 115 secular songs in the *JAF* in 1911. Odum's major study with Guy B. Johnson, *The Negro and His Songs*, appeared in 1925, quickly followed by their *Negro Workaday Songs* (1926), a year after Dorothy Scarborough's fascinating *On the Trail of Negro Folk-Songs*.[10]

African Americans appeared on phonograph records as early as the 1890s, performing the popular coon songs, from both white and black composers, as well as spirituals and much else. The team of Bert Williams and George Walker began recording in 1901, while an increasing number of black musicians entered the recording studios through the nineteen-teens. Various styles and types of blues songs and performers were popular before the 1920s, playing in juke joints, barber shops, and on concert stages. A national commercial breakthrough came in 1920 with

Mamie Smith's OKeh recording of "Crazy Blues," which sparked the blues fad of the following decade and after. Five companies soon dominated the race market: Brunswick, Gennett, Paramount, Victor, and Columbia (which included OKeh after 1926). The female classic blues singers, such as Bessie Smith and Ma Rainey, backed by piano players or jazz bands, originally captured the national market. Until 1927, the female singers dominated the output of race records, although there were a few exceptions. Papa Charlie Jackson, Blind Lemon Jefferson, and Blind Blake recorded for Paramount in Chicago—the company was located in Grafton, Wisconsin—in the mid-1920s, before the floodgates opened after 1926, spurred by Jefferson's popularity. A few rather obscure bluesmen also recorded early for Gennett in Richmond, Indiana.[11]

The last three years of the decade, however, witnessed numerous recording sessions in the South, particularly by Columbia and Victor in Atlanta, Memphis, Dallas, and New Orleans. The rural bluesmen included Blind Willie McTell; the Memphis Jug Band and Cannon's Jug Stompers; Big Bill Broonzy, along with Georgia Tom Dorsey and Tampa Red, who recorded in Chicago for Paramount; and Charlie Patton. The OKeh recording session in Memphis in February 1928 proved particularly productive, including Mississippi John Hurt and Lonnie Johnson; in late December, Hurt traveled to OKeh's studio in New York, where he waxed another dozen sides. Hurt then faded into obscurity in Avalon, Mississippi, not to be heard from again for more than three decades. These bluesmen and their colleagues from Mississippi, Texas, Louisiana, and the Southeast coast mostly came from rural backgrounds, but they early absorbed a modern commercial ethos and easily became professional musicians, at least for a short time. Their songs and playing styles combined tradition and recreation, covering various topics and reaching a national audience.[12]

Phonograph records mushroomed through the 1920s, appealing to a range of tastes, generations, and cultural groups. The major record companies had refined their approach to the expanding markets through establishing separate race (African

American) and hillbilly (white southern), as well as ethnic, lists. Indeed, ethnic records proliferated in the early decades, from both the major companies and independent entrepreneurs, targeting the large foreign-language market and drawing on immigrant performers. Columbia released Polish and Czech records in its green-label ethnic series before the Great War, and the number and variety of performers and styles increased in the 1920s. This was vernacular music but of a particular kind that did not enter the cultural mainstream.[13]

Black and white musicians in the South had long shared their music and sometimes performed together, even within the harsh limits of official segregation—indeed, what marked hillbilly music were the cross-racial influences that long continued, with white musicians such as Cliff Carlisle and the Allen Brothers performing blues-influenced songs—but the record companies had discovered that separate labeling and marketing would prove a commercial gold mine. This business decision depended on racial and ethnic stereotyping, with black and white rural caricatures, while the records were marketed nationally, even as the musicians shared a common musical and instrumental (banjo, guitar, fiddle) lineage. Indeed, there was considerable racial crossover and borrowings.[14]

In 1922, A. C. "Eck" Robertson and Henry Gilliland's Victor recording of "Sally Gooden" and "Arkansas Traveler" uncovered a large hillbilly market. It was quickly followed by Fiddlin' John Carson's OKeh recording of "The Little Old Log Cabin in the Lane" and "The Old Hen Cackled and the Rooster's Going to Crow." Brunswick, Gennett, Paramount, Columbia, and other companies quickly rushed to take advantage of the widening country market, labeling their records as "old familiar tunes," "old-time music," even "Popular Ballads and Mountaineer Tunes" as well as "Southern Melodies." A 1927 Victor Records flyer stated, "Here's another set of 'Southern Specials'—the kind that have been getting more and more popular with each succeeding release. This is perhaps the most diversified list yet to appear. Ballads in 'mountaineer' style, on timely topics, such as Captain Lindberg's Paris flight, the Mississippi flood, sentimental songs, character songs with snappy bits of humor—and each one with a distinct appeal of its own." Some were traditional Anglo-American ballads, songs, and dance tunes, others drawn from the minstrel repertoire dating from before the Civil War and Victorian parlor songs. Many were newly minted event songs, mostly the products of Tin Pan Alley's commercial tunesmiths, that captured the day's headlines. Record company representatives, such as Victor's A&R (artist and repertoire) man Ralph Peer, scoured the South for performers, particularly those with original tunes that could be copyrighted by Peer and his colleagues. The Southern Piedmont, an area of rolling hills stretching from Virginia through the Carolinas and Georgia into Alabama, with Charlotte, North Carolina, as the urban center, proved particularly rich. The area produced Fiddlin' John Carson, Charlie Poole and the North Carolina Ramblers, Dave McCarn, and the Dixon Brothers, among others who represented the hard life of cotton-mill workers.[15]

While scores of musicians appeared on commercial recordings, many others performed only for family and neighbors, on radio shows and in festivals, in fiddlers contests, in local courthouse squares and on street corners, in coal camps and textile towns, in tent and medicine shows, in vaudeville houses, in schools and churches, anywhere people assembled for a social outing. Black and white musicians seemed to be ubiquitous. Fiddle contests began in the eighteenth century, expanding in the modern era with the 1912 Lawrenceville, Georgia, contest, which became the Georgia Old-Time Fiddler's Convention the next year and lasted into the 1930s. Such contests dotted the southern landscape by the 1930s. In 1928, Bascom Lamar Lunsford launched the influential and long-lasting Mountain Dance and Folk Festival in Asheville, North Carolina. Other festivals quickly followed.[16]

There were also numerous country music radio programs by the later 1920s, some reaching a national audience. Pittsburgh's KDKA first aired Berg's String Entertainers in May 1922, quickly followed by WSB in Atlanta, beginning with Fiddlin' John Carson the following September; WBAP in Fort Worth, Texas, launched the first barn-dance show in January 1923.

While the proliferating southern stations rushed to broadcast hillbilly performers, northern stations quickly joined the parade, with WLS in Chicago broadcasting *The Aladdin Playparty* soon after its inauguration in April 1924, which changed to the *Old Fiddlers' Hour* and finally became the long-running *National Barn Dance* in 1926. In late 1925, Nashville's WSM aired its own hillbilly show with Uncle Jimmy Thompson, soon known as the *Grand Ole Opry*. The *National Barn Dance* included performers appealing to a range of musical tastes—although many originally came from the South—such as vaudeville performers, barbershop quartets, polka bands, and cowboy entertainers (including Gene Autry), along with the popular stylings of Bradley Kincaid. The *Grand Ole Opry*, on the other hand, specialized in more hardcore southern hillbilly bands and solo performers, such as Uncle Dave Macon, Deford Bailey (the rare African American on the program, who played the harmonica), and Sam and Kirk McGee. Moreover, there were soon scores of inexpensive country song folios, many featuring the repertoire of the radio stars, making the tunes widely available for home performances.[17]

As electricity continued to spread into rural areas by decade's end, radio programs with vernacular music became increasingly available. Since most phonograph players were still hand cranked, however, even the most remote farmhouse could have access to recorded sounds. Moreover, while the companies focused on selling hillbilly and race records in their expanding southern markets, there also existed a welcoming national audience. Most of the companies, such as Columbia, Victor, and OKeh, had their headquarters in New York City, and indeed that was where most of the studio work was done, with either southern musicians brought to the city or local musicians. From 1923 to 1932, the record companies had about 100 recording sessions on location in the South, but there were more dates in their northern studios, particularly in New York City with Carson J. Robison, Frank Luther, Frank Marvin, Bob Miller, and in particular Vernon Dalhart, all of whom reached a broad public.

Popular artists such as Al Jolson, Bing Crosby, Rudy Vallee, and Ruth Etting, along with the bandleaders Paul Whiteman,

Ted Lewis, and Glen Gray, ruled the northern airwaves and recording studios. They were somewhat challenged, however, by Dalhart and his citybilly colleagues, whose southern-tinged songs found an enthusiastic northern market. Born in Texas and trained as a light-opera tenor, Dalhart recorded "Wreck of the Old 97" backed by "The Prisoner's Song" for Victor in 1924, which sold a million copies and millions more released on nine other labels. By decade's end, he had recorded several hundred songs under various pseudonyms, with sales even reaching to Great Britain and Australia. Carson Robison, born in Kansas, wrote many of Dalhart's topical songs and others for the polished singer Frank Luther after 1928, selling into the hundreds of thousands. Indeed, hillbilly songs, perhaps about train wrecks and various disasters, Charles Lindberg's flight, and other stories ripped from the headlines, while couched in a southern acoustic musical style, had a broad appeal. Hillbilly recordings and radio shows proved decent competition for the products of Tin Pan Alley, because of or even despite the record companies' penchant for using distinctly negative (and popular) stereotypes of backwoods rustics in their advertising and programs. Tin Pan Alley songs featured the role of the individual in modern society, with a heavy emphasis on romantic love. This was in marked contrast to the hillbilly recordings, with their gritty focus on family, community, history, work, and current events.[18]

While Dalhart, Luther, Robison, and their colleagues were crowding the Columbia, Victor, Brunswick, and OKeh studios in New York, a particularly important recording session took place in Bristol, located on the Virginia-Tennessee state line, in late July–early August 1927. Organized by Victor's Ralph Peer, his temporary studio in Bristol attracted nineteen acts, including Ernest V. "Pop" Stoneman and his family, Henry Whitter, Blind Alfred Reed, and, in particular, Jimmie Rodgers and the Carter Family (A. P., Sara, Maybelle). Victor soon issued a number of their recordings. Jimmie Rodgers quickly became widely popular. Born in Pine Springs, Mississippi, in 1897, he had a rather checkered life until winding up in Bristol. Peer quickly brought him to the Victor studio in Camden, New Jersey, where his amazing recording career began, lasting until his early death from tuberculosis in 1933. His combination of traditional and contemporary songs, some written by his sister-in-law Elsie McWilliams, and accompanied by a range of instruments and performers, including a jazz band, Hawaiian guitar, even Louis Armstrong on the trumpet, set the standard for male country performers in the larger realm of popular music. The Carter Family, with their focus on more traditional (including religous) material and presentation, with a family and conservative bent, also had an immense influence on the national music scene for many decades.[19]

Peer had begun his southern field recording in Asheville, North Carolina, in 1925, including Stoneman, Whitter, Lunsford, Wade Ward, and Kelly Harrell. Within a few years, OKeh visited Winston-Salem, North Carolina, while Brunswick conducted hillbilly collecting in Ashland, Kentucky, as well as Knoxville, Tennessee. Columbia's A&R scout Frank Walker's trip to Johnson City, Tennessee, in October 1928 and October 1929 proved particularly fruitful. The recording of Earl Shirkey and Roy Harper's "Steamboat Man" along with "When the Roses Bloom Again for the Bootlegger" sold 75,000 copies in 1929. Walker returned to Johnson City in late October 1929, just in time for the stock market crash, but he had already recorded Clarence Ashley's "The Coo-Coo Bird" and the Bentley Boys' "Down on Penny's Farm."[20]

Record companies essentially targeted southern musicians and their audiences in their race and hillbilly lists, but folklorists were not so geographically focused, as vernacular songs could be found nationwide. For example, Pound compiled *Folk-Songs of Nebraska and the Central West* in 1915, which included songs of Indian, Irish, German, English, and African American background. In New England, Fannie Hardy Eckstorm and Mary Winslow Smyth published *The Minstrelsy of Maine: Folksongs and Ballads of the Woods and Coast* in 1927; two years later, Eckstorm and Smyth, along with Phillips Barry, issued *British Ballads from Maine*. While some collectors had a geographical focus, others specialized in specific genres, such as George Korson's

Songs and Ballads of the Anthracite Miner (1927), based on his field collecting in Pennsylvania; he quickly followed with other compilations of miners' songs. Roland Palmer Gray's *Songs and Ballads of the Maine Lumberjacks* appeared in 1924. "Their resemblance to mediaeval English and Scottish popular ballads aroused my interest," the folklorist Gray explained. "At first thought, it seemed altogether unlikely that conditions in Maine would be favorable to the growth of ballads of the old type. Such favorable conditions, nevertheless, were found to have existed for over half a century." Franz Rickaby's *Ballads and Songs of the Shanty-Boy* (1926) also focused on the occupational songs of lumberjacks.[21]

There were also various vernacular musical styles throughout the country, somewhat out of the mainstream, including Cajun and zydeco, Mexican American, along with numerous labor songs. Joseph Falcon recorded the first Cajun song in New Orleans in 1928, about the same time as the first Mexican American (Tejanos) recordings. The Industrial Workers of the World (IWW), founded in 1905, began publishing *Songs of the Workers*, better known as the "Little Red Songbook," in 1909, and numerous printings appeared into the next century, with songs by Joe Hill and Ralph Chaplin. Harry "Haywire Mac" McClintock, with "The Big Rock Candy Mountain" and "Hallelujah! I'm a Bum," and Goebel Reeves, with "Hobo's Lullaby," helped spread labor songs, with folk-style arrangements, to their audiences. Born in 1882, McClintock had a life filled with various manual-labor jobs around the world, including a longtime career as a trainman; he became a performer in the mining camps of Nevada and the oil-boom towns of California. He joined the IWW soon after its founding, while "Hallelujah! I'm a Bum" became its unofficial theme. His radio career began in San Francisco in 1925 on the KFRC show *Blue Monday Jamboree*, singing songs and telling stories. Soon after, he organized his own band, and he remained on the radio for the next thirteen years. He recorded "Big Rock Candy Mountain" for the Victor company in 1928 and produced thirty-eight titles for the company through

1931. In 1938, the year he moved to Los Angeles, he recorded four songs for Decca, including "The Bum Song."[22]

Socialist songbooks began to appear early in the century and included a variety of compositions and texts, but were seldom based on Victorian/Tin Pan Alley tunes or had any sort of folk music roots, except for the IWW compositions. They were mostly based on religious songs. The Communist Party of the United States emerged in 1919—sparked by the creation of the Soviet Union following the Russian Revolution of 1917—out of some remnants of the Socialist Party and other leftist groups. It quickly fragmented, while mostly driven underground by the federal government's fervent attacks led by J. Edgar Hoover in the Federal Bureau of Investigation (FBI). Various factions merged into the Workers (Communist) Party until 1929, when it officially became the Communist Party, USA. The Young Workers League of America, formed in 1922 as the party's youth wing, published its own songbook, *The March of the Workers and Other Songs*. It contained mostly older socialist songs, as well as Ralph Chaplin's "The Commonwealth of Toil" and Joe Hill's "The Preacher and the Slave" from the IWW songbook. "In this book are collected the songs of the international proletariat, old and new, and all refreshing with their spirit of youth, of the new conquering the old," the foreword explained.[23]

The 1920s were generally a prosperous time, with definite pockets of poverty among many farmers, African Americans North and South, Native Americans, textile-mill workers and coal miners, and southern sharecroppers and tenant farmers, white and black; the rich were getting richer, the middle class moderately so, while everyone else struggled to survive. The eclectic music industry sailed through the end of the decade in good shape, with country stars such as Jimmie Rodgers and the Carter Family doing particularly well. Then came the stock-market crash of 1929 and the hard times to follow. The 100 million records sold in 1929 plunged to only 6 million in 1932. Folk music, along with the larger world of popular music, would take many twists and turns during the Great Depression.[24]

CHAPTER TWO

Depression's Beginnings and Labor Songs

The Depression Takes Root

On November 5, 1931, a delegation from the National Committee for the Defense of Political Prisoners (NCDPP), headed by the left-wing novelist Theodore Dreiser, arrived in Pineville, Kentucky, to investigate the escalating warfare and suffering in "Bloody" Harlan County and the surrounding Appalachian coal towns. John Dos Passos, Samuel Ornitz, and other writers accompanied the author. Organized the previous April by Dreiser, the NCDPP brought together an interracial group of writers and artists to fight for social justice. Two days later, the middle-aged midwife, songwriter, and singer Aunt Molly Jackson (1880–1960) regaled the committee with her stories of the terrible, longstanding hardship among the miners, which she deftly illustrated by singing her roughly phrased song "Hungry Ragged Blues" (aka "Ragged Hungry Blues"):

> I'm sad and weary, I've got the hungry ragged blues
> Not a penny in the pocket to buy one thing I need to use.
> I woke up this morning, with the worst blues I ever had in my life
> Not a bite to cook for breakfast, a poor coal miner's wife!

While labeled a blues, the song had no relation to the structure of African American southern blues. Raw and graphic, it deftly captured the miners' plight from the woman's viewpoint. It was not structured as a sing-along but was the unique creation of a singular voice and songwriter.[1]

Songs had long accompanied labor union organizing and the violence that had ripped through the country's coal fields and towns during strikes since the nineteenth century. George Korson, a journalist in Pennsylvania, began collecting such songs in 1924, first among the anthracite (hard coal) miners, and soon after published *Songs and Ballads of the Anthracite Miner* (1927): "It represents an attempt to salvage from the past a vein rich in the homespun creations of the common people before it is lost forever with the passing of that generation which produced it." He included a number of strike songs, starting with "The Long Strike" dating from 1875 and ending with "Me Johnny Mitchell Man" from a strike in 1902 (Mitchell was the president of the United Mine Workers at the time). In 1938, Korson followed with the greatly expanded *Minstrels of the Mine Patch: Songs and Stories of the Anthracite Industry*, a book that included sixteen strike songs, along with much else, again ending in 1902. Following the publication of his book on Pennsylvania miners, he next tackled the folklore of the bituminous (soft coal) miners from the coal fields of Pennsylvania, Ohio, Illinois, Indiana, Virginia, West Virginia, Kentucky, Tennessee, and Alabama. He found a wealth of strike songs, beginning in 1894 and ending with the 1930s. There were none by Aunt Molly Jackson, however, who was only listed among various "other bituminous miner bards and minstrels" in Korson's *Coal Dust on the Fiddle: Songs and Stories of the Bituminous Industry* (1943). Apparently he avoided mentioning Jackson since she was affiliated with the National Miners Union (NMU), the Communist Party's militant counter to the United Mine Workers (UMW) of America, which Korson strongly supported.[2]

Alan Calmer celebrated Pennsylvania's legacy of labor songs in his 1934 article "Early American Labor and Literature" in *International Literature*. "The folklore that flourished in the anthracite region of Pennsylvania during the last third of the nineteenth century was of a very striking nature," he explained. "Although the custom of balladry and minstrelsy had been transplanted from the British Isles, these homespun songs and poems were rooted deep in the life of the coal miners of the state." Drawing his song examples mostly from Korson's *Songs and Ballads of the Anthracite Miner,* Calmer also quoted from Albert Parsons (tried and executed for the Haymarket riot in Chicago in 1886) and other radical organizers in documenting the legacy of labor writings.[3]

Times were tough in Harlan County, Kentucky, particularly after the 1929 stock-market crash and ensuing national economic depression. Located near the Virginia and Tennessee borders, this had been an agricultural area hidden away in a narrow valley between the Pine and Black Mountains until the first coal mines opened in 1911. By 1930, nearly 20 percent of the Harlan County population (11,920 miners out of 64,000) was working in the mines. In the early years, union organizing had been feeble at best, and then it had disappeared by the mid-1920s due to a combination of fear of the brutal tactics of the mining companies and the generally prosperous times. Soon poverty, disease, and hunger were rampant.[4]

Mary Magdalene Garland, later known as Aunt Molly Jackson, was born in Clay County, Kentucky, in 1880. Her half brother, Jim Garland, was born in 1905, followed five years later by her half sister, Sarah, and both also became singer-songwriters. The teenage Molly married the coal miner Jim Stewart in 1894 and became a midwife. When a strike broke out at the Hughes mine in Ely Branch in 1910, she wrote her first protest song, "Fare Ye Well, Old Ely Branch." Following the death of Stewart, she married Bill Jackson sometime in the 1920s. In February 1931, following another wage reduction, the miners in Harlan County went out on strike; the mine owners immediately retaliated, evicting the miners from their homes, while the miners received scant assistance from the conservative UMW.

In 1928, Jim Garland moved to Harlan County to work for the Peabody Coal Company, and two years later, he switched to the Whitfield Coal Company. By the fall of 1931, he was an organizer for the NMU. "November also saw the Theodore Dreiser Committee's entry into the coalfields," he later wrote. "Dreiser and his group of writers had come from New York to conduct interviews and to evaluate the miners' situation. During one of their meetings . . . my sister Aunt Molly Jackson sang a song she had just recently made up; she called it 'The Hungry Ragged Blues.' The Dreiser people were so impressed by her that they thought she was just about the whole Kentucky strike. In fact, she had done very little in the strike aside from going down into Knox County a time or two to solicit vegetables for the community kitchen." Whatever Jackson's role in the strike, her songwriting captured the mood and plight of the strikers, as did many of her other songs. She was joined in 1931 by Florence Reece, another supporter of the NMU in Straight Creek, whose politically charged song "Which Side Are You On?" quickly became a rallying cry for labor union activists:

> Come all of your good workers
> Good news to you I'll tell,
> Of how the good old union
> Has come in here to dwell.

The song was sharp, gave details about the brutality of the mine owners, and was easy to pick up. It was also optimistic, at a time when there was little good news in the coal fields.

Less than a month after the Dreiser hearings, Jackson fled Kentucky, fearing violence from the mill owners, and arrived in New York City, where the Lower East Side was to be her home for many years. She quickly became popular among the city's communist left, personifying the suffering of the mining families while artistically expressing their hopes and hardships through her lyrics and performances. Labor and radical songs had a long history and increased during the Depression years. Shortly after Jackson arrived, Margaret Larkin, a musician and left-wing journalist, brought her to the Columbia studio, where she recorded the two-sided "Ragged Hungry Blues." A week later, she recorded "Poor Miners Farewell" backed by "I Love Coal Miners," but only the first record was released by the sinking company in a very limited quantity and quickly disappeared, since Columbia was phasing out its country series.[5]

The Music Industry

Poverty had long ravaged the coal fields of Kentucky, but it was equally devastating throughout the South and quickly the rest of the country after 1929. The record industry was particularly hard hit as unemployment soared following the stock-market crash and ensuing Depression. The Gross Domestic Product (GDP) reached a high of $103 billion in 1929 and then began its plunge, hitting a low of $56 billion in 1933, the Depression's nadir. Unemployment took a similar path, beginning at 3.2 percent in 1929 and rising to 25 percent in 1933, then making a slow up-and-down recovery until 1940. The same occurred with federal spending, which roughly stabilized from 1928 to 1933 at around $9 billion, then began its climb, again inconsistently, to a height of $14 billion in 1939, until the beginning of World War II in 1941, when it doubled to $28 billion. The plethora of New Deal programs starting in 1933 certainly helped to stimulate employment, provide spending money, and save the family farm, but they did not end the Depression; that only happened with the onset of defense spending after 1940.

The music industry felt the crippling sting of the Depression. Record sales fell from $46 million in 1930 to $16.9 million within the year, a drop of 90 percent in sales, and the ethnic and race markets were hit the hardest. Only 6 million records were sold in 1932. RCA had purchased the Victor Talking Machine Company in 1929; at the same time, Edison folded its record division. Columbia experienced a series of owners in the early 1930s, when it was selling only 100,000 records a year, and finally survived the decade but in weakened condition. Many of the smaller, budget labels went broke and were swallowed up by the American Record Company (ARC), which controlled Columbia, Banner, Cameo, Conqueror, Melotone, Pathe, Perfect, OKeh, Romeo, Vocalion, and Brunswick, amounting to 60 percent of the market (until it was purchased by CBS on January 1, 1939). In 1932, RCA Victor launched the budget Bluebird label, which proved very popular as it was sold through the Woolworth's chain. Decca Records emerged in 1934, founded by the English investor Ted Lewis as a challenge to ARC and RCA Victor. He hired the experienced Brunswick record company executive Jack Kapp, who lured Bing Crosby and others from his old company. By decade's end, Victor and Decca led record sales, with ARC a distant third. The jukebox industry, although not new, flourished with the reopening of bars and clubs after the ending of Prohibition in December 1933 and purchased a large number of records; there were soon 500,000 of the machines located in restaurants, bus stations, and cafés, along with the juke joints selling liquor. Recorded music increasingly appeared on radio.[6]

The surviving companies continued to record race and hillbilly performers, although on a vastly reduced scale. For example, Victoria Spivey managed to sell a little over 100 copies of "Baulin' Water Blues" parts 1 and 2, the popular black Grand Ole Opry star De Ford Bailey less than 150 of "John Henry," and the Memphis Jug Band about 200 of "Taking Your Place"/"Aunt Caroline Dyer Blues." A good seller might have been Jelly Roll Morton and His Red Hot Peppers' "Strokin' Away"/"Each Day" with around 500 purchased. Some of the major performers continued to record through the decade, however. The Carter Family began with Victor, moved to the ARC labels in 1935 (Columbia, Romeo, Perfect), Decca in 1936, and then OKeh in 1940. Jimmie Rodgers recorded for Victor until just before his death in May 1933 and had immense influence. Gene Autry, one of his prolific acolytes, quickly issued "The Death of Jimmie Rodgers." Big Bill Broonzy began his recording career in the late 1920s and particularly took off after 1934, recording about a record a month until 1942 for RCA Victor's Bluebird brand, as well as for Vocalion and other ARC labels.

Labor Songs

Why Gene Autry, backed by Frankie Marvin, recorded "The Death of Mother Jones" on February 25, 1931, which appeared on various discount ARC labels, is unknown:

> The world today's in mourning
> O'er the death of Mother Jones;
> Gloom and sorrow hover
> Around the miners' homes.

That New York session also included "True Blue Bill," "The Gangster's Warning," "Bear Cat Papa Blues," and "I'll Always Be a Rambler." Born in 1837, Mary Harris "Mother" Jones had by the 1870s become an active labor union firebrand, a role she continued up to her death in late 1930. Autry's recording of "The Death of Mother Jones," while in limited circulation, spread through the South through the work of the labor organizer Tom Tippett. Tippett shared the words with another labor organizer in West Virginia, Walter Seacrist, who adapted the words to a different tune and through a private recording spread the song at union meetings. Tippett brought a copy of the Autry record to Brookwood Labor College in Katonah, New York, where he was a teacher, and this also helped its popularity. From the founding of Brookwood in 1921 until its demise in 1937, the college, partly though its songbook *Brookwood Chatauqua Songs*, promoted labor songs through the country. As for Autry, not known for any left-wing politics, his star began to rise in 1932 with the release of "That Silver Haired Daddy of Mine," recorded for ARC in late 1931, which sold an astounding 500,000 copies. With his career off to a good start, and having dropped his Jimmie Rodgers imitations, Autry moved to Hollywood in 1934 to initiate his phenomenal singing-cowboy film career, beginning with *In Old Santa Fe*, followed by the odd Western serial *The Phantom Empire*; he quickly became the most popular Hollywood musical cowboy, following in the footsteps of Tim McCoy, Hoot Gibson, and Tom Mix.[7]

Most labor songs from the late 1920s and early 1930s did not appear on records issued by the major record companies. A noteworthy exception occurred in 1929 in the North Carolina textile towns of Marion and Gastonia. A series of strikes generated a number of class-conscious songs that were released on commercial recordings. In 1930, Dave McCarn, who was born in Gaston

County and had worked in the local mill until the Great Depression, recorded the jaunty yet depressing "Cotton Mill Colic" for RCA Victor in Memphis, Tennessee, with the chorus,

> I'm gonna starve and everybody will
> You can't make a living in a cotton mill.

McCarn had played guitar with the Yellow Jackets, a jug band in Gastonia, and along with "Cotton Mill Colic," he recorded "Everyday Dirt" for Victor's Ralph Peer on May 19, 1930. The record, appearing in the label's "Old Familiar Tunes and Novelties" series, initially sold well, particularly in the Piedmont textile towns, and over the following year he made ten more recordings for the company, including "Poor Man, Rich Man (Cotton Mill Colic No. 2)" and "Serves 'Em Fine (Cotton Mill Colic No. 3)." These social protest songs, with a comical twist, long remained popular, appearing in numerous song anthologies over the following decades. When McCarn's short-lived musical career ended, he returned to North Carolina, where he worked in a variety of industrial jobs and ended up as a radio and TV repairman until his death in 1964 at the age of fifty-nine, having led a hard life.[8]

McCarn's role in the 1929 Gastonia textile strike is unknown, unlike that of Ella May Wiggins, who wrote the anguished and widely popular "The Mill Mother's Song (or Lament)"—which was published in the *Labor Defender* in October 1929—and more than a dozen others. "The Mill Mother's Song" begins,

> We leave our homes in the morning,
> We kiss our children good-bye,
> While we slave for the bosses
> Our children scream and cry.

A single mother, Wiggins raised her five children while working at the American Mill No. 2 in Bessemer City near Gastonia. Textile workers and their families had always known hard times, living on low wages in company towns, but things were worse by the late 1920s, even before the stock-market crash. The strike in Gastonia was over the long hours, low wages, the stretch-out system (more work for the same pay), and increasing layoffs. Championed by the National Textile Workers Union (NTWU), recently launched by the Communist Party, the strike began on April 1, 1929, and centered at the Loray Mill. Violence escalated until September 14, when Wiggins, noted for her prounion songs, was shot to death by some strike breakers. The strike soon ended, but not before dozens of protest songs had circulated, most by women, including "Up in Old Loray" by the eleven-year-old Odell Corley, herself a striking worker. Margaret Larkin had covered the strike, met Wiggins in August, and promoted her songs. "Meetings, speeches, picket lines, the crises of terror—these developed Ella May's latent talents. The immense vitality of the mountain woman," Larkin wrote, "unquenched by 10 years in the mills, overflowed into 'Song Ballets' about the union and the strike." The Department of Cultural Activities of the Workers' International Relief published a small songbook, *Songs of the Class Struggle: In Memory of Ella May Wiggins and Steve Katovis* (the latter a Communist Party member and union activist who was shot by a policeman in New York). In 1938, Larkin followed up with a further testimonial in the *Daily Worker*: "The grave, beautiful 'Mill Mother's Song'—that classic expression of a working mother's love—was sung at her burial." Wiggins's songs were not recorded at the time, however.[9]

Margaret Larkin devoted much of her life to the work of the Communist Party, while believing that folk songs could promote labor consciousness. She took a different tack in her rich compilation *Singing Cowboy: A Book of Western Songs* (1931), drawing on the collections of John Lomax and others and including both old and new compositions. "If cowboy songs may not be classed as folk lore," she explained, since they lacked ancient roots, "they nevertheless contain some of its elements.... They deal with the fundamentals, with work, fun, danger, love, money.... English and Scottish ballads, Irish reels, Negro spirituals, German *lieder*, and sentimental songs of the day were the sources of the tunes for cowboy songs." They expressed a slight class-conscious nature, however. "There is a noticeable absence of the rich man–poor man theme so common to folk song, in the cowboy's balladry," she noted. "The boss rode with the hands and shared the hardships of the life. . . . The songs record only occasional complaints about the food, and the credit system by which the cowboy drew money in advance against his wages." Her collection, with helpful headnotes for each song, proved to be a popular hit, perhaps because she avoided overt references to her radical politics. In 1937, she married the Hollywood screenwriter Albert Maltz (later one of the Hollywood 10 who went to prison for refusing to testify before Congress).[10]

Strike fever also spread to the destitute mill towns of Clinchfield and East Marion, North Carolina, where the American Federation of Labor (AFL)–affiliated United Textile Workers Union, a militant foe of the more radical NTWU, had organized the workers in the summer of 1929. The strikers clashed with the sheriff's deputies and National Guard troops off and on, resulting in six deaths and many more wounded in September; the strike collapsed soon after. The Marion strike, unlike Gastonia, produced few songs and seemingly none by the workers. The prolific duo of Frank Welling, a vaudeville entertainer, and John McGhee, a lay preacher, using the name the Martin Brothers, composed and recorded "The Marion Massacre"/"North Carolina Textile Strike" for Paramount in 1929. They had no political agenda but used the strike to create event songs to sell records, a common strategy at the time.

Just as the textile workers' strikes failed, so too did those in the coal fields of Kentucky. The Harlan County strike had been crushed by early 1932, but strikes had broken out in Bell and Knox Counties, partly led by the NMU until its collapse in 1933. Harry Simms (aka Harry Hirsch), an NMU organizer in Brush Creek, Bell County, was shot by a deputy sheriff on February 10, 1932. Jim Garland, Aunt Molly's half brother, spoke at his fellow organizer's funeral in New York and soon composed "The Ballad of Harry Simms." Garland had temporarily fled Kentucky, fearing he would be arrested and perhaps even killed. He soon returned but permanently moved to New York in 1935. As for the miners, following the passage of the National Industrial Recovery Act (NIRA) in June 1933, including section 7(a) guaranteeing union representation, the UMW and the coal operators signed an agreement recognizing the union. Despite such apparent success, labor conflicts continued for many years.

Miners' struggles and violence erupted elsewhere, also producing songs. In Davidson-Wilder, Tennessee, for example, strike activity in early 1933 led to the murder of strike leader Barney Graham. His daughter, Della Mae, composed "The Ballad of Barney Graham." Ed Davis wrote "The Wilder Blues," while Tom Lowery, in the neighboring town of Davidson, turned out "Little David Blues." Although the songs from Kentucky and Tennessee did not circulate widely, a few appeared in the *Red Song Book*, issued by the Workers Library Publishers in 1932 (in connection with the Workers Music League). It included not only Aunt Molly's "Poor Miner's Farewell" and Ella May Wiggins's "I.L.D. Song," referring to the International Labor Defense, the Communist Party's legal arm involved in Gastonia, but also "Miner's Song" and "Miner's Flux." They joined the older "Hold the Fort," "The Preacher and the Slave," and the Communist anthem "The Internationale." Margaret Larkin welcomed the appearance of the *Red Song Book*, since a "workers' song book is always a cause for rejoicing, and this one is particularly valuable." She was pleased by the "half dozen songs that have arisen from mass struggle.... These songs stem from native American folk song tradition, both musically and poetically. They are a direct and vigorous expression of the revolutionary spirit of large masses of American workers." Despite her enthusiasm, the songs reached only a few people. Labor songs increased in popularity later in the decade, however, as political and union activism escalated.[11]

Communist Party

Communist Party (CP) members composed and published songs to help foment class rebellion, but with little initial success because of the songs' early modernist structures. The brief 1932 *Song Book for Workers*, issued by the Red Star Publicity Service, included only eleven songs, such as the stilted "Comintern" and "Stand Guard, the Soviets Are Calling," along with Joe Hill's popular "The Preacher and the Slave." In June 1931, a group of activist composers, led by Charles Seeger, Henry Cowell, and Lan Adomian, formed the Workers Music League (WML), a branch of the CP's Workers Cultural Federation. They were inspired by a Federation of Workers Choruses concert that featured seven language groups, representing the party's dominant ethnic membership in New York: Yiddish, Ukrainian, Hungarian, English, Lithuanian, Yugoslav, and Finnish. The Communist Party's membership had originally included a large segment of foreign language groups, predominantly from eastern Europe, each with its own chorus or orchestra. In an attempt to Americanize the membership, the party leadership had officially dissolved these federations in 1925, but they did not disappear.[12]

The CP had struggled through the 1920s, reaching a membership of perhaps 24,000 by decade's end. This was known as the party's Third Period, beginning in 1928 (and lasting to 1935), when the leaders in Moscow ordered that there would be no collaboration with other left-wing organizations. This led to the organization of separate labor unions, such as the NMU and the broader Trade Union Unity League, an unsuccessful rival to the AFL. While the party continued to attract new members, such as writers and composers, its overall membership shrunk to around 6,000 by 1932 because of internal disaffections and external pressures from federal and local governments. With the outbreak of the Depression, the party began organizing the unemployed, while supporting civil rights and a socialist economy.

The WML was affiliated with the Workers Musicians Club in New York, which became the Pierre Degeyter Club, named after the French composer of "The Internationale" who died in 1932. Moreover, a group of composers affiliated with the CP, including Charles Seeger, Marc Blitzstein, Henry Cowell, Aaron Copland, and Elie Siegmeister, formed the Composers' Collective in early 1932, also affiliated with the Degeyter Club. Some had studied in Europe, for example, Blitzstein with Nadia Boulanger and Arnold

Schoenberg, as well as Copland. They were highly influenced by European modernist composers, such as the German Communist Hanns Eisler, in their rather futile search for a musical connection to the laboring masses. Their radical lyrics and compositional complexities, however, with no connection to American folk, popular, or religious music, could hardly find a mass audience. For example, Charles Seeger, soon a champion of native folk music, wrote,

> We are fighting with a host of foes, we do not fear guns or cannon.
> Fascist promises cannot fool us, we will fight them to a finish.

This was hardly designed as a popular sing-along.[13]

The *Red Song Book*, with its inclusion of folk-styled songs that broke with the organization's general (elitist) idea of proletarian music, was one of the WML's earliest accomplishments, along with the first issue of its short-lived periodical the *Worker Musician* in December 1932. "The Freiheit Gezangfarein of New York is greeting the appearance of the 'Worker Musician,' a magazine long overdue, to cover the field of proletarian song and proletarian music in service of the revolutionary workers under the leadership of the Communist Party and to bring closer contact between all our choruses, bands, orchestras, etc.," ran a letter from the Yiddish-language organization. The issue included Hanns Eisler's "Red Front," with English texts by Margaret Larkin, along with Nathan Nevins's generally favorable review of the *Red Song Book*. Nevins did feel, however, that "the songs of the Kentucky miners . . . are immature. It is interesting to note, however, the low musical level, the result of an arrested development, caused by the exploitation by the coal barons." Nevins reflected the group's essentially European, classical orientation, which gave only modest recognition to the compositions of southern rural songwriters such as Aunt Molly Jackson, although this lukewarm assessment soon changed.[14]

A small Communist Party–related songbook, *Songs of Struggle*, in both English and Yiddish, included the required "Solidarity Forever" and "Hold the Fort," along with "Red Flag," "The Army of Hunger Is Marching," and "The Scarlet Banner," the latter designed for choruses. A later, and also bilingual edition, added the more folk-oriented "On the Picket Line" and "The Preacher and the Slave," as well as "Scottsboro" by Siegmeister, which referred to the ILD's defense of nine young black men accused of raping two white women in Alabama in March 1931 (they were all convicted). It also contained the "Soup Song," written by Maurice Sugar, a radical labor lawyer in Detroit, and sung to the popular tune of "My Bonnie Lies over the Ocean":

> I'm spending my nights at the flophouse,
> I'm spending my days on the street,
> I'm looking for work and I find none,
> I wish I had something to eat.
> [Chorus:]
> Soo-oup, soo-oup,
> They give me a bowl of soo-oup.
> Soo-oup, soo-oup,
> They give me a bowl of soup.

Sugar had composed the song in 1931 during his work with the city's homeless and destitute, and he well captured their trials and tribulations. With its familiar music—which made it easy to remember the words, a common tactic among topical songwriters—and jaunty style, it quickly spread throughout the country among union members and their supporters. The NCDPP, as part of the expanding Communist Party's cultural coalition, had also become involved with the Scottsboro boys' defense. Its benefit on May 15, 1932, at the Rockland Palace in Harlem featured a variety of African American musicians, dancers, and speakers, including Taylor Gordon performing songs collected by Lawrence Gellert.[15]

By the time of Franklin Roosevelt's presidential election in November 1932, during the depths of the Depression, a variety of radical and labor-oriented songs were circulating, promoted by an expanding network of organizations and publications but so far only among a small number of trade unionists and political activists.

Popular Songs

During the 1930s, some popular songs touched on the national economic disaster. They appeared on records and sheet music, as well as on movie soundtracks and in Broadway musicals. While devoid of sectarian politics or overt political messages, these songs conveyed the spirit of the times in commenting on the suffering of the masses. In October 1932, Bing Crosby recorded "Brother, Can You Spare a Dime?" on the Brunswick label. Written by E. Y. "Yip" Harburg, with music by Jay Gorney, and having been part of the Broadway musical *Americana*, which ran for seventy-seven performances, it quickly became one of the decade's theme songs. *Americana* depicted a breadline with Rex Weber singing the theme song that well expressed the bitter feelings of the hordes of the jobless who were desperately trying to survive by selling apples on city street corners. The Warner Brothers' popular musical *Gold Diggers of 1933*, by Al Dubin and Harry Warren, opened with "The Gold Diggers' Song (We're in the Money)," which was quickly recorded by the film's star, Dick Powell, on the Perfect label. While many of the film's songs were just as upbeat, this was not the case with "Remember My Forgotten Man," sung at the film's conclusion by Joan Blondell. It was a spectacular ending, with much sadness, that yet had the theater audiences up and cheering. With vocals by Helen Rowland, backed by Freddy Martin and His Orchestra (which included Jimmy Dorsey on saxophone), the song quickly appeared on the Banner label. The Broadway smash musical *Of Thee I Sing*, opening at the end of 1931, was a satire on modern politics, with some glancing blows at the Depression. For example, "Posterity Is Just around the Corner" was a parody of the declaration attributed to President Herbert Hoover that "prosperity is just around the corner." *Of Thee I Sing* won a Pulitzer Prize for the year's best play.[16]

Several blues and gospel artists used their songwriting talents to comment on the painfully hard times. The gospel singer Washington Phillips recorded "The World Is in a Bad Fix Everywhere" in 1929, but it remained unreleased. J. D. Short's "It's Hard Time" appeared in 1933:

> Now we have a little city, that they call "down in Hooverville,"
> Times have got so hard, people ain't got no place (to live).

Two years earlier, the prolific Charlie Jordan had cut "Starvation Blues," with the line "Starvation is at my door." Also in 1931, the pianist Charlie Spand issued "Hard Time Blues" on the Columbia label:

> Well, the time is so hard, the birds refuse to sing
> And no matter how I try, I can't get a doggone thing

Tampa Red (Hudson Woodbridge) released "Depression Blues" about the same time. While these records likely had modest circulation, the lyrics would certainly have resonated with those who bought and listened to them.[17]

Folk songs, broadly defined, had joined with a smattering of Tin Pan Alley tunes in expressing the sour mood of these difficult times. The country was holding its collective breath as President Hoover's disastrous term neared its end in early 1933, and many Americans hoped and prayed that a new political, economic, and social/cultural era would emerge. Through the remainder of the decade, as conditions seemed to improve, there was a continuing flood of hard-luck songs, including references to President Roosevelt's uplifting government programs. Music, in various forms, continued to define the age.[18]

With Roosevelt's election and his launching of a New Deal for the country, the arts were given an economic, political, and cultural boost. The new administration's numerous arts programs were designed both to create jobs as well as to stimulate artistic expression in a plethora of fields, including art, literature, photography, drama, and music. Topical themes gained in popularity as the general (although highly exaggerated) high life of the previous decade, followed by the gloom and doom of Hoover's administration and the Depression's early years, gave way to an upsurge of confidence and an artistic renaissance. This was all bolstered by the coming era of the common man, when vernacular culture, including music, gained a renewed vigor spurred by the increasing popularity of the Communist and Socialist Parties, as well as the expanding labor unions.

CHAPTER THREE

The Early Roosevelt Years

The New Deal Emerges

In November 1932, at what appeared to be the nadir of the Depression, the country elected Franklin Delano Roosevelt, the governor of New York, as president, although he was not inaugurated until the following March. Meanwhile, in Germany, Adolf Hitler became the country's chancellor on January 30, 1933, appointed by President Paul Hindenburg, followed on March 5 by the Nazi Party's official election to head the government; a year later, Hitler ascended to the office of head of state, the führer. The stage was now set for the disastrous clash of economic, political, and military systems for the following decade and more. Once in office, with a majority Democratic Congress, Roosevelt launched a series of governmental programs that were to transform the country, rejecting the generally laissez-faire economic policies of his predecessor, Herbert Hoover, although significant change did not come overnight. The Democrats had a comfortable lead in Congress, with 311 members (compared to 117 Republicans) and 59 seats in the Senate (with only 36 for the opposition). While southern politicians (mostly conservatives who upheld the South's racial hegemony) had previously had a majority of the Democratic seats, this was no longer true, although they continued to hold significant leverage over the committees because of the powerful seniority system. Indeed, southern Democrats remained an essential part of the New Deal coalition until late in the decade. The president quickly initiated the National Recovery Act (NRA), the Public Works Administration (PWA), the Agricultural Adjustment Administration (AAA), and so much more with the intention to stabilize the economy, create jobs, and establish various federal economic controls. In August 1933, the hillbilly singer Bill Cox recorded "The NRA Blues," on the Conqueror label, a celebration of the New Deal's importance to working people:

> The rich men's all on easy street, sweet thing, sweet thing
> The rich men's all on easy street
> And the poor man can't get enough to eat
> Sweet thing, yes, baby mine
> When you all join the NRA, sweet thing, sweet thing
> When you all join the NRA
> We'll all feel happy and all feel gay
> Sweet thing, yes, baby mine
> I've got the blues, I've got them NRA blues
> Lord, I got them NRA blues

The Western swing band leader Milton Brown wrote and performed on his radio show, but never recorded, "Fall in Line with the NRA." In late 1934, the Allen Brothers, a hillbilly duo, cheered the president in their recording of "The New Deal Blues."

Secretary of the Treasury Henry Morgenthau and Harry Hopkins, heading the Federal Emergency Relief Administration (FERA, which soon became the Civil Works Administration and after 1935 the Works Progress Administration) and the short-lived Federal Public Works of Arts Project (FERA/PWAP), initially led the way in funding the varied arts programs. Indeed, the arts were to be an important component of the New Deal's energies through the decade.[1]

The Roosevelt years also unleashed a plethora of political movements, on the right and left, that challenged the fluctuating status quo in various ways. The latter, in particular, stimulated a labor-union-fueled "cultural front" that had a vital affect on music, theater, literature, dance, art, film, photography, scholarship, and journalism through the decade. For example, the American Artists' Congress Against War and Fascism, formed in early 1936, brought together such avant-garde artists as Stuart Davis, Rockwell Kent, Jose Orozco, and David Siquerios and backed the loyalist side in the Spanish Civil War. Moreover, in 1933, the president had finally recognized the Soviet Union, and while not a close ally during the decade, at least there was a diplomatic relationship while the domestic Communist Party expanded.[2]

John and Alan Lomax

In late May 1933, the sixty-five-year-old John Lomax set out on an expansive collecting trip through the South. His traveling companion and collaborator was his youngest son, Alan, then eighteen and a student at the University of Texas, who had transferred back after a year at Harvard. They first stopped at the Smithers Plantation near Huntsville, Texas, where, using their bulky and often recalcitrant equipment, they recorded black tenant farmers. Believing that older African American folk songs, untainted by modern music, could be found in prisons, on June 10, they stopped at the facility in Huntsville, where they were turned away by the administration. Lawrence Gellert, Howard Odum, and Robert Gordon had all made field recordings of African Americans, but the Lomaxes soon established themselves as the most zealous of such collectors. In July, they did gain entry to the Imperial State Prison Farm at Sugar Land, near Houston, where they recorded the fascinating James "Iron Head" Baker and Mose "Clear Rock" Platt. With financial assistance from the Library of Congress and the arrangement that their recordings would be sent to Washington, D.C., they moved on to Angola State Prison Farm near Baton Rouge, Louisiana, on July 16; they were now equipped with a 315-pound disc-cutting machine, fitted into the back of their car along with two seventy-five-pound batteries. Here they recorded Huddie "Lead Belly" Ledbetter. They followed in August with a visit to the Parchman State Penitentiary in Mississippi. Next arriving in Harlan, Kentucky, the Lomaxes stayed with Harvey Fuson, a collector who had published *Ballads of the Kentucky Highlands* (1931), indicating that they were also interested in white rural performers.[3]

Father and son landed in Washington on August 23, and in mid-September 1933, Herbert Putnam, the librarian of Congress, appointed John to the position of "Honorary Conservator of Our Archive of American Folk Song" for a symbolic one dollar a year, replacing Robert Gordon, whom the library could not afford to pay a full salary. The librarian's letter instructed Lomax to continue with the Library of Congress's recording machine, at his own expense, "to record and collect material in the field and, while in Washington, [to assist] in the response to inquiries involving the Archive itself." During the Lomaxes' stay in the capital, they worked on their expansive collection *American Ballads and Folk Songs*, which was published in 1934. Anxious about establishing their credentials as folklorists, both John and Alan soon compiled articles on their southern collecting. The younger Lomax rushed into print with "'Sinful' Songs of the Southern Negro" in the Winter 1934 issue of the *Southwest Review*. "This past summer I spent traveling through the South with my father collecting the secular songs of the Negroes, work songs, 'barrelhouse' ditties, bad-man ballads, corn songs. Our singers classed all these songs to distinguish them from recorded music and from written-out songs in general, as 'made-up' songs," he began. He found "Clear Rock" the most interesting, but with only a slight mention of Lead Belly.[4]

John Lomax quickly followed with the similarly titled "'Sinful Songs' of the Southern Negro," appearing in the April 1934 issue of the *Musical Quarterly*, edited by Carl Engel, chief of the Music Division of the Library of Congress. Perhaps because this was a more scholarly publication than the *Southwest Review*, and certainly due to John's conservative racial and political views (while Alan had been increasingly turning to the left), he added his own personal reflections: "It is well known that the Negro is fond of singing. He is endowed by nature with a strong sense of rhythm.... Moreover, the Negro in isolation, without books or newspapers, the radio or the telephone, sings for his own amusement, to relieve the tension of his loneliness and that of his companions in misfortune." He singled out "Iron Head" as well as "Clear Rock," with no reference to Lead Belly. This soon changed regarding Lead Belly, but otherwise Lomax clung to such views, certainly common among white folklorists at the time.[5]

Since John's early book of cowboy songs, he had mostly devoted his life to working at the University of Texas and as a banker, but with the onset of the Depression, he eagerly returned to folk song collecting and publishing at his relatively advanced age, always joined and prodded by Alan. They long remained highly influential, despite numerous controversies and difficulties, as folk song scholarship picked up during the decade. Father and son, in various ways, pulled together many of the threads that made up the decade's intricate vernacular music tapestry—the role of the Library of Congress and the government in general, radical politics, field collecting, commercial promotion and publications, and racial complexity, for example—while often they disagreed, particularly regarding politics.

The Lomaxes' *American Ballads and Folk Songs*, published by Macmillan, appeared in October 1934. John had settled into his work at the Library of Congress, while Alan struggled to plan his future. The book's musical selections ranged over the country, similar to Carl Sandburg's *American Songbag*, with no particular focus on hillbilly and race songs from the South. "Although the spread of machine civilization is rapidly making it hard to find folk singers, ballads are yet sung in this country," the editors explained in their introduction. "The cowboy, the miner, the tramp, the lumberjack, the Forty-niner, the soldier, the sailor, the plantation Negro (and also his sophisticated city cousin), the sailor on the Great Lakes, and even the boatman in the early days of the Erie Canal, all have 'made-up' songs describing their experiences or detailing situations religious, tragic, sentimental, humorous, and at times didactic." They drew from commercial records, their own field work, and numerous published collections. The scores of songs were divided into twenty-five categories, beginning with "Working on the Railroad," "The Levee Camp," and "Songs from Southern Chain Gangs" and ending with "White Spirituals" and "Negro Spirituals." They somewhat focused on songs derived from African American sources. "In giving ample space to the songs of the Negro, who has, in our judgment, created the most distinctive of folk songs—the most interesting, the most appealing, and the greatest in quantity—we may have put into too narrow limits songs of other types," they admitted. Whatever the case, and despite various flaws, such as the awkward format and rough documentation, the collection received generally favorable reviews and long remained a standard and influential reference.[6]

John was mostly responsible for *American Ballads and Folk Songs*, while the teenage Alan struggled with his identity. Both kept active through 1933 and 1934, with John spending little time at the Library of Congress. They continued their southern collecting trips, traveling around Texas in early 1934 searching for Hispanic materials and in June moving to southern Louisiana, while John kept up a busy schedule of speeches. In July, John, a widower, married Ruby Terrill, the dean of women at the University of Texas, who soon joined him on his collecting trips. That month, Engel resigned from his post at the Library of Congress, to be replaced by his assistant, W. Oliver Strunk, while Lomax's rather tenuous position there continued. Also in July, John and Alan returned to Angola State Prison Farm in Louisiana and again recorded Lead Belly. Grants from the Carnegie Corporation and one much smaller from the Rockefeller Foundation allowed John Lomax to continue his collecting trips, since he received no salary from the government.[7]

An off-and-on-again student at the University of Texas, Alan kept up a steady stream of letters to his father. "I think now that, unless I go red, I should like to look at the folk-songs of the country along with you and do some research in that field from the point of view of sociology and anthropology," he wrote at one point. "You and I are peculiarly well fitted for a partnership in this task it seems to me." The "red" reference referred to his flirting with radical politics while at Harvard, which became a lifetime commitment and which continually antagonized his father, but otherwise they worked remarkably well together. In May 1931, Alan had been arrested at a small rally at the Boston office of the U.S. Immigration Bureau for protesting the deportation of the labor organizer Edith Berkman. For his troubles, Alan paid a small fine and served no jail time, but the incident long remained in his FBI file. At another time, he explained to his father, "I am not ready as yet to lay down my very comfortable living and hurt my very kind father by giving myself openly and wholeheartedly to the cause of the proletariat. Neither are you desirous of gently shoving [me] out the door and telling me to seek my own path in the best way I devise." Therefore, Alan promised to be politically cautious. "It is a pity we quarrel sometime," he concluded. "We are too much alike, I suppose, to avoid that." They continued in this fashion, father and son in somewhat tenuous friendship, until John's death in 1948. Through the fall of 1934, Alan's nagging health problems found him living with his sister Shirley and her doctor husband, Chris Mansell, in Lubbock, Texas. There he learned to read music, play the guitar, and study French, while keeping up his correspondence with Carl Sandburg and others.[8]

One of the Lomaxes most important musical discoveries was Lead Belly. Born in Mooringsport, Louisiana, in 1888, Lead Belly had long lived a troubled life as a gifted musician with a violent streak that often led to various incarcerations. A deadly assault charge in 1930 resulted in his most recent sentence of six to ten years at Angola. He was released from prison in early August 1934, having served his time, which had been reduced by the Board of Pardons. In September, he joined John Lomax and became his driver as they traveled through the South on a collecting trip. They stopped at the Cummins Prison Farm in Arkansas as well as in New Orleans. While still in Lubbock, Alan ended a letter to his father, "My best love to you and my regards to Lead Belly. All the luck in the world fall on your nice bald head." In November, Alan had recuperated enough to join his father and Lead Belly for more collecting before the three arrived in Philadelphia for the yearly meeting of the Modern Language Association (MLA), where Lead Belly performed. Then they moved on to New York City. There Lead Belly caused a mostly positive sensation, while generating such insulting headlines in the local press as "Sweet Singer of the Swamplands Here to Do Few Tunes between Homicides" along with *Time* magazine's article on the "Murderous Minstrel." In March 1935, John hosted Lead Belly's appearance at Harvard, where they were honored by Professor George Lyman Kittredge, who had first met John as a student early in the century. Friction between John and Lead Belly soon led to their parting company, however, with the latter desiring greater control over his life, although the Lomaxes had already signed a contract with Macmillan for a book based on his life. Alan recorded many of Lead Belly's songs, along with information on their origins and much of his autobiography, which appeared as *Negro Folk Songs as Sung by Lead Belly* in late 1936. A number of his songs became folk standards, such as "Goodnight, Irene," about life's difficulties:

> Irene, good night, Irene, good night,
> Good night, Irene, good night, Irene.
> I'll kiss you in my dreams

And there was "Pick a Bale of Cotton," about the hardships of plantation labor:

> Jump down, turn aroun', pick a bale o' cotton,
> Jump down, turn aroun', pick a bale a day.
> Oh, Julie, pick a bale o' cotton,
> Oh, Julie, pick a bale a day.

The Lomaxes and Lead Belly had by now mostly gone their separate ways. Each continued to make his distinctive, long-lasting mark on the folk music world. Lead Belly soon joined the expanding and creative left-wing folk community in New York of which Alan was a part, although they did not remain close.[9]

Communist Party

Left-wing composers continued their challenge to organize and motivate the proletariat, with scant results. The Workers Music League (WML) struggled through the worst years of the Depression, led by classical musicians and composers such as Charles Seeger (using the pen name Carl Sands), Elie Siegmeister (as L. E. Swift), and Aaron Copland. The organization published the first *Workers Song Book* in 1934. "In this volume, with the exception of the Internationale, is presented the first collection exclusively of original revolutionary mass, choral and solo songs with English texts to be made in America," ran the foreword. "With four exceptions the songs were all composed in 1933 as part of the work of the Collective—a group in which conservative and radical musical thought and taste meet in free and vigorous clash upon the question of the definition of a musical style 'national in form, proletarian in content.'" Still under the thrall of the European modernist style, with no connection to familiar folk, religious, or popular tunes, such songs as Sands's "Mount the Barricades" and Swift's "The Scottsboro Boys Shall Not Die" were hardly designed to appeal to a mass audience:

> Mount the barricades!
> Mount the barricades
> For the workers' cause,
> Carry on the fight for freedom,
> Carry on the fight for freedom,
> Carry on the fight for freedom.

The organization's earlier *Red Song Book* had included such folk-style songs as "Hold the Fort" and "On the Picket Line," demonstrating that the members of the WML had some musical flexibility. They soon abandoned their essentially classical/modernist approach, however. The Communist Party had not yet signed on as a member of the president's broad coalition with the formation of the party's Popular Front by middecade, but it was moving in that direction as the New Deal attempted to combat the withering effects of the economic disaster.[10]

As music critic for the *Daily Worker*, Charles Seeger continued his modernist approach for a few years. Welcoming the coming of the Workers' Music Olympiad, held on May 21, 1933, at the City College of New York, Seeger called for "songs [that] should arouse and maintain the will to victory" as well as "have emotional 'drive' and 'life' and be optimistic, not morbid." The Olympiad included a "Children's Concert" and piano and violin musicians performing classical selections, capped by the evening's Workers Music League's choral competition (Finnish, Italian, Ukrainian, Lithuanian, Yugoslav, and American). The Daily Worker Chorus performed Seeger's "Song of the Builders" and Jacob Schaeffer's "Lenin—Our Leader" and "Strife Song." The Olympiad was part of the Communist Party's International Music Buro, organized in Moscow in early 1932. Moscow's First International Music Conference was held the following November; the WML's Lan Adomian and Jacob Schaefer served on the Buro's staff, along with the influential German composer Hanns Eisler. While the Buro stressed the stilted modernist compositions, with no interest in folk songs, in a *Daily Worker* article in early 1934, Adomian suggested that workers' choruses should include "Negro songs of protest, work songs, railroad songs, cowboy and hill songs."[11]

While composers linked to the Communist Party had so far refrained from directly mentioning the Roosevelt presidency and New Deal programs, various blues performers were not so hesitant. In July 1933, Lucille Bogan recorded "Red Cross Man" in New York City, referring to government stores supplying food in Birmingham, Alabama. Others recorded the similar "Red Cross Blues," including Walter Roland and Sonny Scott. The next year, the Houston blues singer Joe Pullum sang "CWA Blues," referring to the Civil Works Administration:

> I was hungry and broke, because I wasn't drawing my pay,
> But in stepped President Roosevelt, Lord, with his mighty CWA.

In July 1934, Roland performed the similar "CWA Blues." By middecade, despite the continuing Depression in the record industry, other blues-tinged, pro–New Deal discs appeared, such as Walter Vinson's "I Can't Go Wrong" in 1935, referring to the NRA, which had ended in May.[12]

Commercial and Vernacular Music

As the decade advanced, folk music included a plethora of grassroots performers throughout the country as well as such commercial musicians as John Jacob Niles. Born in Louisville, Kentucky, in 1892, the young Niles was influenced by the local jug bands and vaudeville performers, as well as the minstrel acts still popular by century's end. When he was ten, the family moved to rural Jefferson County, although he attended high school in Louisville. While in high school, he began collecting folk songs from his family and on trips with his father, including an early version of "Go Way from My Window," to which he added his own verses. This long remained his style, conflating original and composed lyrics. He served in the army during World War I and took voice lessons after his return to civilian life. He then moved to New York, where he mostly developed a writing career. In 1927, *Scribner's* published "Hillbillies," his story about music and moonshining in the southern Appalachian Mountains. He worked closely with Carl Engel, who was serving as president of G. Schirmer while also chief of the Library of Congress Music Division and the editor of the *Musical Quarterly*. He began to publish song collections, starting with *Impressions of a Negro Camp Meeting* in 1925 from the publisher Carl Fisher, followed by a series from Schirmer: *Seven Kentucky Mountain Songs* (1929), *Seven Negro Exaltations* (1929), *Songs of the Hill Folk* (1934), and *More Songs of the Hill Folk* (1936). In 1929, Niles also launched his concert career with Marion Kerby, performing folk and traditional music.[13]

Niles and Kerby were a unique team, both collecting and performing southern vernacular songs. Lorraine Wyman and Howard Brockman had earlier tried something similar, but Niles and Kerby hit the big time, appearing at the Barbizon Hotel in New York in early 1930 and then in London and through 1931 traveling around the country and back and forth to Europe until their act broke up in July 1933. Meanwhile, Niles arranged with the photographer Doris Ulmann a collecting trip in the South, including a visit with Jean Bell Thomas, a collector, promoter, and organizer of the American Folk Song Festival in Ashland, Kentucky, launched in 1930. During the following year's southern excursion, Niles and Ulmann visited with Olive Dame Campbell at her folk school in Brasstown, North Carolina. Moreover, in New York in late 1933, Niles had begun a solo career, which he continued for many decades, including a performance at the White House for the Roosevelts in March 1935. A few months later, Niles and Ulmann were traveling through Kentucky, but he had no interest in the miners' protest songs that were then circulating. "The idea that the Miners have made over the ballads and written in words about oppressive Mine operators is bunk I believe," he wrote. His interest in traditional white and black folk songs, although often modified by his creative editorial hand, long guided his musical life. Niles represented a somewhat traditional approach to vernacular songs, which remained influential through his numerous books and recordings until his death in 1980.[14]

While Niles was deftly popularizing southern folk songs, there was a range of other commercial outlets and products that filled the musical marketplace. Along with phonograph records, there were numerous radio shows featuring country music that had begun appearing in the 1920s, particularly the *WLS Barn Dance* in Chicago and the *Grand Ole Opry* out of Nashville, soon followed by the *Iowa Barn Dance Frolic*, the *Boone County Jamboree* from WLW in Cincinnati, the *Crazy Barn Dance* in Charlotte, WWVA's *Wheeling Jamboree* in West Virginia, and myriad others. They featured live acts and personal appearances, spreading throughout the country a variety of rural sounds that continued for decades. These programs shied away from any overt political statements, while emphasizing the nationalistic (and therefore apparently conservative) substance of grassroots (particularly white) music.

The marketplace had long overlapped with homegrown music through the publication of song folios, along with sheet music and songbooks, which covered a range of folk and country songs, spanning the country, often designed for personal entertainment. Pianos were ubiquitous in many homes, along with guitars, banjos, and even fiddles. For instance, the 1931 folio *Log Cabin Songs by Johnny Crockett*, featuring a photo of the Crockett Kentucky Mountaineers hillbilly band on the cover, included "I Was Born 10,000 Years Ago," "Drunkard's Dream," "Sweet Betsy from Pike," and "Black-Eyed Susie." The year before *Carson J. Robison's World's Greatest Collection of Mountain Ballads and Old Time Songs* appeared. A popular musician who recorded with Vernon Dalhart and Frank Luther in New York, Robison's songbook included "Dying Cowboy," "Hallelujah I'm a Bum," "Letter Edged in Black, and "She'll Be Comin' 'Round the Mountain." *Play and Sing: America's Greatest Collection of Old Time Songs and Mountain Ballads* (1930) featured "Barbara Allen," "Golden Slippers," "Death of John Henry," "That Big Rock Candy Mountain," and "Frankie and Johnny," demonstrating the wide range of country-style tunes, including Tin Pan Alley compositions.[15]

Walter Peterson, known as the "Kentucky Wonder Bean," was featured on the cover of *Sensational Collection of Mountain Ballads and Old Time Songs* (1931), with "Camptown Races," "The Dying Hobo," and "I Am a Jolly Railroad Man." The next year brought *Elmore Vincent's Lumber Jack Songs*, with "Down in That Lonesome Valley," "The Lumberjack and the Pretty Girl," and "Canaday-I-O." Frankie and Johnny Marvin, a popular New York recording duo, issued *Folio of Down Home Songs* (1932) with mostly their own compositions, such as "Go Along Bum," "I'm Ridin' the Blinds," and "I'm Just a Gambler." De Sylva, Brown & Henderson published *Salty Tunes: A Collection of Sea Chanties and Rollicking Sailor Songs* (1932), featuring "Blow the Man Down," "Sam Hall," "Shenandoah," and even the popular "Abdul-A-Bul-Bul Ameer." Bob Miller, the influential hillbilly publisher and songwriter, issued a range of folios, including *Bob Miller's Famous Hill-Billy Heart Throbs* (1934), full of his own compositions. Into the depths of the Depression, radio stations, large and small, promoted their own folios, as did WNAX in Yankton, South Dakota, which issued *Tiny Texas: World's Greatest Collection of Cowboy and Mountain Ballads* (1933, published by the prolific M. M. Cole in Chicago). It included such standards as "Hallelujah I'm a Bum," "Birmingham Jail," "When the Work's All Done This Fall," and "I Wish I Was Single Again." Moreover, numerous folios from the Carter Family and Jimmie Rodgers appeared for many years. Folk songs, in various forms and formats, from numerous popular sources, easily spread through the country as the Depression deepened.[16]

In contrast to John Jacob Niles's high-toned styling of southern roots music—his training as an opera singer can be compared to that of the prolific Vernon Dalhart—most of the commercial interest in vernacular music came from its more rustic-sounding presentations. Folk festivals spread through the decade, presenting various venues for a variety of regional, ethnic, and historical styles, although mostly focused on the South. Jean Bell Thomas's American Folk Song Festival joined Bascom Lamar Lunsford's older Asheville Mountain Dance and Folk Festival in promoting and encouraging regional vernacular music. Festivals would often expand their roster of performers beyond those who had made records or appeared on radio, giving amateurs a chance to gain some public attention while highlighting much of the current state of folk culture. Lunsford ruled the Asheville festival with an iron hand, inviting only "authentic" ballad singers, string bands, and a variety of dancing styles. Thomas, born in Ashland in 1881 and with a background as a script girl in Hollywood, returned to her southern roots in the early 1920s and resumed collecting folk songs. Her festivals featured mountain dancers, singers, and pickers. She aptly characterized one act in 1933 as follows: "The Sloane sisters, Bessie, Ada, and Nannie, from Rowan County, wearing the simple gingham frocks they had worn in the little schoolhouse in Rowan County where I had discovered them, held the audience spellbound with the plaintive sweetness of their ancient ballads, and with their skilled, though untrained, accompaniment on the guitar and banjo." The next year, she presented "warning and wassail songs, frolic and lonesome tunes, sea chanteys, gay ditties, playgame songs and answering back ballads to the muted strains of homemade banjos whittled from white oak with sounding head of coon hide, gourd banjos, and corn shock fiddles." She preferred a seemingly primitive styling and musical presentation. "After that I made more expeditions into the level land with groups of my mountain minstrels, and these expeditions began to bring level-landers into our Southern Highlands," Thomas later wrote. "The country was going wild on ballad hunting." She even invited Marion Kerby, Niles's former partner, to gather folk songs in the Kentucky mountains, launching her own folk career.[17]

Annabel Morris Buchanan, born in Texas with a classical music background, initiated the White Top Festival in southwest Virginia in 1931. About 100 old-time performers, mostly from Virginia and all white, initially competed for awards for the fiddle, harmonica, dulcimer, banjo, ballad singing, group instrumental, clog dancing, and highland fling (but no guitar). The next year, the now two-day event, with 4,000 in the audience, welcomed the seventy-five performers. When Eleanor Roosevelt, wife of the president, attended in 1933, the roads had to be widened to accommodate the 12,000 visitors. In 1934, the 200 musicians had expanded to include Sailor Dad Hunt, an old salt who now lived in the Virginia mountains and possessed a wealth of sea shanties. An accompanying academic conference included the folk song and ballads collectors Robert Gordon, Mellinger Henry, George Pullen Jackson, and Arthur P. Hudson. "The significance of the festival was manifold," Jackson wrote in *Musical America*. "It was apparent that the deep love of singing, playing and dancing was not restricted by either the age or the sex of those who took part. . . . And a definite denial was given by the White Top experience to cynical and unwarranted doubts as to the innate musicality of the Anglo-Celtic racial composite in America." A few years later, Buchanan explained that the White Top Festival did not encourage recent compositions, since "most of these, with the 'chain-gang' song, the 'hill-billy' tunes and slapstick comedy productions, are actually degrading. Humor is welcomed to the festival. . . . Vulgarity is barred. The folk festival is not concerned with products of the streets, nor of the penitentiaries, nor of the gutter . . . but in the presentation of America's finest native material, whether from mountains or lowlands, city or country." Perhaps this was true for many people, but others had a more comprehensive view of the country's folk culture and history, including John and Alan Lomax.[18]

Breaking with the traditions of the Asheville, Ashland, and White Top festivals, Sarah Gertrude Knott, who grew up in western Kentucky and with a drama background, began the National Folk Festival in 1934 in St. Louis. With an inventive, eclectic approach, she made a concerted effort to reach out to include George Pullen Jackson, Jean Thomas, Bascom Lamar Lunsford, and Annabel Morris Buchanan as advisers and participants but also the New England collector Helen Hartness Flanders, the folklorists Benjamin Botkin and George Lyman Kittredge, the African American scholars/writers Zora Neale Hurston, Charles Johnson, and James Weldon Johnson, as well as Arthur Campa, an expert on Spanish culture in the Southwest. She expanded beyond the regional audiences and performers that dominated the southern festivals, although to keep up with the musical times, she attended the Asheville festival in 1933 and the White Top festival the following year. "We couldn't have gotten a National Folk Festival started without Bascom," she explained. "He was the greatest possible influence in helping us to show what the folk festival was to be like."[19]

Despite Knott's reliance on the (white) southern festival promoters, she created an event that was musically inventive and inclusive. Her St. Louis program featured numerous musicians from the Ozarks, Kiowa Indian musicians and dancers, George Pullen Jackson's Old Harp Singers, singers and dancers from Asheville, French Americans from Genevieve, Missouri, Captain Dick Maitland and retired seamen from Sailor's Snug Harbor on Staten Island, plus cowboy singers and lumberjacks from Michigan. There was seemingly something for everyone. While the festival lost several thousand dollars, Knott was not discouraged and the next year moved to Chattanooga, Tennessee, and in following years to Dallas and Chicago. "Thus, with entertainment which had the roots far back in the folklore of other nations, the festivals in America brought home to the spectators the sense of interdependence between nations which makes toward mutual tolerance and understanding," she explained in the *Christian Science Monitor*. The Chattanooga festival, in May 1935, included some of the same performers from St. Louis but also anthracite coal miners from Pennsylvania. Having read George Korson's *Songs and Ballads of the Anthracite Miners*, she invited him to give a talk. Korson was so stimulated that he organized the first Pennsylvania Folk Festival in Allentown, held two weeks before he left for Chattanooga. Korson brought together Moravian Church music, spirituals from the chorus of the Federated Colored Catholics in Philadelphia, Indian folklore, and, naturally, anthracite miners' ballads and stories. While the festival lasted only until 1938, this was a far cry from the antiquated approach of the southern mountain festivals, and it joined the National Folk Festivals in capturing the country's culturally complex past and present as the New Deal developed. The folk festivals mostly bypassed the professional performers in allowing for a variety of amateur musicians and dancers to appear in public.[20]

By middecade, folk music appeared in various guises and commercial formats, while the record industry remained in the doldrums. The proliferating New Deal programs had begun to improve the plight of the unemployed, however, including those in the arts. This situation continued to improve. In particular, John and Alan Lomax, through their books and field recordings, had sparked the work of folklorists, who were increasingly dependent on government funding, in documenting vernacular music. Left-wing composers and performers, with a collection of labor songs, were becoming a vital part of this dynamic mix. Folk music and musicians, including recordings, folk festivals, songbooks, and folios, increasingly served a role in the decade's deepening cultural, economic, political, and social movements.

CHAPTER FOUR

Heart of the Depression

As the New Deal quickened in 1935, the federal government increasingly emphasized job creation along with the promotion of the arts through the Federal Theatre Project, the Federal Music Project (FMP), and the Federal Writers' Project, among others—all part of Federal Project Number One, known as Federal One, under the Works Progress Administration (WPA). In these and other governmental endeavors, such as the mid-1935 Wagner Act, which established the National Labor Relations Board that protected the rights of workers to collective bargaining through their burgeoning unions, the role of the "common man" remained central. Folk music's collectors, musicians, and promoters flourished in this multiracial environment, somewhat connected to the expansion of the Communist Party. There were now broader ideas of citizenship and patriotism, with more of a grassroots, all-inclusive focus. In this heady atmosphere, John and Alan Lomax played an increasingly influential role.[1]

Alan Lomax

Alan Lomax, working closely with his father, had been devoting his folk song collecting and publishing to southern white and African American performers, and he partially continued in this vein during the summer of 1935. In early June he launched a collecting trip with Mary Elizabeth Barnicle, a politically activist professor of English at New York University who had been a champion of Lead Belly when he first arrived in the city. They were joined by her friend the African American folklorist and writer Zora Neale Hurston. Lomax had been highly impressed by Hurston's ethnographic experiences as related in her essay "Hoodoo in New Orleans." The three met up in Brunswick, Georgia, with the twenty-year-old Lomax traveling with two women twice his age. Relying on Hurston's expertise, they began collecting in the black communities they visited, with Lomax informing his father that the "songs fall into the following categories: Spirituals, ring shouts, children's game songs, work songs—which are hereabouts called shanteys—children's hollers, chain gang songs, and a raft of primitive blues and rag-time songs picked on the guitar." Along with his traveling companions, Lomax had eclectic musical tastes.[2]

The trio moved on to Eatonville, Florida, Hurston's hometown, where she was familiar with the local culture. "Miss Barnicle, Zora and I make a reasonable happy combination although at times I have to act as a buffer between the two ladies," Lomax explained to his family. "But Zora is worth a lot to both of us, since she can really tell us and really does tell us about the people we come in contact with." Collecting in Florida proved most successful, including "seventy-five double-faced records consisting of the following types of recordings: Spirituals, chanteys, ring-shouts, folk-tales, jumping dances, work songs, ballads, guitar picking, minstrel songs, praying, sermons," all destined for the Library of Congress, a partial sponsor of the trip. But the trio parted company in Miami because of friction between Barnicle and Hurston, with the latter refusing to continue on to the Bahamas. "I finally decided that it was no use trying to hold the expedition together," Lomax informed his father from Nassau on July 15, "& that Miss B[arnicle] was the best bet in the long run. It was at her insistence & on her money that we flew over Miami." He also kept in contact with Oliver Strunk at the Library of Congress, who had lent him the recording machine: "The material here, besides being interesting in itself, will have great importance in the study of the Afro-American music, since it represents a mixture of African & English cultures at a much earlier stage than can now be found anywhere in America." After a busy time in the Bahamas, a stimulating, exotic experience for

Heart of the Depression 57

the young Lomax, he and Barnicle returned to New York in early September.³

Once back in New York, Lomax, continuing as a student at the University of Texas, began planning his future. First he had to organize the records from his recent trip and deposit them at the Library of Congress. He could perhaps then move to Washington, D.C., for a longer period, working with the Library of Congress's large, unruly collection of field recordings. "It seems to me that the most constructive piece of work and the work that would bring in records fastest and keep everyone better satisfied would be the job that one or both of us could do in six months in Washington," he suggested to his father on September 4. He also began working with Barnicle on recording Aunt Molly Jackson's musical autobiography; these discs were deposited as well at the Library of Congress.⁴

While Alan Lomax still had no regular position or source of income, the Roosevelt administration broadened its approach in dealing with the persistent economic depression, which provided him with some new opportunities. Earlier in 1935, the president appointed Harry Hopkins to head the newly created WPA, designed to put people to work building bridges, dams, and roads. During the summer, Hopkins initiated a program called Federal One, which included creating four separate projects to employ writers, visual artists, musicians, and theater workers. While controversial in many circles, the WPA proved most successful in stimulating (at least temporarily) jobs but also in promoting the arts. Through Barnicle, Lomax met her student Herbert Halpert, a recent NYU graduate who was a recreation worker for the WPA. Lomax gave a presentation to a group of local musicians and obtained assurances that he would get some assistance. He was proposing a project that would include "a class in American folk-music under the direction of some such skilled person as [George] Herzog [of Yale University] to teach musicians how to write down folk-music accurately." Overflowing with ideas, he also suggested to his father "a central clearing house for folk-songs in Washington under your [John's] direction to start the inflow and outgo of songs from and to the whole country." Alan planned on rushing off to Washington, since they would "now have the chance to do something really big, something of lasting value in all sorts of ways both to [them]selves, for this country and for folk-songs. The money is crying to be spent."[5]

Lomax followed up with a detailed letter to Francis McFarland, director of music projects for the WPA, on September 12, 1935. He mentioned the Lomax family's music credentials and gave some details on his proposal for a folk music class, which would produce a "group of experts in the transcription of folk music whose services in the study of primitive and folk music would be invaluable." A week later, he wrote to Betty Calhoun, who also worked in the Music Division, with additional details. He concluded, "Folk song is the natural and easy introduction to both poetry and music insofar as the coming generations will become acquainted with our American folk songs. . . . Speaking for myself, as a young person, I have found folk songs not only an open sesame for the hearts of American people, but also an incentive to my interest in the understanding of these people." While the WPA turned down his request, Alan had demonstrated the creative, expansive nature of his onrushing ideas.[6]

It soon became clear that the FMP would have limited interest in promoting folk music. Hopkins had appointed as its national director the classically trained Nikolai Sokoloff, who had no background in folk music. Sokoloff also wished to avoid any taint of radicalism, since the WPA was already under pressure from conservative elements who thought it smacked of left-wing politics. There would be a slight modification of Sokoloff's initial approach, however, particularly in the western states. Hawaiian musical combos were popular in California, while Hispanic music, in the form of *orquestas tipicas*, was featured in Arizona, Texas, and New Mexico. The Santa Anna, California, FMP promoted a cowboy band, the Western Pals, in 1936, and other hillbilly bands performed for schoolchildren in Los Angeles; cowboy bands were also sponsored in Arizona, New Mexico, and Texas. In 1935, the Colorado Project established the Denver Annual Folk Festival, which lasted into the 1940s. Similar to the National Folk Festival, it featured a variety of ethnic groups. The California Folk Music Project (1938–42), under the leadership of Sidney Robertson Cowell, who had worked with Charles Seeger at the Special Skills Division of the Resettlement Administration, amassed an extensive collection of ethnic recordings and photos. The FMP also worked with Jean Thomas and her American Folk Song Festival in Ashland, Kentucky, while Sokoloff appointed Seeger, now a proponent of vernacular music, as his deputy director in late 1937. Still, folk music essentially remained on the FMP's back burner.[7]

Radical Folk

The shifting political and cultural currents coming from the Soviet Union in middecade had a marked influence on left-wing folk music circles in the United States. With the rise of fascism in Germany, Italy, and Spain, the international communist movement turned from attacking capitalism to joining forces with Western democracies in fighting the common enemy. Georgi Dimitrov, the Comintern (Communist International) general secretary, announced at the organization's Seventh World Congress in 1935 that Communist Parties should work with democratic alliances in popular-front, antifascist governments. Moreover, the party began to accept traditional cultures, including folk music, that would hopefully have a socialist content, deftly connecting the past with the present. As Norman Cazden, a member of the Composers' Collective, later reflected regarding the early 1930s, "in New York at the time, we would not have meant [not just] American [vernacular] folk music, certainly of the hinterland of America. New York City was very largely a city of immigrants." Soon enough, however, "there was a feeling that, if the radical movement was ever to command the support of the majority of people in this country, the radical movement had to learn the language of the people." This development fueled the increasing desire by first- and second-generation ethnics, particularly Jewish musicians and folklorists, to connect, through songs and stories, with the country's Anglo-American and African American roots. In countering the country's widespread anti-Semitism, many Jewish cultural workers were eager to demonstrate their patriotism, now increasingly necessary because of the rise of the deadly, antisemitic Third Reich in Germany.[8]

Pete Seeger and Left-Wing Music

"Then in 1935 I discovered folksongs with teeth," Pete Seeger later recalled, capturing this crucial turning point. "I was sixteen years old and met some folklorists who had spent years collecting songs among the poorest of the working people of the country. Irish miners and railroad workers, Negro cotton farmers from the deep south, and among the most musical were the white settlers, 'backwoodsmen,' who had remained in isolated small mountain communities while the tides of 'civilization' flowed around and past them." He continued, "I had never heard any of these songs before, 95 percent of Americans had not heard these songs." Born in 1919, the son of Charles Seeger, one of the most active members of the Composers' Collective, Pete was attending boarding school at Avon Old Farms in Connecticut at the time. As an infant, he had traveled with his parents through the Southeast, where they first heard mountain fiddles and guitars, but folk music was of no interest to the family at the time. As the Depression deepened, he was influenced by his father's left-wing politics, but it was not until 1936, when he accompanied Charles on a trip to visit Bascom Lamar Lunsford at the Ninth Annual Folk Song and Dance Festival in Asheville, that he discovered the five-string banjo and absorbed its hillbilly past. The banjo and folk music now took over his life, accompanied by an ongoing commitment to radical politics. As he later wrote, "I, born in New York City, started learning songs of Kentucky miners, Wisconsin lumberjacks, and Texas farmers. It appears I was just one of the first of thousands, perhaps hundreds of thousands of Americans from the city, who felt the same way." Seeger was soon familiar with the work of the Lomaxes and other folklorists, as well as the vernacular music available through radio programs, folk festivals, song folios, and recordings, joining an expanding market for such music.[9]

Musicians in the communist orbit had somewhat favored folk songs, but this commitment escalated through the remainder of the decade. For example, the Composers' Collective became independent from the Degeyter Club and launched its short-lived journal *Music Vanguard* in early 1935, with Charles Seeger as one of the three editors. As explained by Earl Robinson, another member of the Collective, "if little music written in the Composers' Collective ever genuinely reached the masses, still we honed our talents for the greater work to come." Tellingly, the first of the two *Music Vanguard* issues began with examples from Lawrence Gellert's article "Negro Songs of Protest." Drawing from his own field research, Gellert concluded that "these Songs of Protest collected throughout the length and breadth of the Southland are of inestimable value if they do no more than give the lie once and for all to that mythical Negro, standing hat in hand while the white folks pass; shouting glory to God, dancing to the Blues—supposedly unruffled by the economic stress of these days." Gellert had indeed collected scores of songs and ballads, but whether they actually contained African American protest lyrics is somewhat doubtful. Gellert had been collecting for some years and even worked with W. C. Handy on discovering songs that Handy could adapt for his compositions. He had already published five articles on "Negro songs of protest" in *New Masses* magazine beginning in late 1930, presenting a sampling of such songs. Many songs in his collection were hardly unknown, however, having been previously collected by others and even appearing on commercial records. Gellert's brother Hugo, a prominent illustrator connected with the Communist Party, certainly had an influence in steering him to publish in left-wing magazines, which perhaps influenced the idea of the songs having a protest agenda.[10]

The Degeyter Music Club of New York launched a new journal in 1935, *Music Front*, which featured Anne Livingstone's article "Negro Music" in the second issue in August. "The

Negro in jail or on the construction or chain gang has an infinite number of songs to sing," she explained. "Most of them seem, at a casual hearing, to be an expression of woeful resignation; it is not until we have begun to understand the Negro's long struggle for freedom that we detect the undercurrent of militant revolt which runs through these songs." The article contained various musical examples but with no mention of Gellert's collections. Still, Livingstone's conclusion seemed to come directly from his work: "The Negro cries aloud for his freedom, for the right to exist. Through his songs he calls upon his people to live."[11]

Whether or not Gellert had uncovered a hidden trove of African American protest songs, his collection was warmly received in Communist Party circles eager to prove native radicalism, particularly in the South. In 1936, the American Music League (AML), which had recently replaced the disbanded Workers Music League and was headed by Lan Adomian, Marc Blitzstein, and Elie Siegmeister, published in book form Gellert's *Negro Songs of Protest*, with arrangements by Siegmeister and illustrations by brother Hugo. Gellert explained in his introduction, "These songs, reflecting as they do the contemporary environment—the daily round of life in the Black Belt—aside from their musical and literary worth, are human documents. They embody the living voice of the otherwise inarticulate resentment against injustice—a part of the unrest that is stirring in the South." One example was "Wake Up Boys":

Wake up boys, spit on de rock
Ain' quite day but its fo' o'clock.
Ah wouldn't call you, but jes' has to,
Ah doesn't wan' you but white folks do.

The book was well received among party members as well as by the mainstream press, such as the *New York Times*, seemingly indicating the possibility of a grassroots movement that was also manifest in the more overt southern civil rights and labor-organizing efforts at the time. Three years later, Gellert followed with the sequel compilation *"Me and My Captain,"* now published by the Hours Press (with two more volumes contemplated but never issued).[12]

Vernacular folk songs and ballads were becoming an increasing part of the left's cultural (and political) movement. Still, the Workers Music League's *Workers Song Book No. 2*, appearing in 1935, adhered to the organization's lingering modernist thrust. The editors proclaimed that this edition included "for the first time, two original Negro songs of protest revealing the rising discontent and militancy of the oppressed Negro people"; both songs were arranged by Siegmeister. The bulk of the songs were again penned by Charles Seeger, Siegmeister, and Adomian, along with Aaron Copland's "Into the Streets May First," but they had more of a folk style and origin than did the songs in the first *Workers Song Book*. Wallingford Riegger (under the name J. C. Richards) submitted "The Red Banner," an arrangement of a Mongolian folk song, while Adomian contributed the antilynching "Look Here Georgia!" (words by Don West) and "The Ballad of Harry Simms" (words by Harry Alan Potamkin), about the NMU organizer in Kentucky murdered in 1932:

> It was a Wednesday that Harry Simms was shot,
> And him but still a growing lad the miners loved a lot.
> And he was killed, was Harry Simms, for no dark evil thing
> But only that he thought men should live while laboring.[13]

At the same time, the Rand School Press, originally part of the Socialist Party's New York school (becoming the Tamiment Institute and Library in 1935) published the large *Rebel Song Book*, which featured an eclectic array of songs, mostly older socialist tunes but many in a folk style, such as "Hold the Fort," "On the Picket Line," "Solidarity Forever," "We Shall Not Be Moved," and Joe Hill's "Casey Jones," a rewrite of the older event song that now celebrated the death of a strikebreaker:

> The workers on the S.P. line to strike sent out a call,
> But Casey Jones, the engineer, he wouldn't strike at all.
> His boiler it was leaking, and the drivers on the bum,
> And his engine and its bearings, they were all out of plumb.

The second (and last) issue of the *Music Vanguard* reviewed both the *Workers Song Book No. 2* and the *Rebel Song Book*. "In the publication of this song book the Workers Music League has notably increased the all too meager store of workers' music," the naturally positive reviewer concluded. As for the *Rebel Song Book*, it "contains a good deal of good, and much—not so good. Such unevenness is to be suspected in a volume which draws from hither and yon, from right and left, in the most eclectic manner.... As such it will interest historians of the future, though it expresses no clearly defined political program and makes no new contributions to the art of song-composition." Such a critical review would be expected for a songbook not connected with the *Music Vanguard*'s Communist Party adherents, but it hinted at a musical development that quickly bypassed the *Workers Song Book No. 2*.[14]

By the end of 1935, the future of radical songs seemed to be somewhat at hand, represented by the fall issue of the New Singers' Timely Records three-record album. Recently launched by the insurance salesman Leo Waldman, Timely Records featured the baritone Mordecai Bauman leading a male chorus, with Marc Blitzstein and Hanns Eisler on piano. Bauman had met Eisler through Siegmeister and had accompanied him that summer on a ten-concert tour. The album included three Eisler–Bertholt Brecht compositions ("In Praise of Learning," "United Front," "Forward We've Not Forgotten"), another by Eisler and V. J. Jerome, Maurice Sugar's "The Soup Song," and an English translation of "The Internationale." "It was the Friends of the Workers School which projected the general idea of records which would carry their message of hope and solidarity into the furthest corners of the United States, as well as to other English-speaking countries," A.G. commented in a review in the *Daily Worker*. "These records can play a great role in popularizing working class music through mass organizations, at meetings and mass gatherings." Despite each record's artistic label, the set had slight distribution, a result of Timely's paltry audience, but it was a landmark in Communist Party–connected recordings. At the same time, New Music Quarterly Recordings released Bauman's single of the stylized "The Strange Funeral at Braddock," with words by the *Daily Worker* columnist Michael Gold and music by Siegmeister. "It is a dissonant work about a steel mill worker who fell into a bucket of molten steel and was buried in the hardened metal," Bauman later explained. "Anna Sokolow choreographed a dance based on the poem; I sang it many times."

> Wake up! Wake up! The furnaces are roaring like tigers,
> The flames are flinging themselves at the high roof,
> Wake up! It is ten o'clock, and the next batch of flowing steel
>   is to be poured in your puddling-trough,
> Wake up! Wake up! for a flawed lever is cracking in one of
>   the fiendish cauldrons,
> And now the lever has cracked, and the steel is raging and
>   running like a madman,
> Wake up! Oh, the dream is ended and the steel has
>   swallowed you forever, Jan Clepak![15]

The combination of modernist song stylings and European choruses dominated the AML's festival in May 1936 at New York's Yorkville Casino, indicating the party's rather slow acceptance of vernacular folk music. The lengthy program highlighted the IWO Band, the German Workers Club Chorus, the Italian Workers Chorus, the New Singers conducted by Lan Adomian, the Furriers Joint Council Band, the Ukrainian Workers Chorus, and the Daily Workers Chorus conducted by Siegmeister, as well as Aaron Copland performing three of his piano compositions. The festival's program also advertised Gellert's newly published *Negro Songs of Protest* as well as *America Sings*. According to the notice, the latter contained "Freedom Songs, Songs of the Abolitionists, Farmers' Songs, Union Songs, Anti-War Songs," and more songs of an older folk nature, which were becoming more acceptable in radical circles.

Unison, the AML's short-lived publication (only five sporadic issues appeared from May 1936 to the winter of 1938), covered a variety of the organization's activities. The first issue praised the WPA's musical activities, since "this timid experiment in collectivism (the people subsidizing its entertainers as against the 'minstrel-age' idea of the 'angel' supporting artists) has already accomplished" much. The issue also praised Adomian's New Singers, who appeared in numerous concerts promoting the music of Hanns Eisler and featured a song from Gellert's collection, "Lice in Jail." Gellert's newly published book "has introduced at this late date an entirely new field of folk music. It has convinced the Lomaxes that the songs they collected are 'white man's songs,' sung under the surveillance of guards, foremen, and the 'bossman.'" The next issue, in June, praised the league's festival at the Yorkville Casino, as well as the *America Sings* songbook and another song from Gellert, "Way Down South." The third number, in November, continued to feature the modernist composers, such as Henry Cowell and Lehman Engel, along with another song from Gellert, "Ku Kluck Klan":

> It say in the de Bible how Lawd he make man, but who in de Hell make Ku Kluck Klan?
> Shaped like a tad-pole, smell like a skunk, hide in midnight sheet like chintz in a bunk.

The fourth issue, dated summer 1937, continued to feature bands and choruses, including the Manhattan Chorus, "one of the first workers' singing groups in New York to devote itself to the performance of American music." The chorus had just recorded an album of folk-style union songs for the Timely company. The magazine continued to cling to its classical and band agenda, but by now such a commitment had generally faded from the activist music scene.[16]

Ray and Lida Auville's *Songs of the American Worker*, published in Cleveland by the John Reed Club in 1934, had been an earlier indication of some Communist Party members trending toward folk music. Southerners who had moved to Cleveland and into the party's orbit, the Auvilles had composed twelve songs in a folk style, including "The Ghost of the Depression," "Painting the Old Town Red," and "The Miner's Son." Mike Gold in the *Daily Worker* praised their collection: "One has this folk-feeling or one hasn't. Joe Hill had it, and the Auvilles have it." Charles Seeger and Elie Siegmeister also welcomed the collection, although they found the songs of limited musical appeal. They had little popular reach and quickly vanished but did indicate a trend toward folk stylings that Gold was one of the first to champion.[17]

The Lomaxes

As the political and cultural landscape was rapidly changing in 1936 with the expansion of left-wing cultural circles and labor union activism, centered in New York and Washington, D.C., Alan Lomax, who was certainly sympathetic to these developments, had become distracted and temporarily far from the action. Having lost the WPA grant, he decided to move on, although as he informed his father, "I and a few of my admirers will always know that they made the mistake of their lives when they lost me, but that is no concern of mine—their loss. I am too glad to come back to Texas and read and study." And he added, always with much praise for his father, "I realize (after two years) that you know a Hell of a lot more about collecting folk songs than I do. Your records stand out far above mine in quality of material performance—if not in recording technique." Alan graduated from the University of Texas in May 1936, with a BA in philosophy, then considered attending graduate school at the University of Chicago to study anthropology. He also took a side trip to Trinity, Texas, to record R. H. Harris and the Soul Stirrers, a popular gospel group, which went on to have a stellar career as performing and recording artists. With slight prospects and no money for graduate school, he decided to study Spanish in Saltillo, Mexico, where he stayed for a while.[18]

In the fall, Lomax returned to the Archive of American Folk Song to work for his father and in late November began receiving a salary as the first special and temporary assistant. He chose not to return to the South for a collecting trip, as might be expected, but rather to visit Haiti, an exotic, poor, and difficult country for foreigner visitors. Lomax would add "to the Library's collection of recorded folk music," Oliver Strunk, chief of the Library of Congress's Music Division, informed the

Haitian minister in Washington, and he would be associated with Zora Neale Hurston. Lomax arrived in Haiti in December and quickly married Elizabeth Harold Goodman, whom he had met in Texas. They stayed until late April 1937, Lomax having collected a vast amount of musical material. Upon returning to Washington, he plunged into the work of the archives, where he remained for some years.[19]

With Alan Lomax off on his own ventures through part of 1937, John Lomax remained busy with his field projects, accompanied by legal issues with Lead Belly. On January 5, 1935, Lead Belly had signed a contract giving John 50 percent of his earnings. A few weeks later, Lead Belly cut his first commercial recordings for ARC, ten songs including "Roberta," "Packin' Trunk Blues," and "New Black Snake Moan." Two sessions quickly followed, for a total of thirty sides, although many were not issued; subsequent ARC sessions into March also remained on the shelves, while at the time, Lead Belly also recorded privately for the Lomaxes in Wilton, Connecticut, where he and his wife, Martha, were staying. ARC had originally paid $250 to John Lomax for an advance on sales, but Lead Belly only received one-third of that sum; and two records were issued within a month, but they sold poorly. Lead Belly continued to travel with John until late March, when Huddie and Martha moved to Shreveport, Louisiana, and from there to Dallas. For a while, he was working in a gas station, but he soon returned to New York. Moreover, he began suing Lomax over the record contract and other financial matters, which worried George Brent at Macmillan, who thought that this legal hassle would hold up publication of *Negro Folk Songs as Sung by Lead Belly*. The book did appear the next year, and a legal settlement was finally reached.[20]

"Every so often one can find a note of mild protest in a few of the Negro blues records which are tucked away in the 'race' catalogs of the Vocalion, Melotone-Perfect, Bluebird, Decca and Champion companies," Henry Johnson explained in *New Masses* in early 1936. "But in general the studio supervisors are careful to see that the blues sound a note of defeat and futility, for it is middle-class whites and large chain stores that distribute records to Negroes in the South." Occasionally a record of political interest would appear. "The most significant of recent 'race' records is 'W.P.A. Blues' (Vocalion 03186), in which Casey Bill Welden expresses mild resentment with existing conditions in relief." Johnson mentioned "Silicosis Is Killin' Me" (Melotone 60551) by Pinewood Tom (aka Josh White). Johnson also included Lead Belly's "Pigment Papa" and "Becky Deem, She Was a Gamblin' Gal." By this time, African American musicians were becoming part of the political upsurge in folk music, in particular Lead Belly and Josh White.[21]

John Lomax continued his field work into 1936, this time with a new featured musician. Lomax had earlier met James "Iron Head" Baker at the prison farm in Sugarland, Texas, and in early 1936 had him paroled for four months so that they could work together. In April, they traveled to Mississippi, Florida, and North Carolina, reaching Washington, D.C., on May 20. After a short and not particularly successful trip to New York, Iron Head returned to Texas and soon after wound up back in prison on a new burglary charge. "Less than a year after the Governor set him free, I found Iron Head in the garden squad of the Ramsey State Convict Farm in Texas," Lomax later explained in his autobiography, *Adventures of a Ballad Hunter*. "He peered past me through the iron bars of his cell. Once more he was a convict longing for the 'free world.'" Soon back in Washington, John accepted a position with the newly formed WPA Writers' Project as "National Advisor of Folklore and Folkways." He now met Charles Seeger, also a new government employee, and they developed a close friendship, despite their glaring political differences. At Seeger's suggestion, Lomax was off on a field trip to North Carolina, where he joined Duke University's Frank C. Brown, with the assistance of the fledgling folklorist Sidney Robertson, who soon launched her own career and married the composer Henry Cowell. In December, Lomax recorded the blind mountain singer Emma Dusenberry in Mena, Arkansas: "For two days Emma Dusenberry sang almost continuously into a microphone from which records were made of eighty-two songs for the Library of Congress.... Among her songs was the greatest number of the 'Child Ballads' were recorded from one person as far as I know." Lomax next returned to Washington, busy with the Writers' Project and the Library of Congress.²²

New Deal Programs

The New Deal Resettlement Administration (RA) was created in April 1935, under the direction of Rexford Guy Tugwell and housed in the Department of Agriculture. A concept that Roosevelt had proposed when he was governor of New York, the RA had a mission to establish new rural communities for uprooted urban and farm families, many located in the South, along with well-run camps for migrant workers in California. Charles Seeger became the technical adviser in the RA's Special Skills Division, which included not only musicians but also painters, photographers, filmmakers, and others in the arts. He placed a few musicians and composers in the new communities, with an emphasis on folk music, rather than classical, to connect with the residents, but they had little success. He also sent out field workers, such as Margaret Valiant, Herbert Haufrecht (a colleague in the Composers' Collective), and Sidney Robertson, to collect recordings. Haufrecht focused on writing down workers' songs in the Southeast. Seeger promoted the use of song sheets to encourage group singing in the new communities, including "The Farmer Comes to Town," "Young Man Who Wouldn't Hoe Corn," and "The Dodger," which was collected by Robertson from Emma Dusenberry in Arkansas:

> Oh, the candidate's a dodger, yes, a well-known dodger,
> Oh, the candidate's a dodger, yes, and I'm a dodger too.
> He'll meet you and treat you and ask you for your vote,
> But look out, boys, he's a-dodgin' for your vote.

The song sheets received a cool reception, however, since the audiences did not seem particularly interested in folk songs, preferring religious, popular, or other genres. Nine song sheets were originally published, with another seven planned but never issued because of program cutbacks and criticisms. These RA song sheets, designed to appeal to the new homesteaders, appeared to be no more popular than Seeger's former promotion of modernist musical styles for the working class. In September 1937, the RA became transformed into the Farm Security Administration (FSA) and moved to the Department of Agriculture; he soon relocated to the Federal Music Project.[23]

Charles Seeger worked for the RA for almost two years. "Musically, I knew what I was doing," he later noted. "I was absolutely sure, and I had enough chance to test it out: that music must serve. That you must use the music that the people got in them already. There's no use pumping foreign music into something that's a perfectly going concern and you can make use of. Socialism in music was what we tried to practice there. But, of course, Congress gradually found out what was happening." He had clearly left behind the modernist idealism of the Composers' Collective. The RA funded the film *The Plow That Broke the Plains* in 1936, written and directed by Pare Lorentz. Designed to show the environmental devastation in the central plains and its man-made causes, the documentary featured a soundtrack by the composer Virgil Thomson, who drew on folk songs for his stirring composition. Two years later, Lorentz used Thomson to score *The River*, another film about environmental destruction, but this time without the folk themes. Moreover, Thomson arranged Marc Blitzstein's score for Joris Ivens's 1937 documentary *Spanish Earth*, about the fascists' terrible destruction of a town in Spain. The Spanish Civil War had broken out in 1936, when General Francisco Franco initiated an uprising against the popularly elected republican government. Franco, backed by the Catholic Church, the rich, and the army, received crucial military support from Hitler's Germany and Mussolini's Italy. The government got some aid from the Soviet Union, while the United States, Great Britain, France, and their allies, still recovering from the devastation of World War I, remained neutral. The Communist Party, along with other left-wing organizations (although they often fought among themselves), strongly supported the government until Franco's victory in 1939.[24]

Seeger, the Lomaxes, and their colleagues quickened their support of folk music, which included Lead Belly, as well as the New York newcomer Josh White. Born in 1914 in Greenville, South Carolina, Joshua Daniel White at a young age began work as a lead boy for local blind musicians, helping them in their travels. By the age of fourteen, he had become an accomplished guitar player and in 1928 accompanied Joe Taggart on four sides for the Paramount and Herwin labels, recorded in Chicago. In 1933, White moved to New York to record for ARC, with twenty blues as well as religious songs, under the name Pinewood Tom, during the first four sessions. By middecade, after he had settled in New York, dozens of his records were circulating on various labels, mostly in the South. Two 1936 songs written by Bob Miller, "No More Ball and Chain" and "Silicosis Blues," appearing on the Perfect label (similar to his Melotone record), were the first protest songs that White released, although many more followed as he connected with the local activist political scene:

> I said, "Silicosis, you made a mighty bad break of me. Oh,
> Silicosis, you made a mighty bad break of me.
> You robbed me of my youth and health.
> All you brought poor me was misery."

A crippling accident to his right hand put White's career on hold in 1936 until the decade's close, however, when he became one of the most popular folk performers and a particular favorite of the Roosevelts.[25]

The controversial Federal Theatre Project under Hallie Flannigan also included a Folklore Department that produced plays with a folk component. In July 1936, Herbert Halpert established a music research unit in the Theatre Project's Bureau of Research and Publication. He worked with the noted anthropologist Ruth Benedict, his adviser at Columbia University for his master's degree and the editor of the *Journal of American Folklore*. "These studies were on a variety of topics: cowboy songs, secular Negro songs, American minstrelsy and the folk rhymes and song games of city children," he explained in the *Southern Folklore Quarterly* in 1938. Halpert made his own field recordings in southern New Jersey, while working with folklorists throughout the country. He soon assisted in publishing Arthur Palmer Hudson's *Folk Tunes from Mississippi*.[26]

As the Depression lingered through middecade, with continuing suffering despite the influx of New Deal programs, folk music became more prevalent among the expanding role of the Communist Party and its fellow travelers. Charlie Chaplin's mostly silent, and prolabor, film *Modern Times* (1936) included the music for the IWW's "Hallelujah, I'm a Bum" on the soundtrack.

> Hallelujah, I'm a bum.
> Hallelujah, bum again,
> Hallelujah, give us a handout
> To revive us again.

This interest in vernacular culture developed as part of a growing nationalism to combat the rise of fascism in Europe. Alan Lomax, John Lomax, Charles Seeger, Earl Robinson, Herbert Halpert, and many others found themselves key players during this time of hope and turmoil, fear and optimism. A wide range of government programs stimulated the collection of folk songs throughout the country, as vernacular music moved from rural to urban areas, promoted by record companies, radio shows, and publishers. Labor schools soon proliferated, while the Archive of American Folk Song, under Alan Lomax's energetic guidance, greatly expanded its collection. In particular, Woody Guthrie emerged as the country's rural bard.[27]

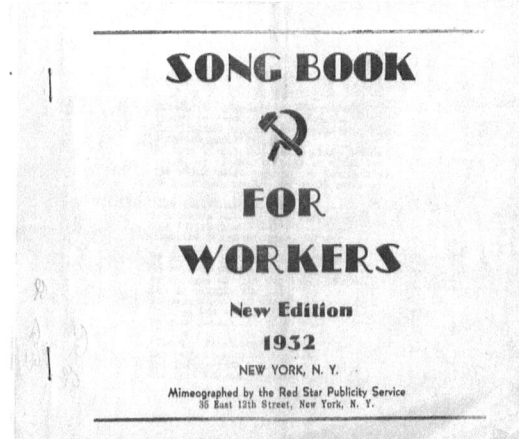

Song Book for Workers (New York: Red Star Publicity Service, 1932). This was one of the earliest radical songbooks affiliated with the Communist Party.

Red Song Book: Prepared in Collaboration with the Workers Music League (New York: Workers Library Publishers, 1932). Another early songbook connected to the Communist Party and the affiliated Workers Music League. It contained a few labor songs with a folk accent.

Pierre DeGeyter, *The Internationale* (New York: Workers Music League, 1934). In 1888 the French composer Pierre DeGeyter added music to Eugene Pottier's 1871 poem, and this song soon became the most popular of all labor songs throughout the world.

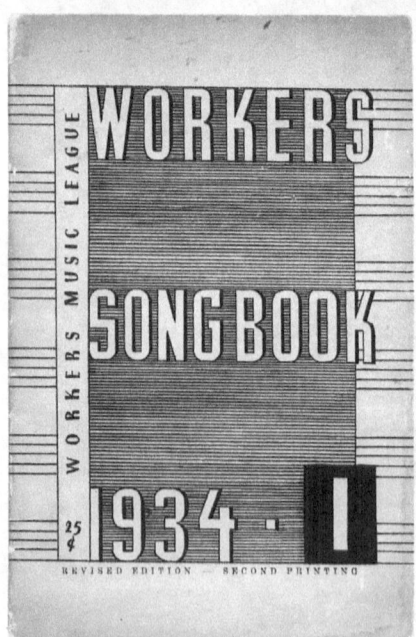

Workers Song Book, No. 1 (New York: Workers Music League, 1934). This songbook by the Workers Music League included thirteen original songs by modernist composers such as Charles Seeger and Elie Siegmeister. Since they were not based on familiar tunes, they did not catch on with workers.

Ad, *Workers Songs*, Timely Recording Company. This ad for the three record, six song, 78 rpm album *Workers Songs* from the Timely Recording Company, included creative illustrations from the record labels. The album sold only a few copies and became very rare.

(below)

Rebel Song Book (New York: Rand School Press, 1935). The Rand School Press, connected with the Socialist Party's school in New York City, included catchy labor songs in its colorful songbook, including "The Soup Song," "Hold the Fort," and "Solidarity Forever."

Lawrence Gellert, *Negro Songs of Protest* (New York: American Music League, 1936). Gellert (1898–ca. 1979) began collecting African American songs in the South in the 1920s, some of which were circulated among Communist Party members in the 1930s through this songbook and other publications.

Harold Rome, "Sunday in the Park," *Pins and Needles* (New York: Mills Music, 1937). The labor musical *Pins and Needles*, written and performed by members of the International Ladies Garment Workers Union, with music by Harold Rome, opened in New York in 1937. It traveled to enthusiastic audiences around the country for four years. This was one of its most popular songs.

Earl Robinson/Alfred Hayes, *Abe Lincoln* (New York: G. Schirmer, [1938]). Earl Robinson (1910–91) wrote the music to lyrics crafted by Alfred Hayes (1911–85) to this and other left-wing songs, in particular "Joe Hill."

Lenin Memorial Meeting Program, Convention Hall, New York, January 20, 1939. This program of a Communist Party gathering in 1939 illustrates the range of music and speakers popular among party members in New York in early 1939.

White Top Folk Festival, August 12 and 13, 1938. The White Top Folk Festival began in 1931 under the direction of Annabel Morris Buchanan (1888–1983). It was a gathering place for southern traditional musicians until 1939.

John A. Lomax and Alan Lomax, *Negro Folk Songs as Sung by Lead Belly* (New York: The Macmillan Company, 1936). John Lomax (1867–1948) and his son Alan (1915–2002) conducted extensive folk music-collecting trips throughout the South. They met Huddie Ledbetter (aka Lead Belly, 1888–1949) at the Angola Prison Farm in Louisiana in 1933. Upon his release the following year, Lead Belly did extensive recording and traveling. The Lomaxes gathered his songs, which would become highly influential, into this publication in 1936.

Bascom Lamar Lunsford and Lamar Stringfield, *30 and 1 Folk Songs from the Southern Mountains* (New York: Carl Fischer, Inc., 1929). Bascom Lunsford (1882–1973), based in North Carolina, was an energetic folk performer on the fiddle, song collector, and festival organizer. This is one of his early song collections.

Carter Family: Album of Old Family Melodies (New York: Southern Music Publishing Co., ca. 1931). The Carter Family (A. P. Carter [1891–1960], his wife Sara [1898–1979], and his sister-in-law Maybelle [1909–78]) were first recorded by Ralph Peer in Bristol, Tennessee, in 1927. Their songs quickly became highly influential among country and folk musicians and audiences.

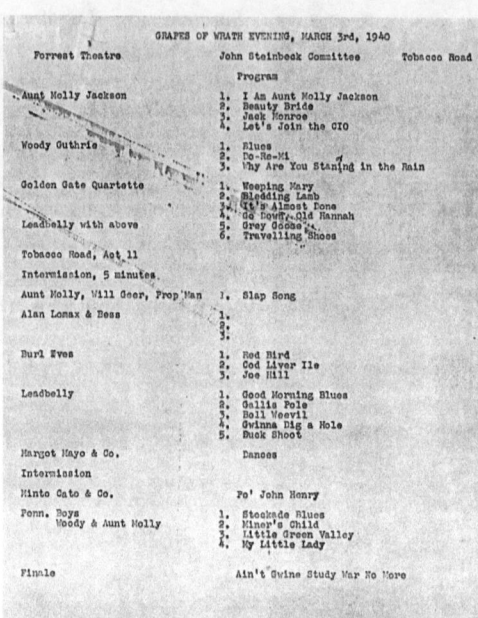

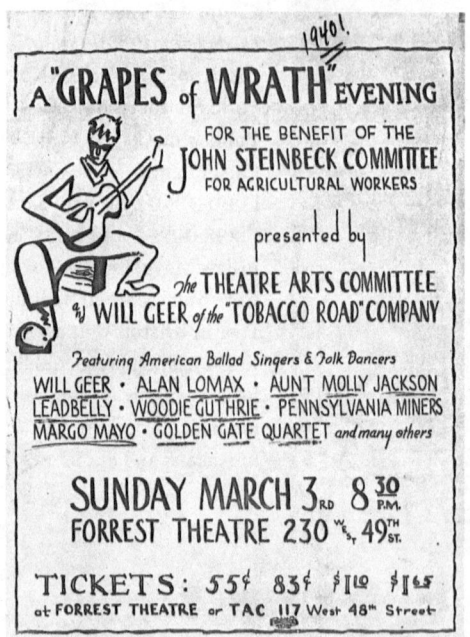

"A Grapes of Wrath Evening," Forrest Theatre, New York, March 3, 1940. This event, organized by the actor Will Geer as a benefit for the John Steinbeck Committee for Agricultural Workers, featured many future influential folk performers, including Woody Guthrie, Burl Ives, and the young Pete Seeger.

CHAPTER FIVE

Woody Guthrie Emerges

Folk music's exposure, publications, and left-wing ties increased through 1937. The Popular Front, with its focus on the folk arts, including painting, music, dance, drama, film, photography, and literature, melded with the New Deal's cultural programs in connecting vernacular culture with the country's urban audiences. John and Alan Lomax, in particular, continued with their field work, joined by numerous others. These were heady times for musicians and scholars, particularly with the rise of labor schools.[1]

Labor and the Left

In a *Daily Worker* review of *Songs of the People*, a songbook published by the Workers Library Publishers, Frederick Adams explained that "America has a musical life of its own, but a life that nobody ever thought it worthwhile to talk about or write down. This life does not concern our music critics nor those who sit on the Board of the Metropolitan or the Philharmonic. In fact, in many cases, this real American music may be dangerous to these gentlemen." Adams's view expressed the definite turn toward folk music by many people with ties to the Communist Party. Beginning with the obligatory "The Internationale," *Songs of the People* included "Casey Jones," "Death House Blues (Scottsboro Blues)" by Peter Martin and Earl Robinson, "Hold the Fort," "Solidarity Forever," and "We Shall Not Be Moved." There was also "In Praise of Learning" by Hanns Eisler and Bertholt Brecht. With some exaggeration, Adams claimed that the collection included "Negro spirituals, cowboy songs, popular

75

ballads, even hymn tunes [as well as] labor, anti-war and antifascist texts which express the thoughts and sentiments of the great mass of Americans today." Perhaps more to the point, the American Music League's smaller *March and Sing!*, also appearing in 1937, featured "Solidarity Forever," "Sit Down," "Write Me Out My Union Card, "Ain't Gwine Study War No More," and S. Karnot and Earl Robinson's "Frisco Strike Saga" (to the tune of "Home on the Range"):

> Oh, hold that picket line.
> We're fighting for jobs and more pay;
> For the longshoreman's right
> To picket and strike!
> And to organize in our own way.

The song referred to the 1934 West Coast longshoremen's walkout, initiated by a general strike in San Francisco, part of a growing number of national labor protests. The booklet's back cover had a notice for Lawrence Gellert's *Negro Songs of Protest*.[2]

The founding of the labor-oriented Ruskin College at Oxford University in England in 1899 stimulated the movement for workers' education in the United States. The country's various labor schools became active in promoting a workers' agenda through folk songs, which had long been part of the union movement. By the turn of the century, socialist songbooks had been circulating, but their stilted compositions had little resonance with the average workers. Things had changed with the Industrial Workers of the World (IWW), founded in 1905, the pioneer in adapting clever lyrics to familiar (often religious) tunes. By the 1930s, its songs were widely circulating, appearing in the new left-wing songbooks as well as the IWW songbook, which continued to be published in new editions.

A variety of labor schools began to issue their own songbooks, drawing on the rich musical heritage to fan the organizing flames, particularly in the hostile white South. A group of socialist and pacifist activists created the Brookwood Labor College in Katonah, New York, in 1921, the first residential school of its kind. Supported by a range of national unions until its demise in 1937, Brookwood produced a handful of songbooks, such as *Brookwood Chatauqua Songs: A Singing Army Is a Winning Army*, not long before the school's demise. *Brookwood Chatauqua Songs* began with "Solidarity Forever," and most of its songs were drawn from the *Rebel Song Book*, including the now ubiquitous "Soup Song," followed by the fresh "Company Union" (to the tune of "KKK Katy, Beautiful Katy"):

> C-C-C-Company, company unions,
> We have met you and your Yellow Dog before.
> All the B-Boss wants is to control us;
> We'll k-kick his company union out the door.

Shortly after the founding of Brookwood, the socialists Kate Richards O'Hare and William Zeuch launched Commonwealth College in 1923, soon located in Mena, Arkansas.[3]

Agnes "Sis" Cunningham had arrived at Commonwealth from Watonga, Oklahoma, as a student in 1931. She soon began working on musical dramas and edited the undated *Six Labor Songs* booklet for the college. Two additional songbooks followed, *Commonwealth Labor Songs* and *Commonwealth Labor Hymnal*, before the college's collapse in 1940. A few years after leaving Commonwealth, in 1937, Cunningham taught at the Southern Summer School for Women Workers near Asheville, North Carolina, where she also compiled a songbook for the students, which included John Handcox's "There Are Strange Things Happening," with additional verses by her father, Chick Cunningham.[4]

The School for Workers at the University of Wisconsin issued a songbook, as did the Pacific Coast School for Workers in Berkeley, California, edited by Caroline Wasserman (1938 and expanded 1939), and the Hudson Shore Labor School in West Park, New York (*Song Book*, 1939). The extensive and unusually eclectic Wisconsin songbook tried to reach a broad audience with four topics: "Union Songs," "Good Fellowship Songs," "Spirituals and Folk Songs," and "Patriotic Songs." The latter included "Lift Every Voice and Sing (Negro National Anthem)," "Marines' Hymn," and the antifascist "Peat Bog Soldiers."[5]

The Kentucky Workers Alliance (KWA), connected with the Workers Alliance of America, which organized the unemployed, promoted labor songs through the work of the activist Don West. Following his work at the Hindman Settlement School in Knott County, Kentucky, in 1930, West graduated from the Vanderbilt School of Religion in Nashville, then briefly collaborated with Myles Horton to launch the Highlander Folk School in Monteagle, Tennessee, in 1932. He was soon working as a Communist Party organizer in the Kentucky coal fields. The KWA was founded in 1936, with West as its organizational secretary and state organizer until his departure the next year. In 1937, the KWA published his small songbook, *Songs for Southern Workers*, which included his friend Jim Garland's "Give Me Back My Job Again" (to the tune of "Greenback Dollar"):

I don't want your millions, mister,
I don't want your diamond ring.
All I want is the right to live, mister—
Give me back my job again.

While West did not stay long with Highlander, it carried on in his absence as the most important of the labor schools, incorporating songs into its curriculum.[6]

Zilphia Mae Johnson, born in the coal-mining town of Paris, Arkansas, in 1910, came under the influence of the local activist minister the Reverend Claude Williams. After attending the College of the Ozarks, studying drama and music, she moved to Highlander in early 1935 to become the school's music director. She married Myles Horton, the school's director, two months later; Ralph Tefferteller arrived about the same time as the square-dance instructor. The school issued a steady stream of songbooks under Zilphia's leadership, including *Workers Songs* (1935), *Let's Sing* (1937), *Songs of the Southern Summer School* (1938), *Songs for Workers* (1939), and *Songs of Field and Factory* (1940). She also edited *Labor Songs* for the national Textile Workers Union in 1939. "Most of the songs in this collection were written by people who work in the mines, mills, factories, and on the farms," she explained in the introduction. "It is hoped that this book will encourage workers to write and sing their own songs." She opened with the patriotic "America," followed by "It's a Good Thing to Join a Union," "We Shall Not Be Moved," and Joe Hill's "There Is Power," although most of the songs were freshly written, such as "Strange Things Happenin' in This Land" (John Handcox's name is not mentioned as the author). The founder and president of the Congress of Industrial Organizations (CIO), John L. Lewis, also president of the United Mine Workers of America, gave the book his hearty, and perhaps surprising for a major union official, endorsement: "A singing army is a winning army, and a singing labor movement cannot be defeated. Songs can express sorrow as well as triumph, but the fact that a man sings shows that his spirit is still free and searching, and such a spirit will not submit to servitude."[7]

The labor schools and their musical agendas were part of the larger industrial-union-organizing drive by middecade, countering the sluggish attitude of the American Federation of Labor (AFL), which had always focused on skilled (white) workers in separate craft unions. The CIO, formed in November 1935, was sparked by a combination of successful strikes in 1934 among the Minneapolis Teamsters, the Auto-Lite workers in Toledo, and the West Coast longshoremen, along with the passage of the National Labor Relations Act, known as the Wagner Act, which became law in mid-1935. Giving federal government protections to labor organizing through the use of strikes and other tactics, the Wagner Act was a powerful tool in establishing industrial unions in the midst of the lingering Depression and high unemployment. The CIO, initially known as the Committee for Industrial Organization, brought together a number of industrial unions, including the Amalgamated Clothing Workers, the International Ladies' Garment Workers' Union (ILGWU), the United Textile Workers, the Oil Workers Union, and the Mine, Mill and Smelter Workers Union. In 1937, it celebrated successful organizing drives at the General Motors Corporation, following a sit-down strike in Flint, Michigan, and at the U.S. Steel Corporation. Many (but not all) of the CIO unions used music as an organizing tool. Following strikes by auto workers against General Motors, Chrysler, and Hudson, Maurice Sugar composed the catchy "Sit Down," which rivaled for popularity his "Soup Song" among workers nationwide:

> When they tie the can
> To a union man,
> Sit down! Sit down!
> When they give him the sack,
> They'll take him back.
> Sit down! Sit down!

Other songs were also composed in response to the Flint sit-in.[8]

The country was soon awash with labor songbooks, filled with songs gathered from a variety of sources, old and new. The ILGWU's *Let's Sing* drew on the popular *Rebel Song Book* but also noted, "You are free to make up your own words to meet your local situation." Moreover, "This booklet is small enough for the vestpocket and the handbag so that our members will always have it handy to sing from at their local meetings, on their hikes, their May Day parades, at their union picnics—and on the picket line." A few other union songbooks were just as handy, such as *Songs*, published by the Textile Workers Organizing Committee, which included "The CIO's in Dixie," but most were not. The larger *Sing Amalgamated* from the Amalgamated Clothing Workers of America (1940) featured "Joe Hill," by Earl Robinson and Alfred Hayes, as well as "Ain't Goin' Study War No More." The CIO's booklet *CIO Songs*, featuring a photo of John L. Lewis on the cover, had T-bone Slim's IWW song "I'm Too Old to Be a Scab" but contained mostly songs with new words to older tunes. The back cover noted, "Keep in the Rhythmic Swing of the Labor Movement—Enliven Your Meetings and Join the Grand March to Victory by Singing."[9]

Lee Hays, born in 1914 in Little Rock, Arkansas, moved as a youth to Cleveland, Ohio. When he returned to Arkansas in 1934, he enrolled at the College of the Ozarks in Clarksville, where he found a mentor in the Reverend Claude Williams. A Christian Marxist, Williams used songs in his ministry, such as "We Shall Not Be Moved" and "Roll the Union On":

> If the planter's in the way,
> We're gonna roll it over him,
> Gonna roll it over him,
> Gonna roll it over him.
> If the planter's in the way,
> We're gonna roll it over him,
> Gonna roll the union on.

Williams and Hays became involved with the interracial Southern Tenant Farmers Union (STFU), organized in 1934 in Tyronza, Arkansas, which used music in its organizing drives. "I became aware of the plight of the Dust Bowl refugees and the sharecroppers and the coal miners first through the work of the great American photographers who went out and photographed the face of America during the 30s, when for the first time America got a great look at itself," Hays later wrote. For a brief time in 1937, he visited Highlander Folk School, and then in the fall joined Commonwealth, now under the direction of Claude Williams, to teach theater. "As a teacher of dramatics at Commonwealth, I had to think up a show for my students to do every Saturday night, when the neighbors were invited," he recalled. "Once in a while we'd get Mrs. [Emma] Dusenberry over and build a show around her. . . . The Easterners didn't think much of Mrs. Dusenberry's high, cracked rhythmless voice, and made no bones about their displeasure. But they had to admit that the neighbors did come to hear Mrs. Dusenberry." Alan Lomax, however, celebrated "blind old Mrs. Dusenberry of the Ozarks, living in a little old log cabin in the hills, holding in her memory nearly two hundred songs and ballads."[10]

The STFU, while battling the brutalities of southern racism along with the iron rule of the planters and their political allies, used songs as a recruiting tool. It attracted various musicians, such as Sis Cunningham and John Handcox. Born in 1904 in the eastern hill country of Arkansas, Handcox became a sharecropper, along with most of his black neighbors, while continually facing hard times. Soon after the launching of the STFU, he became an active organizer and its most prolific poet and songwriter.

The organization barely survived for a few years, with continual violent harassment from the planters and politicians and with scant legal or financial assistance from the federal government. In May 1936, Handcox, fearing for his life, fled Arkansas for Missouri and attended the STFU convention in Muskogee, Oklahoma, in early 1937, as did Sis Cunningham. "Each session opened with singing," she recalled, "usually led by A. B. Brookins or John Handcox or a choir from a local church." Soon after, in March, Charles Seeger, working for the Resettlement Administration, arranged for Sidney Robertson to record Handcox at the Library of Congress. He recorded for posterity his most influential and well-known songs, including "Raggedy, Raggedy," "Going to Roll the Union On," "Join the Union Tonight," "Landlord What in the Heaven Is the Matter with You," and "There Is Mean Things Happening in This Land":

> There is mean things happening in this land,
> There is mean things happening in this land,
> But the union's going on and the union's going strong,
> There is mean things happening in this land.

These songs soon entered the lexicon of labor organizing. Handcox said, "[Singing] is the most inspirational thing you can do to organize labor. I don't know, there's something about songs has more effect than makin' a speech to my mind."[11]

Alan Lomax

Conservative political attacks in 1937 against Federal One, the New Deal's arts programs, suspected of harboring communists as well as wasting government funds, resulted in increased budget cuts, part of a general reduction in federal spending. The national unemployment rate now surged to 19 percent, accompanying a dangerous decline in production.

The Roosevelt administration reacted more with rhetoric than substantive policies, although increased spending led to restoring many jobs. The race horse Seabiscuit, an unlikely champion, excited the country through the year and into the near future, proving some distraction for the Depression-weary population; indeed, the horse was soon more popular than President Roosevelt. Meanwhile the talented, diminutive child actor Shirley Temple reigned as Hollywood's prime star during middecade. The passage of the Hollywood Motion Picture Production Code in 1930 soon led to the mandate that all films have a positive story, certainly a happy ending, personified by Temple's prodigious output and easily fulfilled by the popular screwball comedies, musicals, Frank Capra films, and even crime stories. Hollywood's monopoly of the song-publishing industry also promoted Tin Pan Alley's romance songs, further serving to somewhat distract people from their daily miseries.[12]

There was, nonetheless, a growing emphasis on vernacular culture, through music, literature, dance, film, art, photography, and poetry, particularly including those who were affiliated with the Communist, Socialist, and other left-wing parties. Alan Lomax took advantage of this national fascination from his influential position at the Archive of American Folk Song, which remained safe from the fiscal cutbacks, although its budget remained tiny; Lomax's annual salary as the archive's first paid employee, assistant in charge, was $1,620. The elderly John Lomax had been appointed "National Advisor of Folklore and Folkways" for the Federal Writers' Project in June 1936. His job was to assist with editing the detailed state guides that the project published, while he could not refrain from continuing his collecting trips, this time in Virginia and North Carolina and the next year in Texas, Mississippi, Alabama, Florida, and South Carolina. His WPA position ended in October 1937.[13]

In 1938, the National Service Bureau, a branch of the Federal Theatre Project of the WPA, published Robert Gordon's *Folk-Songs of America*, a compilation of his *New York Times* articles from the 1920s. Along with Gordon's book, the bureau issued a number of other ballad and folk song collections. Phillips Barry's early articles in the *Journal of American Folklore*, the *Southern Folklore Quarterly*, and the *Bulletin of the Folk-Song Society of the Northeast* were brought together in *Folk Music in America* (1939). Also appearing in 1939 were two volumes of

John Harrington Cox's *Traditional Ballads Mainly from West Virginia*, which were additions to his collection *Folk-Songs of the South* (1925). The National Play Bureau, another offshoot of the Federal Theatre Project, published Arthur Palmer Hudson's *Folk Tunes from Mississippi* in 1937, adding to his earlier *Folksongs of Mississippi and Their Background* (1936). These government publications did not get wide circulation, however.[14]

Alan Lomax returned to Washington, D.C., from his collecting trip to Haiti on April 23, 1937, and quickly immersed himself in library and other matters. On July 23, he informed his father, "[I had] a delightful dinner with the Seegers [Charles and Ruth] the other night. [Harold] Spivacke [the new chief of the Music Division of the Library of Congress, having replaced Oliver Strunk] and Seeger seem to have worked successfully with [Robert] Gordon [the former head of the archive] and I am to meet him and show him around the Archive Saturday." Such personnel matters were necessary while Lomax worked on organizing and expanding the collection. He urged his father to hire Ruth Seeger to transcribe the songs for their next songbook, based heavily on their field work, and, he added, by "hiring Mrs. Seeger, you're automatically hiring Charles Seeger as advisory editor." Ruth Seeger did work with the Lomaxes, but delays postponed publication of *Our Singing Country: A Second Volume of American Ballads & Folk Songs* until 1941.[15]

That summer, Alan Lomax planned his next southern collecting trip in the eastern mountain region of Kentucky. As he explained to Spivacke, "It would be sanguine to expect to complete the collecting work in this area in two months, but, on the other hand, it would be dangerous, in any matter as chancy as the collection of folk-songs where Acts of God, bad roads and bad tempers so often intervene to restrict oneself to too small an area." He thought that Mary Elizabeth Barnicle would be in Kentucky at the same time, and it turned out he would be working with her during her brief visit to the coal camps. As Lomax explained in his official report, "Throughout most of this region, especially in the coal-mining counties, the tradition of ballad singing and that which is associated with it—the dulcimer, the five-string banjo, the fiddle, the country dance, the play party, the traditional airs and the oral memory—seem to be in process of rapid degeneration or of transformation. Commercial music via the radio, the movies and the slot phonograph is usurping the place of traditional and homemade music." This saddened him.[16]

Lomax and his wife, Elizabeth, arrived in Harlan, Kentucky, in early September to begin their travels. While he usually made no mention of the local labor troubles, he was certainly aware of the situation, as well as sympathetic with the struggling miners. For example, on September 20, Lomax commented to Spivacke, "Barnicle has just departed. Through her I was able to get in touch with what might be cautiously termed the progressives of this part of Kentucky and to learn all there was to know about the progressive songs of this country." A few days later, he informed his boss, "I have made so far 32 records, some of them quite marvelous, some of them mediocre, but all necessary—ballads, local and otherwise, Baptist hymns, Holiness hymns, blues, sentimental hill billy [*sic*] stuff, radical songs." He always maintained a steady flow of detailed letters to Washington when on the road. He next complained to Spivacke that, sure enough, "the coal camps have turned out to be quite disappointing from the point of view of ballads. Traditional material has been ousted by the influx of records and radios." The recording equipment often broke down, but on September 28, he assured Spivacke, "Machine running. Work booming. But pocketbook empty." In early October, his various problems continued: "We are both exhausted. The roads are terrible in dry weather, but in wet they are something fearsome. The people are very timid, religious and shy about performing." Still, he could report, "Yesterday I recorded some fine ballads from a man who refused to sing for [Cecil] Sharpe [*sic*] when he was here. He says that I am more persistent." Arriving in Salyersville late in the month, Lomax informed his father that Elizabeth had "been quite ill": "This awful food here is enough to make anyone sick. It certainly destroys the ap[p]etite." But his song collecting continued: "I met an old fellow (73) who played the banjo and sang the most delightful jig songs I have ever heard and not one of them was less than fifteen stanzas long—several are slated for your new book.... And one of the town[']s most learned loafers one Harve Porter who sings ballads accurately and well is coming to sing with his two daughters."[17]

Lomax was eager to return to Washington, but Spivacke briefly diverted him to Akron, Ohio, to record Captain Pearl R. Nye. The retired canal-boat sailor had recently been recorded by John Lomax, but Alan recorded him for two additional days singing Child ballads. Then an exhausted Alan and Elizabeth drove home. They returned with over 240 twelve-inch discs, a healthy collection filled with a variety of vernacular musical styles. Lomax summed things up in his generally positive final report:

> The tenacity of the tradition of homemade music even in the mining area, however, is evidence in three ways: in the use of traditional tunes by union-conscious mountaineers in the composition of strike songs and ballads, in the tremendous vogue of "hillbilly" and cowboy music, and in the resurgence of song-making in the Holiness and Gospel churches....
> The "hillbilly" musicians on the air have furnished another outlet for the homemade music of the mountains. Many of them come from rural backgrounds and their hopeful imitators in the hills of Kentucky are legion. The tempos of their square dance tunes have grown faster and their concern with the "mammy" song and the sickly sentimental love song greater, but they also sing some of the indigenous mountain ballads and "blues" and their production of new songs is large.[18]

Lomax's left-leaning politics were made clear in his review, published in the *Journal of American Folklore* in early 1938, of the University of North Carolina folklorist Arthur Palmer Hudson's *Folk Songs of Mississippi and Their Background*. He criticized Hudson for overlooking the role of "class conflict and class hate" in the songs he collected, while stressing the rule and role of the planter class. Indeed, Lomax wrote, Hudson did not "mention the poverty and hopelessness of any of his informants, although I have found that such people are much more eager to talk about the meagerness of their lives than about ballads." Moreover, the author "admitted no Negro songs in a book titled *Mississippi Folk Songs*. . . . For it is precisely at this point—the inter-influence of white and Negro folksongs—that American folk-music as a whole has exhibited and is exhibiting its greatest fertility." Here Lomax displayed his lifelong commitment to exploring the cultural roles and musical influences of poor whites and African Americans, along with the widespread class conflict, not just in the South but across the country.[19]

Some years later, Lomax described the function of folk music at that time: "One of the most interesting of my roles then was to be a kind of entertainer and bard for this New Deal group at Washington parties. The liberals adopted these songs as their culture, it was their literature, it was the art of this new big democracy the likes of which nobody'd ever seen—a country of working class people, of farmers and minorities everywhere with a new, raw, exciting culture rising from its belly. This is what we all felt in our hearts."[20]

Dust Bowl and Woody Guthrie

The stock-market crash on October 29, 1929, known as Black Tuesday, and the ensuing economic disaster had ushered in a decade of hardship, on and off, for the majority of Americans. Its impact was amplified by a devastating environmental catastrophe that shattered lives throughout the country's rural heartland and beyond. Droughts had come and gone throughout the Great Plains, but over the centuries, the short grasses kept the soil from blowing away. Bountiful harvests and the rise of grain prices during World War I stimulated the great expansion of wheat planting through plowing up the grasses, however. The rains continued to fall over the southern plains through the 1920s, although grain prices had plummeted, and then the rains stopped in 1932 for the remainder of the decade. Disaster followed. The first dust storms soon struck, and as the winds picked up, they carried the dry soil across the plains—the dust bowl was centered in the Oklahoma panhandle and the adjoining areas of southwestern Kansas, southeastern Colorado, West Texas, and northeastern New Mexico—and eastward over the country. Woody Guthrie, who became known as the dust bowl balladeer and who lived through the experience in Pampa, Texas, penned a vivid description of the situation in his graphic autobiographical novel *Bound for Glory*: "Oil fields dying out, the boom chasers trickled out down the road in long strings of high-loaded cars. The dust crawled down from the north and the banks pushed the farmers off their land. The big flat lakes dried away and left hollow places across the plains full of this hard, dry, cracked, gumbo mud. There isn't a healthier country than West Texas when it wants to be, but when the dust kept whistling down the line blacker and more of it, there was plenty of everything sick, and made, and mean, and worried."[21]

Woodrow Wilson Guthrie's songs soon painted graphic, memorable pictures of this seemingly unimaginable catastrophe. Born in Okemah, Oklahoma, on July 14, 1912, and named after the Democratic Party candidate for president, Woody, as he became known, lived a rather charmed life at first in his middle-class family. Then a series of disasters struck following World War I. First, his father lost his income due to the collapse of the oil boom, then his mother began to exhibit signs of the onset of Huntington's disease; she soon became incapacitated and was confined in the state hospital for the insane, where she died in 1930. Woody was now pretty much on his own, and he moved to West Texas in 1929 to be near his father, winding up in Pampa. He developed his musical talents early on the guitar and other string instruments, as well as on the harmonica, performing locally until he married Mary Jennings, the sister of his friend Matt, in 1935. They soon had three children and survived in poverty, with Woody picking up odd jobs as the Depression and the dust storms raged. In May 1934, blankets of dust even reached the East Coast, but April 14, 1935, "Black Sunday," seemed to be the worst, with the sun completely obliterated by the mountains of dust over the southern plains. Woody was spurred to compose "Dusty Old Dust (So Long, It's Been Good to Know Yuh)":

So long, it's been good to know you,
So long, it's been good to know you,
So long, it's been good to know you,
This dusty old dust is gettin' my home,
I've got to be drifting along.

Such misery lasted a few more years.[22]

Woody, with his usual wanderlust, relocated to Los Angeles from Pampa in 1937, joining thousands of other Okies and Arkies looking for economic opportunities in the Golden State, despite the hostile conditions they would face. Before their arrival, the predominantly Mexican American and Filipino agricultural workforce had staged massive strikes in 1933 and 1934, which resulted in higher wage rates, but the powerful Associated Farmers organization soon brutally retaliated, just as the Communist Party, for its own reasons, dissolved the militant Cannery and Agricultural Workers Industrial Union. By middecade, the field workers had been crushed, while the 1935 National Labor Relations Act excluded agricultural (and domestic) workers from its protections just as the newcomers were arriving in the state.[23]

Guthrie first began performing in July with his cousin Jack Guthrie on station KFVD's *The Oklahoma and Woody Show*. They joined a long line of country performers on local radio stations, including the Stuart Hamblen Gang, the Beverly Hillbillies, the Bronco Busters, and the Sons of the Pioneers with Roy Rogers. Gene Autry topped the list of singing cowboys in movies. Maxine Crissman soon joined Woody and Jack, and when the latter left in September, the show became the *Woody and Lefty Lou* show (Woody had nicknamed Maxine "Lefty Lou from Old Missou"). They performed many of Woody's new songs, including "Curly Headed Baby" and "Do-Re-Mi." Woody's family soon joined him in Los Angeles. Lefty Lou left the program in mid-1938, with Woody carrying on by himself for a short time.

Woody had arrived in Los Angeles with barely formed liberal political views, but he soon fell under the radical influences of Ed Robbin, who had his own show at KFVD, and the aspiring actor Will Geer. Robbin was a member of the Communist Party, which was growing throughout the country during the Depression years, including in Los Angeles. Robbin had lived in Palestine (pre-Israel) before arriving in Los Angeles in the early 1930s. He became the local editor of the *People's World*, the Communist Party's West Coast newspaper based in San Francisco. "Toward the end of the year [1938], I managed to start a radio program of daily news commentary slanted to the left, in which I talked about the struggles of workers and unions, and against war and fascism," he later explained. "Woody Guthrie with his 'gittar' was on the air just before me." Robbin introduced Woody to the local radical community and in 1939 encouraged him to write a column for the *People's World*. Prior to this, Woody had been a roving correspondent for the *Light*, a weekly paper owned by Frank Burke Sr., the father of the owner of KFVD; the paper promoted the successful campaign of the Democrat Culbert Olson for governor. Robbin summed up Woody's politics at this time (and later): "It didn't matter whether he was talking about Harlan County, Jerusalem, Oklahoma, or Cairo. He didn't bother to read what Karl Marx had written, or Lenin. Woody believed that what is important is the struggle of the working people to win back the earth, which is rightfully theirs. He believed that people should love one another and organize into one big union." As for Will Geer, originally from Indiana, he had begun his acting career in New York and then moved to Los Angeles in the 1930s. He long remained one of Woody's closest friends and a valued political mentor. In 1933, when Geer was present at a National Youth Day Demonstration in San Diego, there was considerable violence. Two years later, while directing two plays by Clifford Odets at the Hollywood Playhouse, he was badly injured by a gang of pro-German thugs.[24]

The dust bowl refugees were made famous in Steinbeck's popular 1939 novel *The Grapes of Wrath*, although the Joad family were tenant farmers who had been forced off their land in eastern Oklahoma, not wheat farmers from the dust bowl. Indeed, most of those who were newly arrived in California were not from the country's dust bowl region. Paul Taylor, an economist at the University of California, Berkeley, had been studying the state's dire migrant-labor situation. Joined by his wife, the photographer Dorothea Lange, they had traveled around the state documenting the situation for a 1935 article in the *Survey Graphic* magazine. They next toured the South and West, resulting in their hard-hitting exposé of rural poverty, *An American Exodus*, published in 1939. Lange also worked for the Farm Security Administration's photography unit, which circulated her iconographic "Migrant Mother" photograph. The popularity of John Ford's film *The Grapes of Wrath* in 1940, starring Henry Fonda, further cemented the connection between rural poverty and California's white, destitute migrant workers.[25]

Among the migrants were some who were soon to become part of the country/western music scene. The sharecropping Maddox family, with their five children, had left Alabama in 1933 and first landed in Oakland. They roamed around as migrant workers until their musical group, the Maddox Brothers and Rose, wound up performing over KTRB in Modesto, while they toured the state's rodeo circuit. In 1938, they won the State Centennial Band competition, landing a sixty-four-station national radio hookup. While more popular than most, they represented the evolution of country music in California by decade's end. They had followed the Sons of the Pioneers, including the young Len Slye (aka Roy Rogers), a western outfit that had established itself in Los Angeles by 1935, when they signed a contract with Decca Records. They soon began appearing in Hollywood films, along with Gene Autry, Tex Ritter, and other singing cowboys. Rogers had arrived from Ohio in 1931 as a migrant fruit picker and in 1937 replaced Autry as Republic Pictures' singing cowboy.[26]

Woody Guthrie, connected with California's country music upsurge, had become attracted to various local Communist Party members and their allies, including numerous actors, film writers, and labor union activists. Still, Southern California remained a hotbed of conservative politics, led by Harry Chandler, owner of the *Los Angeles Times*, in conjunction with many of the film-studio heads, particularly MGM's Louis B. Mayer. The studios shied away from producing antifascist films until late in the decade, for example, to avoid alienating Hitler and losing the lucrative German market. Warner Bros. was considered the most liberal of the major studios and did distribute films about poverty and even the evils of Nazism, starting with *Black Legion* in 1937, followed by *Confessions of a Nazi Spy* in 1939, but it was in the minority. Like the rest of the country, Southern California had deep political fissures between a growing conservative movement and the left-wing alliance of labor unions, Communist and Socialist Party members, and others on the liberal-left.[27]

New York City

While Guthrie was performing, writing songs, and delving into left-wing politics in California, and the dust storms continued to rage, the folk community in New York City flourished. Aunt Molly Jackson resided on the Lower East Side and remained politically active as she composed new songs, such as "Disgusted Blues." Mary Elizabeth Barnicle interviewed her at length and met Aunt Molly's half brother, Jim Garland, who had arrived in New York in 1935. He first picked up odd jobs selling fruit and hot chestnuts, then devoted more time to folk music. "By 1936 I was spending much more of my time singing and picking on the guitar," he recalled. "I was scheduled by the International Workers Order and the Cafe Society to sing before numerous groups, one of them being the Workers Alliance, an organization of the unemployed." He began attending Barnicle's classes at NYU and even lectured there on Kentucky folk life and culture. "Jim Garland of Harlan County, Kentucky, will talk on the social significance of American hill-billy songs at the American Writers Union," the *Daily Worker* noted in March 1937. For a few months in 1938, he had a radio program on NYU's station, *Jim Garland and His Kentucky Mountain Folk Singers*, with a group composed of his sister Sarah Garland Ogan, who had recently moved to New York; Mamie Quackenbush; Dorothy Burton; and his wife, Hazel. They even appeared at the New York World's Fair the following year during Farm Week.[28]

An intense folk scene had been developing in Greenwich Village and the Lower East Side. Along with Aunt Molly and her half siblings Jim and Sarah, this was a busy period for Lead Belly. In the fall of 1938, he had driven Barnicle to Kentucky to pick up Sarah Gunning and her family and bring them back to New York. Through Garland in New York, Barnicle had met Tillman Cadle, another former coal miner from Harlan County and a union activist, and they were soon married. Cadle began to work musically and politically with Lead Belly, with the latter getting jobs performing at local political meetings and rallies, such as for the Workers Alliance, the International Workers Order, the Young Communist League, and Spanish Civil War relief organizations, as he became increasingly politicized. Although Lead Belly never voiced many political opinions, he did write a few political songs, such as "The Scottsboro Boys Shall Not Die" and "Bourgeois Blues," referring to the segregation he encountered in Washington, D.C.:

> (Lord) It's a bourgeois town, it's a bourgeois town,
> Got the bourgeois blues, gonna spread the news all around.

In June 1937, Lead Belly recorded additional songs for Alan Lomax at the Library of Congress, including the event songs "The Hindenburg Disaster" and "Queen Mary."[29]

Besides the nurturing folk music environment in Greenwich Village, former members of the Composers' Collective remained active in the city, although they had mostly switched from a modernist to a folk and/or popular music style. Earl Robinson, for one, had become a prolific composer of folk songs, most notably "Joe Hill." During the summer of 1936, he worked at Camp Unity, an adult camp affiliated with the Communist Party in Wingdale, New York, directing the local chorus and organizing musical activities. He included songs from the IWW songbook as well as those collected by Lawrence Gellert. He worked with the camp's dramatic director, Alfred Hayes. "The afternoon of our Friday-night campfire tribute to the Wobblies [IWW], Alfred Hayes gave me this poem of four-line verses he had published two years before in *New Masses*," Robinson later explained.

"I went into a tent with my guitar, and in about forty-five minutes emerged with a song." Their effort resulted in "Joe Hill," about the IWW bard, which was published by Bob Miller in 1938 and quickly became popular among labor and left-wing circles:

> I dreamed I saw Joe Hill last night,
> Alive as you or me.
> Says I, "But Joe, you're ten years dead."
> "I never died," says he.
> "I never died," says he.

Robinson brought various performers to the camp, including Lead Belly, and he also worked with Hayes on "Abe Lincoln," soon another staple for left-wing audiences. Alan Lomax remembered Robinson collecting songs at the Library of Congress: "He learned these songs, which he then made into concert pieces. Then taking off from that, he composed his great songs of the New Deal era." During 1937, Robinson worked for the Federal Theatre Project and the New Theatre League, with a few weeks in the summer employed at Camp Kinderland, a children's camp connected with the Communist Party. He also founded the American People's Chorus and returned to Camp Unity in 1938.[30]

Robinson met Abel Meeropol at Camp Unity in 1936. A New York high school English teacher and political radical, he went on to compose "Strange Fruit" under the pen name Lewis Allan; the two worked together for years. As Robinson recalled about Meeropol, "His own songs—tunes and lyrics—included 'Is There a Red under Your Bed?,' 'Beloved Comrade,' and a song of the Abraham Lincoln Battalion," then fighting on the loyalist side in Spain. The latter was titled "Abraham Lincoln Lives Again," published by Bob Miller in 1938:

> The Armies of Progress are marching
> At the Fascists they are hurled
> A Government of the People
> Shall not perish from the World!

Lincoln had become a vital symbol not only of the major parties but also of the Communist Party during the Popular Front years.

In late December 1938, Barney Josephson opened Cafe Society in Greenwich Village, an interracial nightclub featuring blues, jazz, and comedy, where Billie Holiday soon made "Strange Fruit" famous. As Lomax later noted, "Only with the New Deal did we get this upsurge of protest and song."[31]

By 1938, folk music had become part of the larger world of popular music, while the depressed economy could not be shaken. Labor schools and people with left-wing ties now used folk-style songs to promote their political agendas—labor unions, civil rights, socialism, and antifascism. The next few years, before the U.S. entry into World War II, provided further proof that the political left would make its musical mark on the country, although not without serious problems. As the clouds of war darkened over Europe, Communist Party members faced a quandary, splitting the peace movement while accompanied by increasing right-wing political attacks on the left. Many New Deal programs were soon abandoned or sharply curtailed. Alan Lomax became increasingly active, however, while Woody Guthrie sharpened his political involvements and musical skills.

CHAPTER SIX

The New Deal Survives

Into 1938 and 1939, folk music took on more popular dimensions. The voice of the "people," expressed through music as well as plays, art, nightclub skits, stage musicals, literature, poetry, movies, radio shows, photography, and dance, became increasingly prevalent. Nonetheless, various New Deal programs began to shrink as the country's political conservatives—northern Republicans allied with southern Democrats—marshaled their forces. The rise of fascism in Europe presented problems that mushroomed into full-scale war in 1939, resulting in a fractured peace movement. The Communist Party's Popular Front agenda, particularly its alliance with organized labor, continued as the Depression lingered, while Alan Lomax played an increasing, and vital, role in the country's musical as well as political life.

Popular Folk Music

"In talking about American folk songs it is best to answer the question of what are folk songs, than to concern ourselves with what is *American*," Herbert Halpert explained in the magazine the *American Music Lover* in March 1938. "In what way do folk songs differ from popular or art songs? . . . A song by Shubert, or Stephen Foster, or George Gershwin differs from a folk song because by and large, although you may sing the song from memory, people who want to sing it correctly go back to the form the author wrote and study it." For Halpert, folk songs had been passed down orally, with no idea of the original author. He was aware of occupational songs—"the songs that sailors, cowboys, miners, lumberjacks, plantation workers sing"—but they were also orally transmitted. The author had first presented his views on the *Exploring the Arts and Sciences* radio show on WQZR, a program sponsored by the Federal Theatre Project.[1]

According to Charles Seeger, "The Music of America is made up of three main currents of activity—a folk, an academic or 'high art,' and a popular music. . . . Each has a repertoire, largely inherited. And each constitutes an idiom, a musical speech as it was, which serves the living musician as the medium for communication of a content to his hearers." Seeger now preferred folk music, having abandoned his previous modernist preference, since "as its name implies, [it] is the possession of the bulk of the people." Originally located in rural areas, folk music had now been brought into the cities: "Without any formal organization, therefore, the folk music has met the patronized drive of academic music and the commercialized drive of popular music with a drive of its own—a surprisingly well-rounded permeation of the city mind. . . . In short, following the lead of painting, poetry, the novel and the drama, urban professional music is discovering America." Seeger's faith in folk music and its growing popularity had developed over the previous few years, a product of his evolving musical values and left-wing political commitments.[2]

Representing the growing link between radical politics and folk music, the Detroit lawyer and songwriter Maurice Sugar, for example, penned "'Bosses and Judges, Lis'n to Me': Song for Scottsboro Boys" in 1938. It was written for Clarence Norris, whose death sentence had just been commuted to life:

Hear my cry a-ringing
Ringing through the land
Hold those bloody fingers
Drop that bloody hand.

"[Sugar] is actively associated with the life of labor and liberal and cultural circles and has himself on a number of occasions written many poems and song," according to a *Daily Worker* article in July 1938.[3]

While Halpert and Seeger, along with Alan Lomax and many others, had a deep and growing conviction in the meaning and importance of folk songs, their historical legacies and contemporary value, most of the country was heading in a different direction. In August 1935, Benny Goodman and his orchestra hit their stride at the Palomar Ballroom in Los Angeles, kicking off the swing-band craze that was to engulf the country for the rest of the decade, particularly among young people. About the same time, George Gershwin's *Porgy and Bess* folk opera opened on Broadway, joining a strong list of film and stage musicals, such as *Big Broadcast of 1936*, *Ziegfeld Follies of 1936*, *Babes in Arms*, *I'd Rather Be Right*, and *The Boys from Syracuse*.[4]

In 1938, Ella Fitzgerald's "A-Tisket, A-Tasket," Will Glahe's "Beer Barrel Polka," and Artie Shaw's "Begin the Beguine" each sold over 300,000 records, the first to reach such popularity in the decade, and all soon topped a million in sales. While the Federal Theatre Project, under conservative pressure, banned the opening of Marc Blitzstein's hard-hitting labor musical *The Cradle Will Rock* on June 15, 1937, after moving to a new theater, it was performed in a truncated version, under the direction of Orson Welles and produced by John Houseman. It lasted on Broadway for 124 performances and remained musically and politically influential; Will Geer served in the cast. Popular songs and performers flooded the airwaves, jukeboxes, and theater stages. There was also a Dixieland jazz revival that somewhat countered the popularity of the big bands.[5]

Alan Lomax

Alan Lomax was particularly aware of the various musical and cultural styles swirling around him in the late 1930s, but he preferred collecting and promoting folk music, with some exceptions. Over the winter of 1937–38, he continued his heavy workload as assistant in charge at the Library of Congress, but he became eager to take off for his next field trip. "The Library is sending me to the meeting of the Hoosier Folk Lore Society in April in Indiana," he informed the folklorist John Harrington Cox at West Virginia University in March, "and since my route lies across West Virginia, I should like to drop by and call on you.

I have found your book [*Folk-Songs of the South*] extremely useful in connection with my work here at the Library in cataloging folk songs." Lomax had also been teaching a class on folk songs for the Federal Workers School, sponsored by the United Federal Workers of America, and in mid-March organized a concert for the union in Washington, D.C.; half of the evening included classical music, and the rest featured Lomax performing songs from his collecting trips in the South and the Caribbean.[6]

Before arriving in Bloomington, Indiana, for the Folk Lore Society meeting, Lomax and his wife, Elizabeth, visited the Ohio Valley Folk Festival at the Cincinnati Music Hall. Sarah Gertrude Knott was moving her National Folk Festival to Washington, D.C., in 1938 and as a prelude invited Bascom Lamar Lunsford and John Lair to stage a preliminary event, the Ohio Valley Folk Festival. Lair had earlier worked with the National Barn Dance on WLS in Chicago, then established the Renfro Valley Barn Dance on WLW in Cincinnati in 1936. Lomax was not impressed by the festival, considering it too commercial. As he wrote to Harold Spivacke on April 1, after arriving in Bloomington,

> After a very stiff, 501 mile, drive over the mountains to Cincinnati Mrs. Lomax and I found a very sloppily run and stupid hill-billy show masquerading under the title "Folk Festival." I recorded only two songs while the festival was in progress and they were hardly worth the acetate. Lunsford, as you might have expected, rather boycotted me, and after the festival was over, dashed away with the hope that he would see me in Washington. He gave me not one scrap of information about who was [a] folk-singer out of the huge drove of yodeling, crooning, Alabama-mooning Kentuckians he had assembled. I was able, however, in the course of the most horrible exhibition of Anglo-American, blond, blue-eyed sentimentalism and musical gaucherie that I have ever endured to single out a few genuine informants.

He was especially disparaging of the professional background of the Coon Creek Girls, whom he did not consider authentic vernacular performers. In his later official report, however, Lomax was more charitable regarding the festival. He had found two fascinating performers, Robert Day of Cincinnati and Pete Steele of Hamilton, Ohio. As he explained, "Cincinnati is at once a center for 'hillbilly' broadcasts and one of the gateways for migration out of eastern Kentucky and West Virginia." These newcomers had brought their music to local radio stations, and through "these programs the prestige of rural music is maintained and various individuals are encouraged to keep their heritage of traditional music fresh in mind." Lomax continued to be critical of folk festivals, which were perhaps a bit too showy for him, seemingly lacking an authentic touch.[7]

From Cincinnati, the Lomaxes traveled to Bloomington for the inaugural meeting of the Hoosier Folk Lore Society. Through the Indiana University folklorist Stith Thompson, Lomax met the ballad collector Paul Brewster, who introduced him to some of his local sources. Next, with the help of the WPA Recreation Project and the Federal Writers' Project, he recorded various informants throughout the state—in Crawford County, New Harmony, Vincennes, and particularly in Goshen with its large Amish population. This was his first collecting trip into the North but far from the last. Upon the Lomaxes' return trip to Washington, they stopped in Hamilton, Ohio, to record Pete Steele, a banjo wizard who was soon to be an important influence on Pete Seeger. They arrived back in the nation's capital in late April.[8]

Lomax, excited by his new prospects, began planning an extensive collecting trip to the Great Lakes states of Michigan, Minnesota, and Wisconsin. First he had much work to catch up on at the Library of Congress, since he usually kept up correspondence with his scattered informants, such as John Umble at Goshen College and Josephine Caney in Vincennes. He attended the National Folk Festival in Washington in May but again came away with various negative reactions. "It was the usual uncritical hash of everything you can think of and Miss [Gertrude] Knott played her ordinary dumb but beautiful role, sweeping across the stage in a long white lace dress and pushing folk singers around like a professional checker player," he complained to his father, who was then traveling in Europe. "If

I get my chance in New York, I think that this wen [Wednesday?], the National Folk Festival, may be carved off the name of American folk song."[9]

Lomax was referring to his stream of suggestions to Olin Downes, the music critic for the *New York Times* and the head of music and dance for the upcoming New York World's Fair, opening the following year. For example, in May, working with Nicholas Ray, soon to be his radio collaborator, he proposed an expansive program for the fair titled "Yankee Doodle Comes to Town," which would feature music from the first Dutch settlements throughout the centuries: "New York City has always been a cosmopolitan town and it will be amusing to portray the arrival of the first Chinaman, the first Negro, and the first Jew." A week later, he refined his notion of music for Downes: "You may not agree with me that the ragtime-jazz-blues-swing tradition is the most important American contribution to sophisticated music, but at least this tradition deserves a great deal of attention. I have encountered a Negro here in Washington who might fit into the World's Fair program very nicely, and who I think could represent this tradition as well or better than anyone I know. His name is Jelly Roll Morton." And he added, "I am recording for the Library all of his compositions, all of the folk tunes that he knows along with very full biographical material." Lomax continued to pepper Downes with sweeping ideas for his proposed pageant, beyond anything that Knott would ever present and certainly stretching any definition of folk music, but he soon learned that he would not be appointed to coordinate the fair's folk music division.[10]

Lomax had given more than just a passing thought to the musical importance of Ferdinand Joseph Lamothe, aka Jelly Roll Morton. Born in the late nineteenth century, Morton early participated in the development of jazz in New Orleans. His composition "The Jelly Roll Blues" was the first jazz tune to be published, in 1915. During the late 1920s, his Chicago-based Red Hot Peppers recorded very popular records for RCA Victor. In the 1930s, with the onset of the Depression, he lived in New York and struggled to survive, then moved to Washington, D.C., in 1935. Upon the suggestion of Alistair Cooke, in 1938 Lomax discovered the now relatively unknown musician, except to a few jazz experts, performing at the Music Box. The British-born Cooke had first traveled to the United States in 1932 to study at Yale and Harvard, then returned to England to work for the BBC as its film and music critic. In 1936, he aired a program of American hobo songs, before returning to New York the next year; he was now producing the BBC show *I Hear America Singing*, drawing on recordings from the Library of Congress.[11]

Lomax was unique in stretching the bounds of musical authenticity beyond the usual collection of cowboy songs, Child ballads, African American spirituals and work songs, Amish songs, sea shanties, and the like. In Morton, he intuited the life and work of a musical genius who had certainly influenced the development of popular music, although he first had his doubts. "He came [to the library] with some friends," Lomax recalled. "At that time, jazz was my worst enemy. Through the forces of radio, it was wiping out the music that I cared about—American traditional folk music." He was soon convinced of Morton's importance. "There was something tremendously appealing about the old jazzman with his Southern-gentleman manners and his sporting-life lingo," he explained in the prelude to *Mister Jelly Roll*, the autobiography he edited and first published in 1950. "I decided to find out how much of old New Orleans lived in his mind." The recording sessions began on May 21, 1938, continued through June 12, and picked up again for a final session on December 14, resulting in nine hours of fascinating music and talk. *Down Beat*, the jazz magazine, published an article on the sessions in June, "Black Diamond Express to Hell" by Sidney Martin, which attracted the attention of Melvin Oathout, a jazz bibliographer in New York. In responding to Oathout's inquiry, Lomax explained, "We hope to add extensively to this material in the future as we encounter other distinguished hot jazz musicians." But, he continued, the "function of the Archive at present, however, is to collect and organize recorded material pertinent to the field of American Folk Song and I don't know whether an extensive bibliography on jazz . . . would fit into our program." Lomax had also interviewed W. C. Handy, the black music pioneer, on May 6. As for Morton, Lomax worked with and supported him, financially and otherwise, until his death a few years later.[12]

Lomax, in the midst of the Morton sessions and his plunge into jazz history, was planning his next field trip, a fresh musical exploration to the Great Lakes states. While the commercial recording companies had focused on roots musicians from the South and West, Lomax was quite aware of the work of northern folklorists who had been exploring the ballad and folk song traditions of their own regions. His work in Indiana and Ohio had whetted his appetite for moving north on a filming and recording expedition. Before driving off at the end of July in his 1935 Plymouth Deluxe four-door sedan, he studied the published sources and reached out to his various contacts. As he explained to Spivacke, "In sounding folklore resources of this region, the Archive will be able to record what remains of the once vigorous lumber jack culture, to explore the musical potentialities of the many foreign language groups of that area (Swedish, Norwegian, Finnish, Gaelic, French-Canadian, etc.) and to observe what have been the results of the mixing of these cultures with the Anglo-American matrix." To obtain assistance in the Midwest, he solicited help from such folklorists as Theodore Blegen at the University of Minnesota (*Norwegian Emigrant Songs and Ballads* [1936]), Earl C. Beck of Central State Teachers College in Mt. Pleasant, Michigan (*Songs of the Michigan Lumberjacks* [1941]), and I. H. Walton of the University of Michigan.[13]

Lomax began his three months in Michigan—the area was so rich that he never made it to Minnesota or hardly into Wisconsin—in Detroit, where he recorded in the Serbian and Hungarian neighborhoods. He also interviewed the jazz-band leader Leroy Smith and an African American guitar player. Unfortunately his recording machine and guitar were stolen from his car, but soon armed with a new Presto machine, he took off for Charlevoix. He began recording lumberjacks—Beck had brought a group of lumberjacks to the recent National Folk Festival in Washington—and the Irish fishermen and sailors on

Beaver Island who even sang bawdy songs, as well as numerous others. He arrived back in Washington in early November. He had collected 250 disc recordings, six linear feet of manuscripts, and eight reels of film from 120 performers. He had a rich collecting experience and, as usual, continued to correspond with a number of those whom he recorded, including Johnny Green on Beaver Island, "one of the most amazing ballad singers who has turned up in America," as he explained in his official report. Unfortunately he never published an account of the trip.[14]

Lomax next turned to expanding his knowledge—he was always searching for intellectual stimulation—by enrolling at both New York University and Columbia University for the spring 1939 semester. In a memo to Spivacke, he outlined his plans: "It is important to the adequate performance of my duties as assistant in the Archive of Folk Song that I have more systematic academic training in anthropology and in the anthropological approach to primitive and folk music." He requested $850 but also expected to "add to the Archive in this period at least two hundred records important in the study of American folk-music." Spivacke agreed to put Lomax on half salary from February to June while he and Elizabeth were living in New York. First, however, Lomax made a quick trip to New York to attend John Hammond's "From Spirituals to Swing" concert on December 23 at Carnegie Hall, sponsored by the left-wing magazine *New Masses*. The all–African American night featured the Count Basie Orchestra, the Kansas City Five, boogie-woogie pianists Albert Ammons, Pete Johnson, and Meade Lux Lewis, gospel star Sister Rosetta Tharpe, Mitchell's Christian Singers, Big Bill Broonzy, Sonny Terry, Sidney Bechet, and the Golden Gate Quartet. The eclectic evening highlighted a mixture of gospel, jazz, and the blues. The following day, Lomax was able to interview and record Ammons, Johnson, Lewis, and Terry in a local studio for the Library of Congress, demonstrating his ever-expanding conception of folk music. A year later, in late December, Hammond organized a second, this time racially mixed, concert, with the Benny Goodman Sextet (including Charlie Christian, Lionel Hampton, and Fletcher Henderson),

James P. Johnson, Ida Cox, Sonny Terry, the Count Basie Orchestra, the Kansas City Six, and Big Bill Broonzy.[15]

The Peace Movement and Political Songs

Throughout the 1930s, a strong isolationist impulse ran through the country, made up of a variety of ideas and movements, often with clashing political agendas. Universal Studios remade Erich Maria Remarque's popular and chilling 1929 antiwar novel *All Quiet on the Western Front* into a movie the next year, which received Academy Awards for best picture and director; the film's star, Lew Ayres, became a pacifist and performed noncombat duties during World War II. Four years later, Fox Film Corporation released *Cavalcade*, also with a clear peace message, which won the same Academy Awards. There were a few Tin Pan Alley peace ditties, such as Howard Johnson and Willie Raskin's 1935 composition "If They Feel Like Having a War Let Them Keep It over There." Harold Rome included the hard-hitting "The Yanks Aren't Coming" for the 1939 version of the left-wing musical *Pins and Needles*. Many people in and around the Communist Party, which gained increasing popularity up to 1939, were quick to use music to promote nonintervention in European affairs, except regarding Spain. Indeed, the Republican cause during the Spanish Civil War, 1936–39, generated numerous prowar songs, often by the same left-wing individuals and groups who otherwise supported an antiwar agenda. The American Student Union, a coalition formed in 1935 to promote peace, began to discard this platform by 1938 as the threat of European fascism loomed.[16]

The American League Against War and Fascism, formed in 1933 and changing its name to the American League for Peace and Democracy (ALPD) in 1937, united various groups on the political left into a broad coalition. While the peace movement was heating up by middecade, books filled with peace songs were quite rare, except for the American Student Union's *Patters for Peace*. Similar to many of the left-wing songbooks of the time, however, many of the ASU's songs were difficult to sing, since they were not based on familiar tunes, and only one included music. Moreover, not all twenty-seven songs were about peace, such as "Joe Hill," "Peat Bog Soldiers," and "Strange Fruit," but there was the college cry "ASU—Students Fight for Peace" and the biting "Spring Song" (music by Earl Robinson and lyrics by Harold Schachter):

> Oh, I wonder will there be a war this spring?
> Will we be fighting while the robins sing?
> Will the bayonets be bristling and bullets do the whistling
> When the world is all in bloom in the spring?
> Oh, I just want an ordinary spring
> With people laughing just because it's spring.
> Let's have a celebration with folks from every nation
> 'Cause it's great to be alive in the spring!

"As it fit in with our anti-war policy, I sang this song around quite a bit," Robinson recalled. "American Peace Mobilization used 'Spring Song' in an independent film, called *Says Youth*, and Paul Robeson recorded it on Keynote." Affiliated with the Communist Party, the short-lived American Peace Mobilization was formed at decade's end until Germany invaded the Soviet Union in June 1941. On the other hand, the well-organized right-wing isolationist movement, led by Charles Lindbergh, was unconcerned about using music to promote its agenda, relying instead on its ability to generate much publicity.[17]

In 1938, an alliance of left-wing film, theater, and radio entertainers formed the Theatre Arts Committee (TAC), an offshoot of the Theatre Committee to Aid Spanish Democracy. For almost two years, it staged a variety of politically charged shows, with a weekly midnight cabaret beginning in May 1938; performers included Will Geer, Francis Farmer, Imogene Coca, Tony Kraber, and Michael Loring doing "Casey Jones," along with the satiric "Capitalistic Boss" and "Old Paint (The Horse with the Union Label)":

> Old Paint, Old Paint
> A prouder horse there ain't

'Cause my Old Paint
Is a horse with a union label.

TAC published a monthly magazine and promoted a variety of recordings, radio programs, and the weekly cabaret in New York with a heavy anti-Nazi flavor but with an antiwar message. The TAC Radio Division wrote and published the song "It Shall Not Come to Pass," probably in 1939, with the refrain,

We, who are this nation say: We will not go to war
We have said it oft before;
But now we command it!
It Shall Not Come to Pass![18]

Alan Lomax in New York

Alan and Elizabeth Lomax arrived in New York in early February 1939, and he quickly plunged into the local musical and political scenes, while soon attending anthropology classes at Columbia and New York University. He joined Cabaret TAC at the Young Men's Hebrew Association (YMHA), as noted in the *New York Times*: "You'll get some idea of what TAC would like to do by scanning the list of compositions and performers: 'I Hear America Singing' text by Walt Whitman, cantata setting by George Kleinsinger; Earl Robinson's 'Ballad for Americans,' words by John La Touche, sung by Michael Loring and the American People's Chorus; Henry Brant's tone poem, 'The Marx Brothers—Three Faithful Portraits,' Morton Gould, composer; Alan Lomax, American balladeer; and the Clarence Profit Trio, in some jazz improvisations, or—to coin a word—swing." Lomax continued to work with TAC and did a series of lecture-performances at Cafe Society.[19]

Lomax also began collecting the older commercial hillbilly and race records from the past decade, many now out of circulation, for a discography he was compiling for the Library of Congress. As he informed Spivacke, "I saw John Hammond on Tuesday and he told me about the outcome of your visit to Columbia [Records]. He said that besides the classical records affair, he believed that in the next two weeks Columbia would have agreed to send you their race list—in all about five or six hundred records. Naturally they have many more than this out of print. Upon hearing this I suggested my old plan of making a bibliography of commercial folk recordings, including those of which the masters have not been destroyed." With Hammond's assistance, Lomax visited the Columbia factory in Bridgeport, Connecticut, and discovered it had over 24,000 masters of race and hillbilly records, but unfortunately many of the commercial shellac records had already been scrapped. From Columbia, he soon searched the Decca, Vocalion (part of ARC), Paramount, RCA Victor, and Bluebird catalogs and recordings. As he informed Spivacke, the commercial companies "have done a broader and more interesting job of recording American folk music than the folklorists and . . . every single item of American recorded rural, race, and popular material they have in their current lists and plan to release in the future should be in our files." He also considered reissuing some of the older records from Columbia and thought Musicraft might be interested in new recordings by Aunt Molly Jackson and Lead Belly. Lomax had hundreds of records shipped to the Library of Congress for preservation and research purposes, although in April, Spivacke warned him to "refrain from dumping quantities of records on the Library at the present time. Our present staff cannot cope with it at all." In September 1940, Lomax published the "List of American Folk Songs on Commercial Records": "After listening to three thousand odd commercial records of white and negro songs and tunes from the South, I have compiled this list of three hundred and fifty representative titles in order that the interested musician or student of American society may explore this unknown body of Americana with readiness." In selecting this rich compilation, Lomax had been assisted by his sister Bess and the young Pete Seeger.[20]

The New York World's Fair opened on April 30, 1939, but without Lomax's involvement. "I learned this afternoon that [Olin] Downes has definitely bought the Labor Stage show 'Evening of Negro Music' for the world's fair," he informed

Spivacke on April 8. "Lead Belly was featured in this show—at my suggestion—and the rest of it stunk—although it did get good reviews. I feel a little sore at Downes for not having at least let me know about this or mentioned me in connection with it and I wonder whether a little from you might not help." He also complained that Sarah Gertrude Knott, who conducted the National Folk Festival, which had moved to Washington, D.C., in 1938, had "scheduled her show significantly for the end of April. I wish there was something that we could do about keeping it out of the fair." Lomax's references are unclear, since the festival had not yet opened, and there is no indication that Lead Belly performed in conjunction with it. Jim Garland and his sister Sarah Ogan, however, did appear with a small group representing Kentucky's rural folk culture. As for Lomax, he was now preoccupied.[21]

On March 5, 1939, Lead Belly was arrested in New York for assault for having stabbed a man who was climbing into his apartment window. Lomax came to his rescue, posting $50 for part of the $1,000 bond, and Lead Belly was released pending his initial court appearance on May 4. "I quit Columbia [University] to become his defense committee to raise his legal fees," Lomax later explained. "One of the ways I found money was to arrange a recording for him with Music Craft [sic]. That was in 1939 and they paid us $350 for this first commercial pure folk music album, 'The Sinful Songs of the Southern Negro [*Negro Sinful Tunes*].'" Samuel Pruner had launched Musicraft in 1935, initially to produce classical records. Lead Belly was sentenced on May 20 to less than a year on Riker's Island, but he was released after eight months. His new album included "Fannin Street," "Frankie and Albert," and in particular "Bourgeois Blues," one of his most political songs about racial discrimination in Washington, D.C. "We sat up last night until well past midnight listening to the Lead Belly records," Spivacke informed Lomax. "To say that we enjoyed them would be putting it mildly indeed. The Bourgeois Blues is the finest song that I have heard in years. Your fears regarding this song are unfounded. We Americans have a good sense of humor and can take it."[22]

With Lomax having resolved the Lead Belly matter and having ended his renewed college career, he moved on to new ventures while remaining in New York for a while longer. In May 1939, he recorded Captain Dick Maitland singing sea chanteys at the Sailor's Snug Harbor home on Staten Island and then spent some time with Aunt Molly Jackson recording her songs and memories: "Story led to song and song to story. There are representatives of every type of tune sung in the mountains—English ballads, feud ballads, banjo tunes, fiddle tunes, sacred tunes, love songs, etc., with an exhaustive discussion of each type by Aunt Molly, who can tell stories as well as she can sing." He returned briefly to Washington on June 8 to perform "The Old Chisholm Trail" and "Git Along, Little Dogies" for a state visit by King George and Queen Elizabeth of England. Lomax paired the Coon Creek Girls, Nell Hunter and the North Carolina Spiritual Singers, Kate Smith, Marian Anderson, and Lawrence Tibbett in a program partly organized by Charles and Ruth Seeger. A few days earlier, an Associated Press article had explained, "In a little Greenwich Village apartment, young Allen [*sic*] Lomax threw back his head, thrust his fingers fasted across the face of his blood-red guitar and sang a low, throaty lament ['The Chisholm Trail']. . . . He was just running over a song he will sing for the President and Mrs. Roosevelt and the King and Queen of England." The article went on to explain, "He goes into isolated mountain ranges, valleys and slumbering seaports of the country, carrying along a phonographlike arrangement by which he gets the unrehearsed music of the most obscure of all Americans." Lomax vividly recalled the White House evening: "Roosevelt was on the front row with his head cocked over, smiling and swinging in time to the music. . . . This presence and the vitality that poured out of him made that concert, I think, one of his peak moments." A week later, Lomax spoke at the left-wing Third American Writers' Congress, alongside Dorothy Parker, Dashiell Hammett, and Thomas Mann. The FBI had now begun to compile a file on Lomax, a file that grew substantially over the next thirty years.[23]

Lomax's New York leave now over, he returned to Washington in early summer and began preparing for new research trips as well as his breakthrough with a national radio program. He gave the details to Spivacke:

> The Columbia Broadcasting Company [CBS] has asked me to supervise their musical program on the American School of the Air during its next season of twenty-four weeks, beginning October 10th and ending the second or third week in May. According to the present plan I am to act as advisor on script, commentator and in some cases singer on this program. The series is designed to reach school children during school hours and I am told it goes to more than 120,000 classrooms across the whole country on their coast-to-coast hook-up. It provides, I feel, at once a rare opportunity for stimulating a general interest in American Folk Song, but also will create a situation in which the Archive of American Folk Song can begin at once to play a vital role in American culture. I might add that it is planned to commission twenty-two of America's leading composers to write brief works especially for presentation over this program.

Lomax, using his creative energies, bolstered by his friend Nicholas Ray, was about to bring folk music to a national audience. As he explained to Davidson Taylor at CBS on June 16, "In outlining the two series that I did, I avoided a great deal of contemporary social documentation which someday I hope the songs will be given over the air. As I told you, my experience in collecting has been with poor farmers, workers, etc., in the main." For Lomax, progressive politics was never far from his mind, although he knew he had to walk a fine line when appearing before a national radio audience.[24]

The 1934 Communications Act, which established the Federal Communications Commission, spared the radio corporations—CBS and NBC (with its red and blue networks)—along with the hundreds of local stations from government ownership but did mandate that they devote a significant part of their schedules to civic education. What this meant was not entirely clear, but it resulted in a wide variety of programs, including classical music, discussion groups, academic lectures, government announcements, and much else. In 1930, CBS had already initiated *American School of the Air*, one of a number of such educational programs reaching into the country's homes and schools, often focusing on music appreciation. Lomax's plan was to incorporate folk songs and classical arrangements, a rather unique idea, although classical music had been widespread through much of network programing. He was now part of radio's traditional civic function—it was much more than just an entertainment source—because of as well as despite its private ownership.[25]

A lengthy article in the *Dallas Times Herald* gave a detailed account of native-son Lomax's radio debut. "Next Tuesday over the Columbia Broadcasting System and KRLD will begin a series of programs which are likely to turn up as unexpected results and to be as far reaching in their consequences as any programs that have ever been offered on the radio," John Rogers proudly effused. After a detailed discussion of the collecting work of John and Alan Lomax, the article explained that since the BBC and even the French Broadcasting Company had been programming American folk recordings, "Americans began to wonder if they were passing up something worth while, and as a result of conferences with Mr. Lomax, this series of programs for the Columbia School of the Air was arranged. In this case, there is no intention to use records, but for Mr. Lomax to sing the songs himself or be assisted by singers," along with short orchestral works.[26]

Spreading the Folk Music Gospel

While Alan Lomax worked hard to promote folk music, he was not alone as the world faced increasing conflicts. The Spanish Civil War ended on April 1, 1939, with the fascist defeat of the loyalist forces, a crushing blow to the left. Almost four months later, in late August, representatives from the Soviet Union and Nazi Germany signed a nonaggression pact (known as the Nazi-Soviet Pact), allowing Adolf Hitler to invade Poland on September 1 without worrying about retaliation from Joseph Stalin (who could then invade Poland from the east two weeks later), followed by the German takeover of France and much of western Europe the next spring. The Communist Party supported nonintervention until the German invasion of the Soviet Union on June 22, 1941. In Asia, Japan now occupied much of China and was poised for further expansion.

On the domestic front, following the CIO's successful labor contracts with General Motors and U.S. Steel, other organizing drives slowed in and after 1937. There were a few exceptions, such as in the coal fields of Kentucky, where the United Mine Workers had some victories. More promising was the increase in rainfall in the Central Plains in 1938, with the dust storms beginning to lessen into 1939, but it was not until 1940 that the dreadful drought finally ended. As for southern sharecroppers, black and white, their lives experienced little improvement. In the summer of 1936, the writer James Agee and the photographer Walker Evans traveled to Alabama on assignment from *Fortune* magazine to investigate the lives of white farmers. Their report, "Cotton Tenants: Three Families," was not published in the magazine, but in 1941, an expanded book version, *Let Us Now Praise Famous Men*, appeared. It received only scant attention, however, since the war and improved economic conditions now occupied the public's interest. "[The cotton tenant's] circumstances are merely local specializations of the huge and the ancient," Agee originally wrote, critically and sadly, "all but racial circumstance of poverty: of a life so continuously and entirely consumed into the effort merely and barely to sustain itself; so profoundly deprived and harmed and atrophied in the course of that effort, that it can be called life at all only by biological courtesy." Southern rural poverty did not lessen until World War II.[27]

While the Depression lingered, Republicans and their conservative congressional (southern) Democratic allies were slashing government programs. Federal One had been under scrutiny, and in March 1939, the House of Representatives approved an investigation of the Works Progress Administration

(WPA). In June, Congress cut WPA spending, abolished the Federal Theatre Project (FTP), and mandated loyalty oaths for government workers. The FTP had already staged a successful swing production of Gilbert and Sullivan's *Mikado*, as well as the theatrical revue *Sing for Your Supper*, opening on March 24, including "Ballad of Uncle Sam" by Earl Robinson and John La Touche. "The infamous Dies Committee on Un-American Activities ... leveled its most violent attacks on the [Federal Theatre] Project, in particular *Sing for Your Supper*," Robinson later wrote. "They made sweeping public accusations that the press dutifully played up with little or no refutation, though at the core I believe that they principally objected to black and white actors dancing together in the show." The House Committee on Un-American Activities was established in May 1938 to investigate perceived subversives on the left or right, but mostly the former, and chaired by the Texas Democrat Martin Dies. As for the shrunken WPA, it would now focus on national defense until its demise in 1943.[28]

There was scant leftist theater now to be found in New York or throughout the country, except the revised version of *Pins and Needles 1939*, quickly followed by *New Pins and Needles*. The gospel and blues singer Josh White had been recording for the ARC company in New York since 1933, except for a few years while his hand healed, and he now performed in *John Henry*, a musical based on Roark Bradford's 1931 book on the fictional black hero. The show starred the world-famous actor, singer, and political activist Paul Robeson, who had recently moved back to the United States from England after living there since the late 1920s, with White playing the fictional blues guitarist "Blind Lemon." The show opened on Broadway on January 10, 1940, and closed a week later, having generated poor reviews and little interest. The mounting political repression and other distractions served to produce a rather dismal progressive cultural situation as the decade waned.[29]

Still, folk music continued to be presented in its many forms, rural as well as urban, North and South. In 1936, Benjamin A. Botkin and Charles Seeger had visited Bascom Lamar

Lunsford's Asheville folk festival, along with Charles's son Pete and Sidney Robertson, who then worked as a fieldworker for the Resettlement Administration. In the spring of 1938, Botkin was appointed national folklore editor for the Federal Writers' Project (FWP), replacing John Lomax. With an undergraduate degree from Harvard College and a master's in English from Columbia, Botkin began teaching at the University of Oklahoma in 1921. Through his numerous publications, he soon became one of the pioneers of folklore for the masses. Botkin took a leave of absence from Oklahoma to move to Washington, D.C., and never returned. In the summer of 1938, he visited the South with Charles and Ruth Crawford Seeger. As he wrote to his wife, Gertrude, in August, "The mountain dance festival was in the true nature without the frills and fun of Miss Knott's show. . . . The children have the same sad faces as their parents, but all seem glorified by the spirit of the dances and songs." A few months later, Botkin and Seeger, now the deputy director of the Federal Music Project, established the Joint Committee on Folk Arts of the WPA to coordinate their activities, with Alan Lomax and Sidney Robertson as the assistants. Herbert Halpert, who headed the Folksong and Folklore Department of the Music Division of the National Service Bureau in the FTP, functioned as the primary fieldworker. The conservative attack on the WPA forced Botkin in 1939 to move to head the Writers' Program Unit at the Library of Congress for the next two years. He had been questioned by congressional investigators for suspected left-wing activities, and some of his New York City folklore materials had been confiscated.[30]

Folk song and ballads collectors, scattered around the country, pursued their work, despite the rapid shrinking of the federal cultural programs. In July 1939, for example, Alan Lomax planned a collecting trip to Vermont. To the local folklorist Helen Hartness Flanders, the upper-class wife of the state's future U.S. senator Ralph Flanders, he wrote, "I finally received your letter of June 2nd, and in the same mail the issue of the Proceedings of the Vermont Historical Society which contains the article and check list on Vermont folksongs." She had already published

Vermont Folk-Songs & Ballads (1932) and *Country Songs of Vermont* (1937). That fall, the two spent over a week on a collecting trip around the area.³¹

Lomax and Flanders collected from vernacular musicians, while there were numerous professional country and western performers throughout New England appearing on radio, in town halls, and at the various performance ranches. There were few recordings, although Hank Keene and His Connecticut Hillbillies appeared on the Brunswick, Bluebird, and Banner labels. The list included Bud Bailey and His Downeasters, Don Fields and His Pony Boys, the Down Homers in Hartford, Connecticut, Al Rawley and His Wild Azaleas, Pappy Howard and His Connecticut Kernels, and particularly Hal Lone Pine (aka Harold Breau) and Betty Cody. Lone Pine first appeared in 1932 with two friends on WABI in Bangor, Maine, one of the many local radio stations airing country performers. Others moved to New England from elsewhere, such as Bradley Kincaid, the star of Chicago's WLS *Barn Dance*, who relocated to Boston in 1935, performing on its powerful station WBZ. Numerous performers were barnstorming throughout the region, such as Jerry and Sky, as well as the Ken Mackenzie Tent Show. The musicians included not only cowboy and folk songs but also representations from the rich mix of New England's ethnic and working-class populations—French, Italian, Polish, Greek, German, and Portuguese.³²

During this time, Stetson Kennedy was compiling African American folklore, including songs, in Florida. Born in Jacksonville, Florida, in 1916, he developed early as a writer. The young Kennedy was hired by the Federal Writers' Project in 1937 as the acting local supervisor in Gainesville, and a year later, in December 1938, with Botkin's support, he became director of the Folklore, Life History and Social/Ethnic Studies Unit of the Florida Writers' Project. The civil-rights-minded Kennedy found himself trying to oversee the research and writings of the headstrong Zora Neale Hurston. During this time, Kennedy collected bits of black song lyrics, and in the summer of 1939, he was briefly transferred to the Federal Music Project in Jacksonville. He lost his job when the federal programs passed under the more conservative state control. He was one of the many casualties of the mounting right-wing backlash.[33]

While Lomax, Kennedy, Flanders, and so many others continued their folklore collecting and publishing, but with decreasing government support, Woody Guthrie was expanding his political and musical agenda. He remained in Los Angeles through most of 1939, writing his column "Woody Sez" in the Communist Party's *People's World*, beginning in May, and with Will Geer toured the state's migrant-worker camps. They worked for the John Steinbeck Committee to Aid Farm Workers, while facing an escalating backlash against the influx of Okies and Arkies from the state's agricultural and industrial leaders. "I saw the hundreds of stranded, broke, hungry, idle, miserable people that lined the highways all out through the leaves and underbrush," Guthrie wrote. "I heard these people sing in their jungle camps and in their Federal Work Camps and sang songs I made up for them over the air waves." While Woody was involved with various musical and political projects, Sidney Robertson had begun working for the California Folk Music Project in late 1938; two years later, she issued *The Gold Rush Song Book*. As for Woody, he was honing his musical skills before moving to New York in early 1940; there he joined and influenced a thriving folk community.[34]

The decade wound down with continued left-wing cultural and political activities, partly connected with the ongoing interest in collecting, recording, and publishing folk materials. Alan Lomax had remained one of the centers of this activity, although he was hardly alone in his zeal for promoting folk music as part of the country's grassroots nature and history. Indeed, Lomax's work expanded as the country edged toward war into 1940. The conservative onslaught had crippled many government programs, but folklorists throughout the country continued their work in collecting, publishing, and performing folk music.

CHAPTER SEVEN

Decade Ends

The Wider World of Folk Music

Folk music performance and collecting entered the waning year of the 1930s with somewhat renewed vigor but with reduced federal government support. Of increasing importance, a group of professional musicians, including Woody Guthrie, Lead Belly, Burl Ives, and Josh White, emerged to capture a popular interest in folk music, particularly in New York City. Alan Lomax's CBS programs brought a variety of folk performers into homes and schools throughout the country, and the music's connection to the Communist Party and organized labor continued as the country edged closer to war.

"Were Walt Whitman living today, he would add to his list of workers singing joyously of their occupations, the WPA laborers with their rousing ballads of what a pink slip does to a poor man trying to live on $48 a month," Richard Randall explained in the *Daily Worker* in September 1939. He went on to discuss the many workers' choruses springing up in Chicago, New York, Michigan, and elsewhere. "The balladry of the unemployed, has, as yet, received little interest from those with a commercial interest in music," he continued. "But Decca has made two exceptional recordings of some dealing with relief—'The WPA Blues' and 'Working on the Project.'" "Big Boy" Teddy Edwards recorded the former in 1936, although Big Bill Broonzy quickly followed with his version on the ARC label:

Everybody's workin' in this town
And it's worrying me night and day,
Everybody's working in this town

And it's worrying me night and day,
That's that mean hard working crew
Says, that work for the WPA.

Peetie Wheatstraw recorded "Working on the Project" for Decca in early 1937. But as Randall noted, these songs seemed the exception to the commercial rule, particularly as the decade waned.[1]

In late 1939, the journalist and music critic Paul Rosenfeld, in an article in *Modern Music*, described the wider stirrings of an interest in folk music among scholars and the public at large after attending the White Top folk festival in Southwest Virginia:

> Of the sessions of the recent international congress of the American Musicological Society [AMS] in New York, a whole one, on comparative musicology, was devoted to North American primitive and folk-music. Three of the concerts presented to the congress, were composed of performances of American folklore—Alan Lomax's atmospheric presentation of ballads accompanied on his guitar; the Nashville Old Harp Singers' costume-concert charmingly featuring, together with bits of the Puritan psalmody, some of Wesley's hymns and Billings' fugueing-tunes, and white spirituals and folksongs; and the sprightly recital on the part of Aunt Molly Jackson of Harlan County and three wizened "pinies" from southern New Jersey, of racy ballads, shanteys and lumberjack-songs. . . . The emergence into full view of the American folksong, if not the main musical event of the present, is its main American-musical one.

This was a real stretch for the American Musicological Society, which had only embraced European concert music. Rosenfeld noted with pleasure "that a revolution has been occurring in the consciousness of American society; an occult revolution the cause at once of the folksong's emergence and our sudden sensitiveness to it. The apparent source of the emergence is of course the activities of collectors and musicologists." But these songs were not frozen in time, a fact that must be accepted. "The modern age has terminated the isolation of the mountaineers," he explained. "It has reduced the status of numbers of these nice people to tenancy. The traditional music it has rendered obsolescent. The radio has transmitted a new music; the young are singing hillbilly songs to guitar-accompaniment, and their guitar-technic is not conducive to modal effects." This was all to the good: "The American folksong, like the American people, in the meanwhile continues; showing the often beautiful visage of a vigorous creature born of the free interplay and interchange of groups and influences drawn from many parts, and thus, to those with an eye for it, the image of the American idea." Alan Lomax would surely have agreed, with his expansive, wide-ranging musical views.[2]

Alan Lomax and the Left

Alan Lomax shared the modernizing approach of Rosenfeld, focusing on the role of folk music in an urbanized world, rather than the romantic, parochial nostalgia of his father and various other folklorists and writers. By August 1939, he had been in touch with Davidson Taylor at CBS to produce twenty-five weekly *Folk Music of America* programs, each Tuesday morning from October into May for half an hour starting at 9:15 and aimed at schoolchildren. The network had developed the *American School of the Air* series in conjunction with the New York Board of Education. The concept was for Lomax or others, including Aunt Molly Jackson, to sing folk songs, while various modernist composers—such as Ruth Crawford Seeger, Roy Harris, Aaron Copland, Ferde Grofé—would create companion pieces. Lomax had his doubts that the series would work; but the opportunity to air folk music nationally was too good to pass up, and he was anxious to reach young people. "In writing a request for a regular schedule of leave without pay, so that I can work on the folk music series," he wrote to Davidson in mid-August, "it occurred to me that I have as yet no contract with Columbia." This matter was soon settled, but there were other issues as October approached.[3]

Lomax began arranging the programs with the appropriate songs, such as "The Chisholm Trail," "Santa Anna," "I Married Me a Wife," and "The Boll Weevil," as well as writing the contents for the companion manual for teachers to use in their classrooms. "I am leaving today for New York for my first real encounter with the dragon," Alan wrote to his father in Texas on September 28, as the German and Soviet armies rolled through Poland. "I have been terribly busy getting ready for it for the past week or two.... Listen in Saturday night, WABC New York station Columbia Broadcasting System, for the preview of the American School of the Air series. I am going to have a five-minute spot on this program and would like your frank opinion of how I sound." Once the programs started, John would give his candid, often nitpicking, opinions. Alan now took two days a week of unpaid leave from the Library of Congress, being paid roughly $30 a week, with another $100–$150 coming from CBS, for an annual total around $4,500 (about $65,000 in current dollars).[4]

CBS aired a preview show on October 1, with the regular schedule to begin on the tenth. "I'd like to hear your verdict on the first performance," he inquired of Harold Spivacke, his boss at the Library of Congress. "Personally I feel much relieved that it's over and much surer about going ahead with subsequent performances.... Unless you need me urgently, I think I'd better stay here and rehearse and write steadily until after the tenth. I really need a week to get my soul set for the first show." Each show would have a theme, such as lumbermen, as he informed the Michigan collector Earl Beck, when he inquired if there were "any biographies, diaries, or stories about lumberjacks that would contain more than straight informational material about the process of lumbering and would give more about the men and their recreations." As usual, Lomax took his new educational position most seriously. Moreover, his selections drew folk songs and ballads not just from the South—the focus of the commercial record companies—but nationwide, with all the songs in English. He used songs from the books he compiled with his father and from his own collecting experiences.[5]

Despite Lomax's new broadcasting obligations, his recent excursions through Indiana and Michigan had whetted his appetite for at least one more northern trip, this time to Vermont. He could have selected upstate New York, which had a rich vernacular music culture. Fred Woodhull had established his family in Elmira, New York, in the 1890s, and by the 1920s, with his three sons, Woodhull's Old Time Masters had emerged to play for nearby dances and other occasions. They were quickly joined by other upstate string bands, such as the Hornellsville Hillbillies of Hornell, Ott's Woodchoppers from Oneida, the Rusty Reubens in Wellsville, Woody Kelly's Old Timers from Perry, and Old Dan Sherman and His Family from Oneonta. There was also a thriving vernacular music culture in the Catskill region, soon connected with the left-wing Camp Woodland, a summer camp in Phoenicia opened in 1939—indeed, no part of the country was lacking folk/country performers and songs. Lomax chose to work with the experienced Helen Hartness Flanders in nearby Vermont and into New Hampshire, however. "In a field trip authorized by the library from November 3 to November 14 I made with Miss Flanders' assistance seventy-six recordings of Vermont folk songs," he informed Spivacke later in the month. This was to be his last collecting trip for the year, as his radio programs and library work absorbed most of his time.[6]

In early December, Lomax sent copies of "There Are Mean Things Happening in This Land," the recording of John Handcox made by Sidney Robertson for the Library of Congress, to Sheldon Dick. A Farm Security Administration photographer and documentary filmmaker, Dick was working on a film about the working and living conditions in the Tri-State Mining Area of Kansas, Missouri, and Oklahoma. The film *Men and Dust* was released in 1940, with Will Geer as one of the narrators. The Handcox song was used at the film's opening. Lomax had also suggested including Josh White's (as Pinewood Tom) recording on the Perfect label of "Silicosis Is Killing Me":

> I said, "Silicosis, you made a mighty bad break of me.
> Oh, Silicosis, you made a mighty bad break of me.
> You robbed me of my youth and health.
> All you brought poor me was misery."

As the year drifted to an end, Lomax contacted Alec Saron, who worked with Cabaret TAC: "After you called I spoke to Peter Seeger and Lawrence Gellert in regard to the folk music program we discussed. Gellert knows Negro singers in Harlem and that should round out our program completely. I suggest that you give Mr. Seeger and Mr. Gellert full leeway in planning the program until I return on the second of January." If this was not enough, he was also planning a lecture tour, promoted by Columbia Artists, to increase his outreach and income.[7]

Woody Guthrie

By November 1939, Woody Guthrie's KFVD show in Los Angeles had been canceled, considered by the station's owner too left-wing. Will and Herta Geer had meanwhile moved to New York, with Will starring in the Broadway hit production of *Tobacco Road*. The Guthrie family now returned to Pampa, Texas, but Woody knew he had no future there; there were no jobs. The airwaves were filled with patriotic songs on November 11, Armistice Day (now Veterans Day), particularly Kate Smith's rendition of Irving Berlin's "God Bless America," which the popular singer had debuted a year earlier on her radio show *The Kate Smith Hour* and recorded in March 1939 for Victor. Bing Crosby and Gene Autry followed with their own recordings.

Geer invited Guthrie to come to New York, where there might be a part for him in *Tobacco Road*, and he could join the emerging local folk music scene. In midwinter, Guthrie used twenty-five dollars to buy a bus ticket to Pittsburgh and from there wound up hitchhiking during a freezing snow storm. While on the road, and reacting to Smith's rendition of "God Bless America," Guthrie apparently began to compose a rebuttal before he arrived on February 16, cold and hungry, at the Geers' plush apartment on Fifty-Sixth Street and Fifth Avenue. Guthrie began to explore the city, including the skid-row area around the Bowery, and write numerous songs, particularly "This Land Is Your Land," his counter to "God Bless America," which he typed out on February 23. He borrowed the tune from the Carter

Family's recordings of "When the World's on Fire" and the similar "Little Darling, Pal of Mine."[8]

Feeling uneasy in the comfort of the Geers' apartment, Guthrie quickly moved to a grubby but affordable room in the Hanover House, a boarding house on West Forty-Third. He quickly fell into welcoming company. Lomax recalled, "I'll never forget the first time I saw Woody [Guthrie]. We were doing a benefit for the Spanish cause, the Spanish Loyalists who were fighting against Franco, and Woody was on the show. It was one of the first nights he was in New York. He stepped out on the stage, this little guy, big bushy hair, with this great voice and his guitar, and just electrified us all.... Well, here was Mr. Anonymous singing to me." Geer had invited Guthrie to participate in the benefit for the Spanish Civil War refugees held on February 25, which included a workers' chorus performing Russian folk songs along with the baritone Mordecai Bauman. Guthrie also picked up writing his column "Woody Sez" for the *People's World*, which continued into November, as well as a similar one for the Communist Party's local *Daily Worker* beginning on March 19, which also lasted through the year's end. The first notice of his performing in the city appeared in the *Daily Worker* on March 1, and on March 17, Art Shields introduced the paper's readers to Guthrie in a long sketch about "a balladeer from the 'Okie' country." Guthrie's arrival had an immediate and lasting influence on Lomax's work and life, as well as on the local and national folk music scene.[9]

Commercial folk music was not yet particularly popular. Tin Pan Alley tunes and the large swing bands, particularly the Glenn Miller Orchestra, which had emerged in 1938 and recorded for RCA's Bluebird label, had captured the national mood. Decca records boasted a catalog of seven thousand titles and a long list of popular artists, including the Andrews Sisters, Bing Crosby, Woody Herman, and Guy Lombardo. While Crosby remained the most popular crooner, Frank Sinatra was emerging as a big-band boy singer and recording artist, particularly favored by young women. Broadway musicals were still flourishing through 1939, such as *The Straw Hat Review* with Imogene Coca and Danny Kaye. The next year, the all-black *Cabin in the Sky* did well starring Ethel Waters and Todd Duncan, with lyrics by John La Touche and music by Vernon Duke, as did *Hold on to Your Hats*, featuring Al Jolson, with lyrics by E. Y. Harburg and music by Burton Lane.

On March 3, the Theatre Arts Committee (TAC) along with Will Geer presented a "'Grapes of Wrath' Evening" as a benefit for the John Steinbeck Committee for Agricultural Workers at the Forrest Theatre. John Ford's film *The Grapes of Wrath* had just opened and drew large crowds. Starring the newcomer Henry Fonda, it captured the continuing suspicion of greedy capitalists and tyrants, joining a similar 1938 major Hollywood film, *The Adventures of Robin Hood*, and 1939's *Jesse James*, which also starred Fonda, this despite the Production Code of 1930, which banned presenting outlaws in a positive way. In "The Ballad of Pretty Boy Floyd," written in early 1939, Guthrie had given his own views on the subject: "Some will rob you with a six-gun, / Some with a fountain pen."[10]

Geer, working with Alan Lomax, assembled a stellar cast of folk performers for the concert: Lead Belly, Aunt Molly Jackson, Bess Lomax, Burl Ives, Josh White, Pete Seeger, the Golden Gate Quartet, Richard Dyer-Bennet, Woody Guthrie, and dances by Margot Mayo—all of whom were to play significant roles in the developing folk music revival, locally and nationally. New York had now become a magnet for folk performers. "I was allowed to sing one song on the program because my friend folklorist Alan Lomax insisted on it," Seeger explained. "I wasn't entirely welcome, it was a full program and there were a lot of dependable performers part of it. . . . So the director gave me one song to sing. . . . I got a smattering of polite applause. Woody was the star of the show." As for Alan Lomax, meeting Guthrie had an enduring impact on Seeger's life. Geer had earlier praised Guthrie and sent Seeger a copy of his mimeographed songbook "On a Slow Train through California," so Guthrie was no stranger to Seeger when they first met.[11]

Pete Seeger, son of the famed musicologist Charles Seeger, had enrolled at Harvard College in 1936, just after visiting Bascom Lamar Lunsford's Asheville folk festival, but he dropped out after two years and moved to New York. He joined the Young Communist League and became involved with a group of young artists. Spending much of his time practicing the five-string banjo, he got his first notice in the *New York Times* in April 1939 playing for a dance program by Margot Mayo and the American Square Dance Group (ASDG). That summer he joined the Vagabond Puppeteers, who toured upstate New York for three months performing for the hard-hit farmers.

Over the winter of 1939–40, Alan Lomax hired Seeger to catalog and transcribe the Library of Congress's commercial hillbilly recordings, while he lived in a nearby boarding house. Seeger was particularly influenced by the banjo pickers he was listening to, such as Dock Boggs, Buell Kazee, Wade Ward, Lily May Ledford, Pete Steele, and Uncle Dave Macon. He even assisted Lomax in a field trip to record Ward in Galax, Virginia. "Life down here is always full of a lot of talk," he wrote his grandmother in early February. "New projects, books, shows, trips, jobs, etc., etc.?" He soon returned to New York for the Grapes of Wrath concert, which he anticipated being "much different from what was originally envisaged. I have a good deal smaller part, but it is all for the best, and may lead to more programs of folk music in the future." He also mentioned that he would be performing at the Progressive Education Association conference in Washington, D.C., on March 8. "About the same type of songs I sung at the Earl Browder meeting last fall, which you remember, but what a far cry it is! Well, we shall see what the future brings."[12]

Seeger's work at the Library of Congress soon ended, and in May, he hit the road with his new friend Guthrie. They traveled by car through Virginia, visited the Highlander Folk School, met the Communist Party organizers Bob and Ina Wood in Oklahoma City, stopped for a short stay with Guthrie's wife, Mary, and family in Pampa, Texas, then returned to New York. Seeger next took off on his own for another trip to the West, hitchhiking and riding the freights, then returned to New York, but in October, he was again on the road to Kentucky and Alabama. He now had his first article published, "Pete and His Banjo Meet Some Fine Mountain Folks," in the *Southern News Almanac*, an obscure labor publication, November 14, 1940. He followed in the same paper on December 5 with "No More Labor Wanted until Further Notice: Camp Blanding, Florida." In the latter article, Pete explained that workers were lured to Florida with the hope of a job building an army base but were left jobless and homeless. In November, he was back in New York.[13]

Lomax's Radio Programs

Alan Lomax was now devoting much time to crafting and airing his creative radio shows, which garnered substantial support. Helen Hartness Flanders assured Lomax in December 1939, shortly after their own collecting trip, "Since your CBS programs have been on the air, I have written all my coast-to-coast club [General Federation of Women's Clubs, for which she chaired the club's Folk Music and Folk Festivals committee] contacts urging them to listen and also to speak of your programs at the club-meetings." Two months later, she continued, "I think your last broadcast was particularly fine. Giving America her folk-music and its applied themes, in orchestration, must be tremendously illuminating. The popularity of your broadcast is certainly nationwide." Blanche Lemmon posted a glowing review in *Etude* in April. "American youth are privileged this year to dip into a veritable treasure chest of Americana" because of Lomax's show, she began. And she concluded, "It is the hope of those concerned with the Folk Music of America broadcasts that by them youth may be served, and that by means of the comprehensive outlines offered in the programs increased interest in and appreciation of our great variety of folk songs may be stimulated."[14]

"A significant development in America's cultural coming of age is a growing appreciation of the richness of American folk music," Lomax explained in the *Teachers Manual and Classroom*

Guide for his live CBS show. "It will be the purpose of this series to map the main outline of American folk song in English and to indicate the part it has played in the life of the people and in the growth of America. By stimulating the interest of students in this music, and much of which is still current in their communities, by dignifying it and making it understandable, they will develop the sense that music is a part of living and that this musical heritage is a part of their lives." The entire year's weekly schedule was listed, including such subjects as "On the Trail," "Around the Campfire," "Sea Shanties," "Songs of the Gold Rush Period," "Lumberjack Songs," "Teamster Songs," and "Courting Songs," with a sample of songs selected from the published collections with his father. The 1940 schedule featured "Nonsense and Animal Songs," "Play Parties and Negro Reels," "British Ballads in America," "Negro Spirituals," "Outlaw Ballads," and "Poor Farmer Songs." For the latter, Lomax included "The Boll Weevil," "Po' Farmer," and "Cotton Mill Collect [Colic]," with the explanation, "in the last quarter of a century, as economic and other difficulties beset the farmer, he has composed songs to tell about his particular troubles":

> I'm a gonna starve and everybody will
> You can't make a living in a cotton mill.
> Patches on my britches, hole in my hat,
> Ain't had a shave since my wife got fat.

Although Dave McCarn's "Cotton Mill Colic," written in 1930, referred to working in a textile mill, which Lomax well knew, there was a genuine connection with the business of cotton cultivation. Lomax was naturally cautious about injecting much of his radical politics into the programs, but through the emphasis on working-class songs—his idea of the music of the "common people"—he hoped to get the message across. While Lomax and the accompanying orchestra did most of the shows, he had an occasional guest, such as Wade Ward and the Bogtrotters on January 9 ("Square Dances"), Aunt Molly Jackson on January 23 and 30 ("Love Songs" and "British Ballads in America"), Woody Guthrie on April 2 ("Farmer Ballads"), and Lead Belly along with Guthrie and the Golden Gate Quartet (which accompanied Lomax on numerous programs) for the season's last show on April 23, 1940 ("Final Review").[15]

The program's 1940–41 season, starting in October, under the new title *Wellsprings of Music*, featured a host of fresh voices, such as Burl Ives, Josh White, and Pete Seeger. The format was also changed, as Lomax explained in the new teachers manual: "To show the relationship between good music and the people who make it this series combines two groups of thirteen programs each: one dealing with the folk music of the Americas; the other, on alternate weeks with a part of the symphonic repertoire which will have a strong and immediate appeal to children. . . . The concept basic to the entire series is that good music, whether the spontaneous product of the folk or the consciously elaborated work of the trained composer, is never a thing apart, but a result of man's experience and a common function of daily living." Bernard Herrmann would be conducting the Columbia Concert Orchestra for the art-music programs. For example, the November 26 program, "Animal Songs," was followed a week later by classical compositions from Saint-Saëns, Debussy, and Wagner. The shows ended the following April with "Railroad Songs," such as "John Henry," and compositions by Richard Strauss and Richard Wagner. The value of the programs to students depended on the enthusiasm of their teachers and the access to radios in the country's classrooms, but there were numerous positive signs in the teachers' and students' letters to the network. While Charles Seeger and his colleagues in the Composers' Collective had generally dropped their modernist inclinations in order to educate the masses, Lomax believed that traditional classical music still had a value in reaching the country's students.[16]

Along with the weekly shows in New York and continuing Library of Congress obligations, Lomax became deeply involved with Woody Guthrie. Following the Grapes of Wrath concert, Lomax invited Guthrie, whom he recognized as an unusually talented performer as well as self-made activist, to Washington, D.C., to record his songs and stories at the Library of

Congress. Three sessions took place, on March 21 and 22 for Alan, then on the March 27 for his wife, Elizabeth. They soon returned to New York, and Guthrie appeared on Lomax's CBS show on April 2.

Lomax next contacted R. P. Wetherald at RCA Victor to arrange a commercial recording session for Guthrie. Guthrie had many songs that he had just recorded for Lomax, but he now composed a new one, "Tom Joad," based on Steinbeck's *Grapes of Wrath*, using the typewriter of one of Seeger's friends. On April 26 and May 3, he recorded the seventeen-verse song, along with a dozen selections, for Victor. "Woody came down Friday morning, and we recorded twelve sides," Wetherald informed Lomax. "I am planning to put these out in two albums of six sides each. If you have any thought on the possible groupings, I would appreciate your indicating them to me." Guthrie's two albums, titled *Dust Bowl Ballads*, volumes 1 and 2, appeared in July 1940 to rave reviews. "These albums are not Summer sedatives," Howard Taubman explained in the *New York Times*. "They make you think; they may even make you uncomfortable though not as uncomfortable as the Okie on his miserable journeys. But they are an excellent thing to have on records." Taubman listed the songs, including "Talkin' Dust Bowl Blues," "Do Re Mi," "The Great Dust Storm," "I Ain't Got No Home in This World Anymore," and "Vigilante Man," before concluding, "They reflect the life of the migratory workers, their wanderings, their aching search for a job, their illness, their enemies. Woody does not romanticize." At the same time, Lomax worked with Victor on recordings by Lead Belly along with the Golden Gate Quartet, cut on June 15 and 17.[17]

Paul Robeson, Josh White, and Others

The African American performers Paul Robeson and Josh White also produced progressive-themed albums at this time, including songs promoting racial justice and economic democracy. After many years in England, Robeson returned to New York in October 1939 and immediately continued his political and musical activism. He began to perform the lengthy "Ballad of Uncle Sam," with words by John La Touche and music by Earl Robinson; it was soon renamed "Ballad for Americans" by Norman Corwin when Robeson performed it on his CBS radio show, *The Pursuit of Happiness*, on November 5. The program generated rave reviews, leading Victor to record the album *Ballad for Americans* at year's end, four sides of two 78 records. It was even featured during the Republican Party's June 1940 convention, performed by Ray Middleton and a chorus (while the Democrats opened their convention with "God Bless America"). "Until New Dealers twitted them about it, the Republicans were apparently unaware that Ballad for Americans was written originally for a WPA Theatre Project show [*Sing for Your Supper*] in Manhattan," *Time* magazine pointed out. "Nor did they seem to have reflected that Paul Robeson and the authors of the Ballad ... are well-known Leftists." To prove the point, *Ballad for Americans* was used at the Communist Party's 1940 convention. RCA featured the album in its exhibit at the reopened world's fair in New York, and by year's end, it "had sold more than 40,000 copies," Robinson happily recalled, "enough so that RCA dropped the price from $2 to $1.50."[18]

While appreciating the renown, Robinson did not lessen his political involvements, which soon provoked the interest of the FBI. "During that period I appeared at Moose Hall in Seattle for the anti-war Washington Commonwealth Federation, mentioning how I'd rather have my songs sung before that group than before any other political party," he later wrote. "A leaflet promoting the event stated that a manuscript of *Ballad for Americans* had been sold off to benefit the Communist Party's magazine *New Masses*," or so someone informed the FBI. Over the next four decades, FBI agents shadowed Robinson and assembled a file filled with thousands of pages on his political and personal life.[19]

On June 4, 1940, a month after Guthrie's breakthrough recordings for Victor, John Hammond produced an album featuring Josh White and a quartet, the Carolinians, for Columbia Records. Selecting songs from Lawrence Gellert's books, such as

"Nine Foot Shovel," "Chain Gang Boun'," and "Told My Captain," the album was titled *Chain Gang*. It met stiff resistance in the white South following its release in August but generally reached a welcoming audience in other parts of the United States. Howard Taubman in the *New York Times* found that some record companies "recent releases have had a generous seasoning of unhackneyed material.... To the latter category belongs *Chain Gang*.... Columbia believes that these songs are 'perhaps the most genuine folk music of our time.' Certainly they have an authentic ring." The Carolinians had a polished sound, unlike the chain gangs recorded by the Lomaxes in the field, which would appeal to a popular audience. Taubman continued, "Like *Dust Bowl Ballads*, issued by Victor recently, *Chain Gang* reports on a gloomy phase of American life. There is no superficial cuteness to commend it to those who wish to be entertained but not disturbed. But the album is a must for those who are not afraid to discover some of the dark places of life and those who care about music that rises spontaneously from the hearts and throats of humble and unfortunate men." Taubman also commented on the album that Bing Crosby, accompanied by the Ken Darby Singers, recorded for Decca, titled *Earl Robinson–John La Touche: Ballad for Americans*: "Since it took the nation by storm last Winter, the rise in popularity of 'Ballad for Americans' has been undiminished."[20]

While Lomax was involved with his radio programs and recordings, he continued to work on various book projects. Production was dragging on the new book with his father, *Our Singing Country: A Second Volume of American Ballads and Folk Songs*, with musical transcriptions by Ruth Crawford Seeger. Finally published in 1941, with all the songs drawn from their collecting trips, the Lomaxes explained in the preface, "The function of this book is to let American folk singers have their way with the readers. Most of these singers are poor people, farmers, laborers, convicts, old-age pensioners, relief workers, housewives, wandering guitar pickers. These are the people who still sing the work songs, the cowboy songs, the sea songs, the lumberjack songs, the bad-men ballads, and other songs that have no occupation or special group to keep them alive." Although designed for a popular and not specifically left-wing audience, the book included songs by Dick Maitland, Aunt Molly Jackson, Emma Dusenberry, and Woody Guthrie ("dust-bowl ballad-maker, proud of being an Okie, familiar with microphones and typewriters, familiar, too, with jails and freight trains").[21]

When the three men were together in Washington, D.C., in early 1940, Alan Lomax (compiler), Pete Seeger (transcriber), and Woody Guthrie (note writer) pulled together an extensive book of labor and protest songs, to be titled *Hard Hitting Songs for Hard Hit People* (although it was not published until 1967). This was a labor of love for the three. As Guthrie explained in the introduction, "Here's a book of songs that's going to last a mighty long time, because these are the kind of songs that folks make up when they're a-singing about their hard luck, and hard luck is one thing that you sing louder about than you do about boots and saddles, or moons on the river, or cigarettes a shining in the dark. There's a heap of people in the country that's a having the hardest time of their life right this minute." John Steinbeck agreed in the book's foreword, "The songs of the working people have always been their sharpest statement and the one statement which cannot be destroyed. You can burn books, buy newspapers, you can guard against handbills and pamphlets, but you cannot prevent singing."[22]

Publishers didn't think the time was ripe for such a songbook, however, even though Seeger, the youngest of the trio, didn't want to give up too easily. "I returned to New York City in the fall of 1940," he recalled, and then "I tackled the problem of the manuscript to the book, *Hard-Hitting Songs*, and wondering whether I should try and find a publisher for it. At that time, somebody told me that a man named Lee Hays, who used to teach at Commonwealth College, was in New York, also trying to find a publisher for a book of union songs." Hays had recently arrived in the city after fleeing southern political repression. The previous year, he had put together a book proposal, including 150 songs. A third comprised "union songs—anti-war—anti-fascist etc.," with the rest spread among "International Workers songs," "Negro songs," "Old Left section," "Jail-Convict-chain gang," and the like. He was drawing on his earlier ten-page mimeographed pamphlet "Commonwealth Labor Songs—A Collection of Old and New Songs for the Use of Labor Unions," which had sold for five cents per copy. "Approximate cost should be no more than 15 to 25 cents per copy," Hays proposed for the new book. "The low cost should encourage widespread usage—making it available to workers and workers organizations without an exhorbitant [sic] price." Although both book projects fell through, Seeger and Hays soon joined forces in the Almanac Singers.[23]

During the summer of 1940, as Guthrie and Seeger toured the country and the major labels released politically oriented albums by Guthrie, Robeson, and White that could reach a wide audience, an enthusiastic Alan Lomax was preparing a second radio program for CBS, along with *Wellsprings of Music*, this one aimed at adults. "Well, we finally settled on Kip [Clifton] Fadiman as M.C. for 'I'm a Stranger Here Myself.' We still are questioning the title because, as I pointed out, it doesn't quite tell you what the show is about and requires a bit of explaining," Davidson Taylor at CBS informed Lomax in mid-July. "Suggestions on that are still in order." Fadiman was a noted book editor and the host of the long-running NBC radio quiz show *Information Please*. Lomax worked closely with his friend Nicholas Ray on the show's scripts. "Nick's and my program, called 'I'm a Stranger Here Myself'" with Clifton Fadiman, M.C., will be given a dress try out on C.B.S. on August 19," Lomax informed his father on July 26. "I'm going to be tearing around pretty rapidly between now and then. If the program sells, my end will be writing the scripts here in Washington which ought to be fun."[24]

Nick Ray (born Raymond Nicholas Kienzle in 1911 in Wisconsin) began as a drama student, then studied architecture with Frank Lloyd Wright. By 1935, he had moved to New York and performed in a play along with Earl Robinson, *The Young Go First*, codirected by the talented Elia Kazan for the left-wing Theatre of Action. The following year, he appeared in the short-lived play *Who Fights This Battle?*, which raised funds for the

Ministry of Education of the Spanish Republic just before the civil war erupted; Robinson performed the music composed by Paul Bowles. In early 1937, Ray moved to Washington, D.C., to head local theater activities in the Special Skills Division of the Resettlement Administration, working with Charles Seeger. Ray traveled around the country interviewing lumberjacks, farm laborers, and others, then composed plays and songs performed by the local informants. His pageant at Penderlea Farms in North Carolina attracted six thousand spectators, including Eleanor Roosevelt. Through his work, he met Alan Lomax, and they became close friends. "When I met Nick in Washington in the 1930s he was certainly one of the most splendid young men in the whole world," Lomax recalled. "He seemed to me to be the person I'd always dreamed of being. . . . I was the only person who had been out there with the Blacks, the Mexicans, the Cajuns and all the rest. And Nick was one of the people who came and listened and took it seriously." Through Lomax, Ray plunged into the emerging folk music scene, particularly after his government job ended in late 1939.[25]

Lomax and Ray's first radio show, now titled *Back Where I Come From*, part of the summer CBS series *Forecast*, featured the Golden Gate Quartet, Guthrie, Ives, and White, a good sampling of Lomax's expanding stable of folk singers. "I'm going to New York tomorrow night to stay up a week with Nick's and my radio program called 'Back Where I Come From,'" Lomax continued to his father. "My estimate at this point is 'only fair.' A lot of compromises have had to be made, such as having Clifton Fadiman as the MC. The only reason for this was the hope that his presence will make the program a commercial possibility." The show began its regular nightly coast-to-coast run, for fifteen minutes three times a week, in late September, although it lacked a sponsor. Lomax had soon patched up an initial falling out with Fadiman, as he explained to him: "You know we locked horns the first time we met, and, being young and childish, I took the battle very seriously. Working with you for two weeks in the back country completely revised this edition. The whole cast came around and expressed the same opinion about you.

I'm no good at this, but it was good to know you." Then Lomax came up with a suggestion: "At the behest of various friends of mine I had been thinking of myself in the mc's shoes and I want to know what you think of it. The material and the performers might sell the show." He had already lined up the jazz musician Sidney Bechet, the Coon Creek Girls, and the hillbilly banjo player Wade Mainer. Fadiman remained as the MC.[26]

Back Where I Come From began its regular season on September 25, and two days later, the second show featured Guthrie and Ives with songs on "war and soldiers." Born in Illinois in 1909, Burl Ives learned traditional ballads as a child from his family, particularly his grandmother. He attended Eastern Illinois State Teachers College, although he never graduated, and after a struggle to survive, with a brief stay in Indiana, he arrived in New York in 1933. He initially performed classical songs but soon connected with the city's left-wing cultural workers and the local folk music community. After viewing *The Cradle Will Rock*, he met Will Geer, who played the character Mister Mister, and Ives quickly identified with radical politics, including supporting the government in the Spanish Civil War. When asked if he would "sing some ballads at a party to raise money for the Abraham Lincoln Brigade," he said, "'Certainly. Where?' . . . After that [he] did many benefits for many causes," including the Theatre Arts Committee. While nurturing his acting and singing skills, Ives toured the country with Geer, presenting agitprop (radical) skits and along the way met Alan Lomax at the Library of Congress. In 1939, he visited in Los Angeles with Geer, who had relocated from New York for his movie career, and then through Geer, Ives met Guthrie.[27]

Ives's appearance at the March 1940 "'Grapes of Wrath' Evening" was no fluke but the result of his vital musical and political friendships, particularly with Geer. Lomax later testified, "Will Geer's sponsorship of folk music, as a leading actor, his own warmth, and wide appreciation and love of the material, displayed in his parties, his entertainments, and his friendships were an important spiritual force in the whole early period of the [folk music] revival. All of us loved him and trusted him and depended on him for these things." The following June, Ives launched his own weekly *Burl Ives Show* on NBC radio. "I felt more convinced than ever of the truth in the idea that folk songs are an expression of the People. I was of the people, getting strength from them, singing for them," Ives believed. The next year, he recorded his first album, *Okeh Presents the Wayfaring Stranger*. He also made a short film with Will Geer and Josh White, *Tall Tales*, about folk songs. Ives became a major film and folk star after the war.[28]

"I've just got back from New York where I did my first School of the Air broadcast and several others also," Lomax informed his father on October 12. "Spent the night with Mrs. Eleanor Roosevelt in Hyde Park. She's a very nice lady. I'm working my head off and I'm delighted to know that you're having such good luck." As war approached, Lomax began preparing to get the Library of Congress involved—in September, Congress passed the first peacetime draft, with the registration of men between the ages of twenty-one and thirty-six slated to begin in October—although the Communist Party continued to promote an isolationist foreign policy. As Lomax had suggested to Harold Spivacke, he wished "to make it possible for the American people to explain for themselves what America means and has meant to them." More specifically, he suggested that the Archive of American Folk Song "draw upon its large stock of tunes and songs for material for song books for [army] camps.... I feel, for example that where any large group of second-generation Polish conscripts are located, Polish songs should be sung. The same for Negro, Mexican, Greek, Finnish, etc. conscript groups." Lomax further believed that "'God Bless America' and Kate Smith are both extremely dull and mediocre," but he felt "a pamphlet containing a succinct account of the origin of the *Star Spangled Banner* should be issued at this time."[29]

Back from Where I Come From, before it ended in February 1941, featured not only Guthrie, Ives, White, and Bechet but also Lead Belly, Earl Robinson, and Pete Seeger. Bess Lomax, Alan's sister, then a student at Bryn Mawr College, often visited New York and the show: "My time spent watching rehearsals of *Back*

Where I Come From turned out to be some of the most influential hours of my life so far. . . . The script was almost entirely composed of what nowadays might be called 'folk speech'; it was somewhat Sandburgian in style, with long strings of jokes, proverbs, and hilarious traditional sayings." Late in 1940, Alan had a feeling that the show was in trouble at the network. "I'd like some (friendly, *unofficial*, not in the slightest contractual) assurance from you that BACK WHERE I COME FROM has a clear road ahead for some time," he wrote to Davidson Taylor at CBS. "Morally and artistically, I feel it should have, although I know its many problems for all of us. I also know of its many strong points." Whatever the issues, the time was running short for his evening program.[30]

Lomax had initially become a strong booster of Ives, who was also picking up stray acting jobs. "The most charming singer of old world ballads that I know of—not in any particular authentic American style, but in a characteristic Irish style of his own which is extremely captivating is Burl Ives," Lomax informed R. P. Wetherald at RCA in September. "I think his albums of songs will far outshine those of [John Jacob] Niles and the other dulcimer players on Columbia, whose names I can't recall at the moment." Lomax soon had his reservations concerning Ives's appearances on his radio show, as he explained to William Fineschriber at CBS in early 1941: "I hope that you've found out that Burl Ives had been pretty hard to handle on Back Where I Come From. He's a nice fellow but convinced of the fact that he's the best singer in the world. He can make Back Where I Come From impossible by refusing to take direction and you can make it possible by making him feel that he does not have to." Ives's attitude, a least according to Lomax, could be explained by the fact that by mid-1940 he had already landed his own show on an NBC affiliate. He began to feel increasingly independent, and his emerging film career furthered his independence.[31]

Guthrie, as his popularity expanded, soon had a falling-out with Nick Ray over Lead Belly's involvement in *Back Where I Come From*. Ray urged Lomax to drop him because of Lead Belly's thick southern accent and apparent inability to read the script. Guthrie exploded and quit the show. "I am indeed sorry that you're no longer on Back Where I Come From," Lomax wrote to him in early November. "The first program that you failed to appear on just about broke my heart and I don't know yet how I'm going to plan the script without imagining you taking lines." He also inquired how Guthrie was doing on his autobiography. Guthrie soon cooled down and was back on the show, appearing on "Cowboy Songs" on November 20 with the usual cast of Ives, Lead Belly, and the newcomer Tony Kraber. Two days later, Guthrie joined Ives, Lead Belly, and White in singing about death and then next on "The Jailhouse" program. His last shows were in late December, "The 13th Amendment" and "Christmas," after which he returned with his family to California. In early February 1941, Lomax updated Guthrie, now back in Los Angeles, about his radio programs: "I really miss you a lot on 'Back Where I Come From.' The program has become very 'merry' and 'jolly' since you left us. We don't have anybody who can come out and speak his mind with sincerity and honesty the way you can. Pete [Seeger] is on very regularly and his banjo playing adds a lot."[32]

Woody Guthrie

While Guthrie was on the Lomax shows, he had other media outlets as well. Starting on July 13, he began appearing on Henrietta Yurchenco's local WNYC show *Adventures in Music*; the program lasted until late April 1941. Married to the painter Basil "Chenk" Yurchenco, Henrietta Yurchenco had become part of the New York arts community by the late 1930s, when she began working at the municipally owned WNYC starting with classical music. *Adventures in Music* first featured ethnic music, but, she recalled, "soon American folk music became my chief interest." "With Franklin Roosevelt's election in 1932, Americanism was in the air, and one of its consequences was the birth of city interest in traditional country music. Toward the end of the 1930s, a colony of folk musicians from various regions settled in New York, primarily to raise money for political causes." Her program, titled *Kentucky*, included Guthrie, Jim Garland, and Sarah Ogan

(Gunning): "We heard first-hand about the dismal life in company-owned towns, their fight against company-hired Chicago gangsters, and government compliance.... Woody brought the program to a close with the ballad 'Tom Joad.'" The announcer concluded the show: "With the singing of 'Tom Joad' by Woody, we come to the end of our second adventure in the folk music of Kentucky and Oklahoma.... Tonight we have heard songs of humor, Holy Roller Songs, Dust-Bowl Songs and labor songs, sung by Jim Garland, Sary Ogan and their friends, Mamie Quackenbush, Fanny, and Woody, who plays that guitar."[33]

Guthrie introduced Lead Belly, his close friend, to Yurchenco in a letter on October 3: "You might be interested to know that Leadbelly and me have been working on a lot of things together and we'd like to have you hear them and arrange some programs in Adventures in Music—because I honestly believe that of all the living folk singers I've ever seen that Leadbelly is ahead of them all." He continued, "You are one of the only persons that knows folk and you know that it is wrong for the people of the air waves not to hear Huddie." Yurchenco became convinced and arranged for Lead Belly to have his own show on WNYC, *Folk Songs of America*, fifteen minutes every Wednesday evening beginning on November 7 and going to late February 1941. He would arrive at the studio in a double-breasted gray suit, white shirt, and bow tie, his usual attire. "Once on the air," Yurchenco explained, "Leadbelly would ad lib commentaries about his life, his youth on Fanning Street, a red-light district, his experience with cocaine, backbreaking field work, his sexual exploits and disappointments, and his years on prison farms." Each show had a theme—such as railroad songs, workhouse songs, river songs, and square-dance songs—with Lead Belly beginning and ending with his theme song "Goodnight Irene," and all seemed to include Guthrie. On December 12, for example, Guthrie was singing "Jesse James" and "John Hardy." Lead Belly kept up a busy performing schedule, having also appeared on Elaine Lambert Lewis's WNYC *Songs of the Seven Million* program in August 1940, at Cafe Society in late October, and at the Palm Gardens in New York in a benefit program for the Southern School and

Commonwealth College in November. In early December, he performed at a benefit for the Highlander Folk School at Pierce Hall in Washington, D.C.[34]

Guthrie's friend from California Cisco Houston now arrived in New York, and they resumed performing together at Jimmy Dwyer's Sawdust Trail and other night spots. In September, CBS approached Guthrie about appearing as a host and singer on the network's *Pipe Smoking Time* program. His weekly income was now over $300, which allowed him to send for Mary and their three children. His first CBS show on November 25 opened with Guthrie singing the theme song based on "So Long, It's Been Good to Know You," backed by Ray Bloch's orchestra. Such commercial success also prodded Guthrie into dropping his column in the *Daily Worker*—the last appeared on November 4—since the Communist Party was experiencing increasing scrutiny and criticism (his final column in *People's World* was published on November 25). Letters had already been received at the *New York Sun* questioning his loyalty, responding to the flattering August article by Malcolm Johnson, "Okie to Sing at Jimmie Dwyer's Sawdust Trail," soon followed by a second, longer profile. At year's end, after seven *Pipe Smoking Time* programs, in which he was forced into playing the rube, following the script without any spontaneous jokes, Guthrie had had enough, and the family quickly departed for California.[35]

Folk Music Collecting

Alan Lomax carefully nurtured and promoted the careers of Guthrie, Ives, White, Seeger, the Golden Gate Quartet, Lead Belly, Sonny Terry, and Brownie McGhee—all of whom were to become significant figures in the coming folk revival. He had entered the world of commercial radio, records, books, and talks, but he never abandoned his work for the Library of Congress and his interest in field recordings by vernacular musicians. "We asked for songs. Antique collectors are a serious lot. Stamp collectors are given to frantic appeals.... But the gathering of old songs is by far the simplest and one of the most satisfying forms of the collecting mania," Sidney Snook (an alias?) explained in *Etude*, in an apparent satire. "Up in the Kentucky mountains we soon were hearing the 'song ballets,' telling their tales of high adventure and tragic love, which have resounded in the hills since the day the grandmothers and grandfathers, and great-grandmothers and great-grandfathers of the singers came over from England and Scotland." Whatever the author's apparently humorous intention, he concluded that the song collector "will discover there are many kindly, obliging people in the world who like to sing. He will listen to brave tales of olden days. He will hear strange words and music. And he will find it altogether entrancing."[36]

Lomax strongly agreed that folk music was "altogether entrancing" as he continued promoting field work through his position at the Library of Congress. In January 1940, he had received a letter from Charles Todd: "I was doing some writing for the New York Times on the migratory Labor Camps in Imperial Valley [California] and in the course of my wandering I picked up a number of old 'Okie' ballads—along with others not so old. I managed to make recordings of some of these and I think you might be interested in hearing a few of them." Lomax immediately responded: "Did you work with Margaret Valliant [*sic*] of the F[arm] S[ecurity] A[dministration] last summer? She made records of the camps about the same time. I should like to hear your recordings and talk with you about Okies and folk lore." Todd had studied literature in college and while living in Greenwich Village had met Lomax at the Village Vanguard. He was now working with Robert Sonkin in the Department of Public Speaking at City College of New York. During July and August 1940, the two made recording trips for the Library of Congress to the Arvin, Shafter, Visalia, Firebaugh, Westley, Thornton, and Yuba City FSA camps in California.[37]

In late July, Lomax had sent Todd and Sonkin a list of detailed instructions for their upcoming field trip. For example, "As you know, valuable material is to be had from comparison of different performances of the same songs in the same community by different regions. So also, are different performances of the same songs in the same community by different singers or the same song by different members of the family or the same song by the same performers at different times." What was most important was to remember that "the great beauty of field recordings is that performers take their own time and do things their own way, feeling that if they make a mistake, they can try again. The results are such that no commercial recording company can ever hope to achieve." After completing a successful expedition, Todd and Sonkin published their experiences in the *New York Times*. "With other nations torn by war and hostile ideologies, America is becoming more and more conscious of her priceless possessions," they began their article. "Among other things we are slowly discovering our heritage of song." They found that it was "a somewhat bewildering experience to travel a few miles inland from the modern, sophisticated cities of the California coast to the hot valley of the San Joaquin, where many of the Okies have made their homes in government camps[,] private camps or in roadside tents and shelters." They discovered a plethora of songs and musical styles, both old and new. "There is no need to fear that a people who can sing as these people do will vanish from the earth," they concluded. "They may be 'dusted out' and 'tractored out,' but they are not down and out—not so long as they go on singing songs like these." Todd and Sonkin returned for two more months the next summer, then played some of their recordings for the Roosevelts at the White House.[38]

Margaret Valiant, born in Mississippi, began as an opera singer and fashion model in Paris but during the Depression became involved with promoting folk cultures throughout the country. She had met Ruth Crawford in 1931 (before the latter's marriage to Charles Seeger), and they remained close friends. In 1936, Valiant worked with Charles in the Special Skills Division of the Resettlement Administration (RA), beginning at Cherry Lake Farms, near Madison, Florida, and later in North Carolina, Tennessee, Alabama, West Virginia, and then Camp Bakersfield in California. She staged theatrical productions along with musical events and field recordings for the local residents. In November 1937, Valiant performed with the "Resettlement Folk

Singers" (along with Ruth Seeger) in "An Evening of American Music in Conjunction with the Exhibition of Rural Arts" organized by Charles Seeger in Washington, D.C. Late in the decade, with the demise of the RA, she joined the National Youth Administration and formed the National Youth Orchestra with the conductor Leopold Stokowski.[39]

Along with Valiant, Sonkin, and Todd, John Lomax, now in his early seventies, tried one more collecting trip starting in September 1940, following up on a similar venture the previous year. He traveled a total of six thousand miles through Louisiana, Mississippi, and Alabama, where Ruby Pickens Tartt assisted with supplying local singers in Livingston; after Atlanta and then South Carolina, he ended in Washington, D.C., in mid-November. He had amassed over seven hundred recordings, as well as photographs of their informants, and for the next three months, they worked in the Archive of American Folk Songs organizing their collections. The Library of Congress had established the Radio Research Project, and John compiled, with Alan's assistance, ten broadcasts of his field recordings with commentaries, titled *The Ballad Hunter*, that were distributed on transcription discs to radio stations throughout the country (and later issued on LP records). Herbert Halpert had also been recording in the South in 1939, with a stop at the Mississippi state penitentiary. He captured African American female prisoners singing a cappella, as well as the white banjo player Thaddeus Willingham and the fiddler W. E. Claunch.[40]

While there was a progressive side to folk music promoting racial equality, labor unions, and economic democracy, it remained mostly connected with traditional, grassroots America along with somewhat of a patriotic tinge. This was evident in the numerous field recordings, songbooks, folk festivals, and radio programs popular throughout the country that had no overt political agenda. "The WPA projects of the 1930s also meant a rediscovery of roots," the composer and folk music fan Norman Cazden testified. "It's the hoedown, the local songs, the narrative about a girl in the nineteenth century who got murdered by her sweetheart, the story about Old Joe Clark and his love for chicken pie. This is not political content: self-consciousness in the sense of recognizing that there was indeed a repertoire of song and story and tradition and music of their own; that, yes."[41]

The Conservative Political Backlash

The New Deal years seem to have been a time of liberal politics, radical movements, and labor activism, but there was a contrary conservative current that had crippled or killed off many of the government's programs by decade's end. During the 1938 fall elections, Republican candidates captured eight Senate seats, eighty-one additional House seats, and twelve governorships. The House of Representatives Un-American Activities Committee, along with the assistance of J. Edgar Hoover's FBI, kept busy with its attack on the Communist Party and other such assumed subversives. The Fair Labor Standards Act, passed in 1938, which established a minimum wage (twenty-five cents per hour the first year, rising to forty cents within six years) and maximum hours (forty-four per week in the first year and forty hours within two years), was the last gasp of the old New Deal coalition.

Southern congressmen, now allied with northern Republicans, were becoming increasingly obstructionist. In 1939, the House of Representatives, controlled by southerners, created the House Special Committee to Investigate the National Labor Relations Board (NLRB), headed by Virginia's conservative Representative Howard Smith. The committee opposed both the NLRB's support for the CIO unions and its attacks on companies hostile to unions. Moreover, the country was turning slowly toward a military posture as the European war escalated, further undermining any hope for expanding domestic programs. In 1940, Congress easily passed the Alien Registration Act, known as the Smith Act after the same Rep. Smith, which instituted a peacetime sedition law that J. Edgar Hoover had sought since 1919. As a result, simply advocating the overthrow of the government by "force and violence," not just participating in violent acts, was enough to be tried and convicted. The Smith

Act was long used to prosecute left-wing leaders and members. Labor strikes led by the CIO in 1940 heightened fears of radical activism, particularly in defense-related industries. The conservative AFL union leaders had already hopped on the anticommunist bandwagon.[42]

Various state legislatures throughout the country were adopting a similar conservative thrust. The strong right-wing segregationist and anti-labor-union coalition of Democratic politicians, businesspeople, land and mill owners, dirt farmers, and so many others in the South had been gathering steam, but they were not alone. For example, the Tenney committee in California led the conservative attack in that state. Having served in the First World War, Jack Tenney worked as an attorney while writing songs, such as "Mexicali Rose," before being elected as a Democrat to the California State Assembly in 1936; in 1941, he moved to the state senate, where he chaired the California Senate Fact-Finding Subcommittee on Un-American Activities. In conjunction with Martin Dies's HUAC, Tenney spearheaded a vigorous attack on the Communist Party, focused on the Hollywood film industry, an attack that had begun as early as 1938.[43]

In New York, the Rapp-Coudert committee, officially the Joint Legislative Committee to Investigate the Educational System of the State of New York, functioned in a similar vein, particularly after the signing of the Nazi-Soviet Pact in 1939 brought the Communist Party under intense scrutiny. Established to look into school finances, the committee soon switched to investigating Communists among high school and particularly college teachers in New York City. Between 1940 and 1942, the committee's work led to firing more than fifty teachers, most from the City College of New York (CCNY). During the 1930s, the four Foner brothers—Phil, Jack, Moe, and Henry—had formed a dance band and become involved with the Communist Party, and late in the decade, the oldest three worked at CCNY. "Phil, Jack, and I were suspended and then, in 1941 fired," Moe Foner later wrote. "In the unsuccessful protest campaign that followed, a group was formed called Friends of the Foners. . . . After we were suspended, we changed the name of our band to Suspended Swing."

Their theme song had become "Joe Hill." The Foner brothers were not alone in feeling the sting of the mounting conservative backlash.[44]

The middle of the country was not spared the anticommunist attack, with an especially aggressive purge taking place in Oklahoma. Sis Cunningham had originally left Oklahoma to become active as a performer at Commonwealth College and the Southern Summer School for Women Workers near Asheville, but had returned to Oklahoma City in the late summer of 1939. In 1936, Bob Wood, a labor organizer in the South, had moved to Tulsa to launch the state's Communist Party. Two years later, he was in Oklahoma City and opened the Progressive Book Store. Wood recruited Eli Jaffe to assist him with statewide organizing. They welcomed Pete Seeger and Woody Guthrie when they stopped on their cross-country trip in the summer of 1940. Ina Wood, Bob's wife, encouraged Guthrie to write "Union Maid" (to the tune of "Red Wing").[45]

When Cunningham returned to Oklahoma City, she joined the fledgling Red Dust Players, a ragtag musical and dramatic group that traveled the state helping to organize the United Canners, Agricultural, Packing and Allied Workers of America (UCAPAWA). Cunningham explained, "Soon we had skits and songs ready—enough for a show—and Doria, our director, had us booked solidly every Saturday for months ahead.... Red Dust Players performances were free." The group kept busy until the following spring. "The effectiveness of the Red Dust Players—especially our work with the oil union—was borne out by the reaction that came with suddenness and cut off our activities entirely," she bitterly recalled. "We came back from a strenuous weekend late one night in April or May of 1940 to find the homes of some of our members broken into, their letters and papers strewn about, household stuff in a shambles, and books missing."[46]

Anticommunist fervor had been building among the state's politicians and in the press, allied with the American Legion and even the Ku Klux Klan. On August 17, the police raided the Progressive Book Store, where they seized thousands of books and pamphlets; the local office of the Communist Party; and five private homes. Ina and Bob Wood and Eli Jaffe, along with a few others, were arrested and charged with violating the state's 1919 criminal syndicalism law. Their trials dragged into the fall of 1941, with the conviction of the Woods, Jaffe, and Alan Shaw. But then the furor calmed down, and the convictions were reversed; none served a prison sentence. A frightened Cunningham had gone into hiding with her parents. In March 1941, she met Gordon Friesen from Weatherford, a journalist who was active in the Oklahoma Committee to Defend Political Prisoners and the author of the pamphlet *Oklahoma Witch Hunt*. The two Communist Party members were married four months later and in November fled the state, seeking political refuge in New York and a new musical life.[47]

John Lomax's conservative views alerted him to the dangers that his politically active children faced in this unfolding new world. He was particularly concerned about Bess as she finished college in 1941. "During her three years in Bryn Mawr she had the reputation of being a Communist, her most intimate friends among the students were extreme radicals," he wrote to Alan in June. Moreover, he continued, "I understand from your talk with me in Galveston that you were aware of the peril to your welfare that your record, politically, had placed you. I know, too, that Bess Brown has absorbed from you and your associates, at least in her early adoption of radical tendencies, her devotion to Communistic ideals. . . . The public mind, as you must know, is becoming more and more inflamed against enemies (extreme critics), without and within. We may be approaching a period of unreason and persecution." Bess and Alan, despite their father's fears, however, did not yet suffer from the political backlash.[48]

Folk Music at Decade's End

In 1940, the classical composer Roy Harris, originally from Oklahoma, finished his *Folksong Symphony*. "Many of our folksongs began as transplantations from European music," he explained in the article "Folksong—American Big Business," appearing in *Modern Music* in late 1940. "In a sense our popular music is *urban* folk music. Both performers and audience have folksong characteristics.... For years collecting of American folksong has quietly been going on. Credit must be given to such distinguished collectors as Cecil Sharp and to many others less acclaimed. But to the house of Lomax, father John and son Alan, goes the honor of bringing to records folksongs as they actually sound and of placing before the public such folksingers as Leadbelly, Aunt Molly Jackson, Woodie [*sic*] Guthrie and [Willie] Johnson of the Golden Gate Boys [Quartet]." Harris employed his knowledge and love of folk songs to predict that "all this mushroom exploitation of folksong will neither greatly aid nor hinder it. After the era has run itself out there will remain those composers who have been deeply influenced by the finest, clearest, strongest feeling of our best songs." Taking his own advice, during 1940, Harris completed *Folksong Symphony* for orchestra and chorus, drawing songs from the Lomaxes' *Cowboy Songs and Other Frontier Ballads* and Sandburg's *The American Songbag*. The seven movements included "Western Cowboy," "Mountaineer Love Song," "Negro Fantasy," and "Johnny Comes Marching Home." On December 26, the Cleveland Orchestra previewed the finished work. The *Time* critic quoted the review that appeared in the local *Plain Dealer*: "Forty-five minutes swept by like a second and left one listener with the excited consciousness of having heard something like the American continent rising up and saying hello. This music is nothing if not 100% U.S.A." Harris later explained, "In those days, in New York, famous folk singers used to gather in our house, amongst them Alan Lomax, Burl Ives, 'Lead Belly,' the singers of The Golden Gate Quartet. They came to visit, eat, drink, and make merry which included singing folk songs.... Most of us agreed that folk songs were all things to all people."[49]

While Harris was weaving folk music into his composition, Alan Lomax was explaining his field collecting to a young female audience and encouraging their own involvement. "It's a cool summer evening and you're seated around the campfire, just talking lazily and singing songs," he began "Music in Your Own

Back Yard," an article appearing in the *American Girl*, a publication of the Girl Scouts, in October 1940. "One of the girls has brought her guitar and she's strumming it softly. Then she starts to sing.... It's just a pleasant way of passing the evening, the way of the cowpuncher on the Western plains, of the Kentucky mountaineers gathered around the smoky oil lamp. And when you sing a song about your own lives, you are doing the same thing they do—you are making folk music." Lomax went on to explain something about his own growing up in Texas and the early field trips with his father, including their discovery of Lead Belly, and his later meeting Aunt Molly Jackson. He concluded, "These are the places to look, among the back roads in your own home town, and while you're out on camping trips. Ask around home, do a little detective work, and then go out looking for songs. There's music in your own back yard."[50]

Franklin Roosevelt was reelected to a third presidential term in November, defeating the moderate Republican Wendell Wilkie. Carl Sandburg, a passionate Roosevelt supporter and folk music enthusiast, had penned this election song (not performed at the time):

> Goddamn Republicans
> Scum of the earth
> We will meet them
> And beat them
> And show them what we are worth.
> Out of Wall Street
> Came a Wilkie.
> He's a silkie
> S.O.B.
> Goddamn Republicans
> The G-e-e-e O-h-h-h P-e-e-e!

It was not until December 1943 that the president announced that "Dr. New Deal" had been replaced by "Dr. Win the War," but the momentum for this shift was already well under way. Domestic programs would not vanish, but they would increasingly take a backseat to war mobilization, although the country was not yet willing to become directly involved in the escalating conflicts in Europe and Asia.

Folk music, commercial, vernacular, and otherwise, had come of age during this politically, socially, culturally, and economically dynamic decade and would continue as the new world was forming. Alan Lomax, Pete Seeger, Burl Ives, Josh White, Woody Guthrie, Lead Belly, Gene Autry, the Carter Family, and so many others would shape and promote folk music in the coming decades, along with the numerous record companies, journalists, club owners, and publishers. Folk music did not lose its left-wing gloss, however. While New Deal programs had been greatly curtailed, popular culture continued to include progressive themes, particularly racially inclusive musical shows during the war.[51]

Epilogue

While World War II, emerging full blown for the United States in December 1941, along with the rise of conservative politics, served to devastate the New Deal's social, economic, and cultural programs, much of the Popular Front's agenda managed to survive for a while. Popular culture included a visible interracial agenda, with folk music playing a vital role. Organized labor through the AFL and CIO unions mostly adhered to a no-strike pledge, in order not to disrupt the war effort, but wildcat strikes continued to break out. This was a frightening, confusing, yet also liberating time.[1]

"The publication of *A Treasury of American Song* [by Olin Downes and Elie Siegmeister] gives us the most rounded picture of the growth and importance of American folk music to date," Lou Cooper commented in the left-wing magazine *New Masses* in early January 1941. "Across the centuries this music leaps into our times reliving for us the pain, struggle, and joys of other days, rekindling the traditions which will light the future. In the larger sense, all America wrote this exciting and colorful book."[2]

First Lady Eleanor Roosevelt agreed. The White House asked Archibald MacLeish, the librarian of Congress, to organize "A Program of American Songs for American Soldiers." Alan Lomax met with Mrs. Roosevelt, and they staged the event in the East Room of the White House on February 17, with Lomax as master of ceremonies. He drew on the regulars for his CBS program *Back Where I Come From*: Josh White, Burl Ives, the Golden Gate Quartet, Wade Mainer and his band, and John M. "Sailor Dad" Hunt. Along with the headliners, Lomax "went out to the local boot camps and after a few days found two or three marvelous country and western groups who could really sing and play up a storm," he recalled. "We designed a program booklet full of Davy Crockett mottoes and pictures from the era of the America frontier. We did this because at that point there was a problem about American morale. . . . The most urgent matter at that time was to stop fascism, and we were all part of that." In October 1942, Lomax left the Archive of American Folk Song for the Office of War Information (OWI), where he was generally unsuccessful in attempting to use folk music to promote the war effort. As he later recalled, "Everyone congratulated Mrs. Roosevelt, Archie [MacLeish] and me, but we did not get our program of folk music into the camps. The Pentagon considered the morale of the armed forces a strictly military matter." This was a slight exaggeration. For Mrs. Roosevelt, as she wrote in her newspaper column, she hoped "these evening's songs spread thru all the branches of the services. . . . I think it would serve to make us conscious of our own rich background of folk literature and music."[3]

During early 1941, while the escalating world conflicts and the mounting conservative backlash were capturing the headlines, a group of creative folk musicians, each with an interest in the Communist Party's issues and concerns, were going their own way in New York. They marked a musical trail that would continue through much of the century and into the next. Pete Seeger, Lee Hays, and his roommate, the journalist Millard Lampell, began to form a loose group, the Almanac Singers, in January. Two months later, they recorded the album *Songs for John Doe*, filled with acerbic peace songs criticizing the president's moves toward war. It was issued by Erik Bernay's Keynote Records, a contact they had through Alan Lomax. The Almanacs lived a communal lifestyle in Greenwich Village, and the group eventually expanded to include Bess Lomax, Woody Guthrie, Pete and Butch Hawes, Josh White, and Sis Cunningham. After the German invasion of the Soviet Union in June, following the Communist Party's line, they switched to a prowar stance, although this was not enough to avoid their increasing political criticism in the press. They next recorded two albums of traditional folk songs, followed by the prowar album *Dear Mr. President* during the following winter. Soon the members scattered into various forms of war work—Seeger, Ives, and Lampell joined the army, Guthrie and Cisco Houston entered the Merchant Marine. Alan Lomax first went to work for the OWI and then entered the army, while his sister, Bess, worked at the OWI under Nick Ray. Lead Belly, Lee Hays, Josh White, and Aunt Molly Jackson stayed behind to continue performing, with White often appearing at the White House. Sis Cunningham and Gordon Friesen moved to Detroit, where Gordon was a journalist while the frail Sis tried factory work. All the former Almanacs continued to perform through the war, and their group style musically reverberated for a long time.[4]

In mid-1941, Chester Kallman covered numerous current folk albums in *Harper's Bazaar* in a detailed survey of the field: "Let the cynical but listen to the extraordinarily fine recordings of Americana that have recently been made available: hearing our country sing its hilarities and dejections, its trials and triumphs, from the earliest days of our history to the present, it is impossible not to concede that these are the rich, authentic utterances of a people. . . . These record albums give us a picture of America that cannot be found in books." He included Carl Sandburg, Woody Guthrie, John Jacob Niles, Lead Belly, the Golden Gate Quartet, Josh White, Paul Robeson, Earl Robinson, and various others from all sections of the country. The folk singers found stiff competition in the commercial marketplace, however, from such popular performers as the Andrews Sisters, Tommy Dorsey, Glenn Miller, Bing Crosby, Benny Goodman, Frank Sinatra, and Ella Fitzgerald. "Thar's Gold in Them Thar Hillbilly and Other American Folk Tunes" proclaimed an article in the *Billboard Band Year Book* in September 1942. "Incidentally, it is interesting to note that the war is tending to aid the folk music field," the article concluded. "Placing greater and great importance upon all things that are indigenously American, it is attracting more and more attention to the great field of folk records, which is entirely composed of distinctive and down-to-earth American music—strictly American music." The writer covered Burl Ives, as well as Gene Autry, Bob Wills, Carson Robison, Montana Slim, and Elton Britt, in his roster of the folk musicians. A year later, *Billboard* added an explanation for the heightened interest in folk music in the Midwest: "The influx of war workers, soldiers and sailors from rural communities to Chicago is given as the basic reason for the upsurge since folk from rural communities like to hear their 'native' music away from home."[5]

The American Federation of Musicians (AFM) launched a strike on the major record companies in August 1942 over royalty payments. Added to the shellac shortage that limited record production, this helped to temporarily cripple the major labels and opened the door to Moses Asch's companies, Asch, Disc, and Asch-Stinson, as well as other fringe labels that specialized in country, folk, and African American styles. Decca settled after a year, as did the fledgling Capitol Records; RCA and Victor capitulated in late 1944. Despite the recording ban, a wide range of commercial music thrived during the war, including classical. In late December 1944, Walter Kerr and Elie Siegmeister's stage musical *Sing Out, Sweet Land: A Salute in American Folk and Popular Music* opened on Broadway to positive reviews. It featured Alfred Drake and Burl Ives, and a cast album appeared in 1946.[6]

While the armed forces remained racially segregated, along with much of the country (and not just the South), various stage shows broke racial barriers with black themes and even interracial casts. The color line was pretty firm in Hollywood films, radio programs, and much else but was somewhat flexible on the stage. Racial mixing in New York, such as at the Village Vanguard and Café Society nightclubs, was a vital component of the continuing progressive political agenda. The opening of the successful Broadway production of *On the Town* at the end of 1944—music by Leonard Bernstein, choreography by Jerome Robbins, and the book and lyrics by Adolph Green and Betty Comden—was particularly significant. Created by political progressives, it included an interracial cast and orchestra.

It followed a handful of other shows, such as *As Thousands Cheer* (1933), *Run, Little Children* (1933), *The Cradle Will Rock* (1937–38), *Cabin in the Sky* (1940), and *Carmen Jones* (1943–45), which had interracial or all-black casts. While they did not include folk music, they joined the legacy of Popular Front racial mixing, which included many folk performers.[7]

The most devastating war in history ended in 1945, first in Europe in the spring, then in Asia in August, with 50 million deaths and injuries overall, 24 million in the Soviet Union alone. Much of the world had been destroyed, with millions of homeless refugees and continuing domestic political and ethnic struggles. The United States had emerged physically undamaged, with 400,000 military deaths and a flourishing economy. It was a time of rejoicing and much sorrow, as well as hope for a better future.[8]

Pete Seeger returned from his tour of duty on Saipan in the Pacific in December 1945 and immediately plunged into organizing a new singing progressive labor movement, to be called People's Songs. "In 1945 Americans came home from the war," he later wrote. "We dived enthusiastically into long-deferred projects. A number of us who loved to sing folk songs and union songs thought it the most natural thing in the world to start an organization which could keep us all in touch with one another, which could promote new and old songs and singers, and in general bring closer the broad revival of interest in folk music and topical songs which we felt sure would sooner or later take place." Many of his old friends signed on, such as Woody Guthrie, Lee Hays, Sonny Terry and Brownie McGhee, Alan Lomax, and even Burl Ives, who was now pursuing his film and professional music career. Josh White continued with a busy concert and recording schedule, while not hesitant about appearing at events sponsored by the left-wing People's Songs. Lead Belly also kept musically connected to his friends until his death in 1949.[9]

Folk music was also flourishing in the nightclubs and on the radio stations of New York. After returning from the army in 1945, Oscar Brand launched his WNYC radio show *Folk Song Festival*, which joined *Tom Glazer's Ballad Box* on ABC. There were numerous folk music concerts, while Richard Dyer-Bennet appeared at the trendy Blue Angel. Even Seeger performed at the Village Vanguard in late 1946—"an enormous young ex-G.I. who looks like a telescope also sings, accompanying—or, rather, encouraging—himself on a banjo," according to the *New Yorker*. "He has many of the engaging qualities of the amateur—a fresh, contagious enjoyment of his work and a desire to please that even the most resistant audience must find flattering." But he would always prefer a political rally to a nightclub audience, even when his quartet, the Weavers, hit the top of the charts in 1950— Fred Hellerman, Ronnie Gilbert, and Seeger's old friend Lee Hays. The mainstream record labels, such as Decca, continued to churn out folk (aka "country") records, joined by the Asch and Stinson companies, as well as Young People's Records situated in New York. People's Songs faded away in 1949.[10]

The stage was now set for the blossoming folk revival of the 1950s and after, spearheaded and symbolized by the movers and shakers of the Depression years: Woody Guthrie, Burl Ives, Pete Seeger, John and Alan Lomax, Josh White, Lead Belly, and so many others. The Depression and dust bowl caused devastation for many people in the United States, but these disasters also created the conditions under which artistic and cultural creativity flourished in diverse genres, including the visual arts, music, dance, theater, photography, film, novels, and even creative radio. The artists were in many cases influenced by left-wing politics, and folk music often served as a vital catalyst or ingredient, such as for the young Harry Belafonte, whose popularity soared in the 1950s. Many of the performers and works that emerged had a powerful influence and enduring impact for decades to come. The roots of the future folk music revival had now been deeply planted.[11]

The immense popularity of folk music in the mid-1960s, led by the Kingston Trio, Bob Dylan, Joan Baez, Peter, Paul and Mary, and scores of others, fueled by the numerous record companies, folk festivals, radio programs, folk clubs, and so much else, drew from the legacy of the Depression years. There were substantial differences in the decades, of course, with the federal

Epilogue 157

government now playing a small role, aside from the work of the Library of Congress's Archive of American Folk Song—later renamed the Archive of Folk Culture as part of the American Folklife Center—and the Smithsonian Institution's summer Folklife Festival, launched by Ralph Rinzler in 1967. Moreover, in 1987, the Smithsonian's Center for Folklife and Cultural Heritage obtained the Folkways Records collection, which launched the Smithsonian Folkways label that has released boxed sets of Guthrie and Lead Belly recordings, as well as so much else.

While Woody Guthrie was confined to his hospital bed from the mid-1950s until his death in 1967, his influence was substantial and personified by his friends, particularly Pete Seeger. Commercial folk music had long been identified with racial justice, world peace, economic equality, and strong labor unions. There remained, however, black and white vernacular music—white string bands, African American blues performers, ballad singers, ethnic groups, and the like—which also continued to be popular, not just in rural areas but increasingly in northern communities. This mix of commercial and grassroots performers and musical styles, with a history dating back to the 1920s, continued through the century and into the next. Folklorists, particularly Alan Lomax, who died in 2002 after a long and fruitful life, had worked hard to connect the two since the Depression years. The 1930s vibrant cultural legacy long endured.[12]

Notes

Introduction

1. Ronald D. Cohen, *Folk Music: The Basics* (New York: Routledge, 2006), 1–3.
2. Michael Denning, *The Cultural Front: The Laboring of American Culture in the Twentieth Century* (New York: Verso, 1996), xvii–xviii.
3. Morris Dickstein, *Dancing in the Dark: A Cultural History of the Great Depression* (New York: Norton, 2009), xiv; Ira Katznelson, *Fear Itself: The New Deal and the Origins of Our Time* (New York: Liveright, 2013), 261.
4. Nick Taylor, *American-Made: The Enduring Legacy of the WPA: When FDR Put the Nation to Work* (New York: Bantam Books, 2008).
5. Erik S. Gellman and Jarod Roll, *The Gospel of the Working Class: Labor's Southern Prophets in New Deal America* (Urbana: University of Illinois Press, 2011), 4.
6. Shirley A. Weigand and Wayne A. Weigand, *Books on Trial: Red Scare in the Heartland* (Normal: University of Oklahoma Press, 2007).
7. Rich Remsberg, *Hard Luck Blues: Roots Music Photographs from the Great Depression* (Urbana: University of Illinois Press, 2010); Charles C. Alexander, *Here the Country Lies: Nationalism and the Arts in Twentieth-Century America* (Bloomington: Indiana University Press, 1980), 205–6; Kenneth J. Bindas, *All of This Music Belongs to the Nation: The WPA's Federal Music Project and American Society* (Knoxville: University of Tennessee Press, 1995); Jerrold Hirsch, *Portrait of America: A Cultural History of the Federal Writers' Project* (Chapel Hill: University of North Carolina Press, 2003). See also Richard Barrios, *A Song in the Dark: The Birth of the Musical Film* (New York: Oxford University Press, 1995); Ethan Mordden, *Sing for Your Supper: The Broadway Musical in the 1930s* (New York: Palgrave Macmillan, 2005). The literature on jazz, pop, and other musical styles is very extensive.
8. See Ronald D. Cohen and Rachel C. Donaldson, *Roots of the Revival: American and British Folk Music in the 1950s* (Urbana: University of Illinois Press, 2014); Ronald D. Cohen, *Rainbow Quest: The Folk Music Revival and American Society, 1940–1970* (Amherst: University of Massachusetts Press, 2002).

Chapter 1

1. Tin Pan Alley was the area in New York City where the popular song composers and publishers were based, originally located on West Twenty-Eighth Street between Fifth and Sixth Avenues, then spreading outward.

2. Louise Pound, *American Ballads and Songs* (New York: Scribner, 1922), xii–xiii.

3. Carl Sandburg, *The American Songbag* (New York: Harcourt, Brace, 1927), vii; Penelope Niven, *Carl Sandburg: A Biography* (New York: Scribner, 1991).

4. Debora Kodish, *Good Friends and Bad Enemies: Robert Winslow Gordon and the Study of American Folksong* (Urbana: University of Illinois Press, 1986).

5. Robert Gordon, "The Folk-Songs of America: A Hunt on Hidden Trails," in *Folk-Songs of America* (Washington, D.C.: National Service Bureau, Federal Theatre Project, Works Progress Administration, 1938), 1, 2.

6. Bruce M. Conforth, *African American Folksong and American Cultural Politics: The Lawrence Gellert Story* (Lanham, Md.: Scarecrow, 2013), chaps. 2–3.

7. Frank Shay, *My Pious Friends and Drunken Companions* (New York: Macaulay, 1927), 11; Nolan Porterfield, *Last Cavalier: The Life and Times of John A. Lomax* (Urbana: University of Illinois Press, 1996). Shay also published *Iron Men and Wooden Ships: A Collection of Sailor Songs and Chanties* (New York: Doubleday, Page, & Co., 1924). Scott B. Spencer, ed., *The Ballad Collectors of North America: How Gathering Folksongs Transformed Academic Thought and American Identity* (Lanham, Md.: Scarecrow, 2012); Richard Polenberg, *Hear My Sad Story: The True Tales That Inspired "Stagolee," "John Henry," and Other Traditional American Folk Songs* (Ithaca: Cornell University Press, 2015).

8. The *Journal of American Folklore* (*JAF*) included numerous articles on folk songs and ballads, including Kittredge, "Ballads and Rhymes from Kentucky," (vol. 20, no. 79 [1907]: 241–50); and Perrow, "Songs and Rhymes from the South," (the first appearing in vol. 25, no. 96 [1912]: 137–55, and the last in vol. 28, no. 108 [1915]: 129–90). Loraine Wyman and Howard Brockway, *Lonesome Tunes: Folk Songs from the Kentucky Mountains* (New York: H. W. Gray Company, 1916); Josephine McGill, *Folk-Songs of the Kentucky Mountains* (New York: Boosey, 1917); Loraine Wyman, *Twenty Kentucky Mountain Songs* (Boston: Oliver Ditson Company, 1920).

9. Benjamin Filene, *Romancing the Folk: Public Memory and American Roots Music* (Chapel Hill: University of North Carolina Press, 2000), chap. 1.

10. Howard W. Odum, "Folk Songs of the Southern Negroes," *American Journal of Religious Psychology and Education* 3, no. 3 (July 1909): 265–365; Odum, "Folk-Song and Folk-Poetry as Found in the Secular Songs of the Southern Negro," *JAF* 24, no. 93 (1911): 255–94, and *JAF* 24, no. 94 (1911): 351–454; Odum and Guy B. Johnson, *The Negro and His Songs: A Study of Typical Negro Songs in the South* (Chapel Hill: University of North Carolina Press, 1925); Odum and Johnson, *Negro Workaday Songs* (Chapel Hill: University of North Carolina Press, 1926); Dorothy Scarborough, *On the Trail of Negro Folk-Songs* (Cambridge: Harvard University Press, 1925).

11. Bruce Bastin with Kip Lornell, *The Melody Man: Joe Davis and the New York Music Scene, 1916–1978* (Jackson: University Press of Mississippi, 2012).

12. Tim Brooks, *Lost Sounds: Blacks and the Birth of the Recording Industry, 1890–1919* (Urbana: University of Illinois Press, 2004); Peter C. Muir, *Long Lost Blues: Popular Blues in America, 1850–1920* (Urbana: University of Illinois Press, 2010); W. Fitzhugh Brundage, ed., *Beyond Blackface: African Americans and the Creation of American Popular Culture, 1890–1930* (Chapel Hill: University of North Carolina Press, 2011); David Gilbert, *The Product of Our Souls: Ragtime, Race, and the Birth of the Manhattan Musical Marketplace* (Chapel Hill: University of North Carolina Press, 2015); Marybeth Hamilton, *In Search of the Blues: Black Voices, White Visions* (London: Jonathan Cape, 2007); Elijah Wald, *Escaping the Delta: Robert Johnson and the Invention of the Blues* (New York: Amistad, 2004), 98–102; Ted Gioia, *Delta Blues* (New York: Norton, 2008); David Evans, ed., *Ramblin' on My Mind: New Perspectives on the Blues* (Urbana: University of Illinois Press, 2008); Alex van der Tuuk, *Paramount's Rise and Fall* (Denver: Mainspring, 2003); Rick Kennedy, *Jelly Roll, Bix, and Hoagy: Gennett Studios and the Birth of Recorded Jazz* (Bloomington: Indiana University Press, 1994); Paul Oliver et al., *Yonder Come the Blues* (Cambridge: Cambridge University Press, 2001); Phillip R. Ratcliffe, *Mississippi John Hurt: His Life, His Times, His Blues* (Jackson: University Press of Mississippi, 2011); Bob Riesman, *I Feel So Good: The Life and Times of Big Bill Broonzy* (Chicago: University of Chicago Press, 2011).

13. Victor Greene, *A Passion for Polka: Old-Time Ethnic Music in America* (Berkeley: University of California Press, 1992); Victor Greene, *A Singing Ambivalence: American Immigrants between Old World and New, 1830–1930* (Kent, Ohio: Kent State University Press, 2004); James P. Leary, *Polkabilly: How the Goose Island Ramblers Redefined American Folk Music* (New York: Oxford University Press, 2006); William Howland Kenney, *Recorded Music in American Life: The Phonograph and Popular Memory, 1890–1945* (New York: Oxford University Press, 1999), 74–87;

James P. Leary, *Folksongs of Another America: Field Recordings from the Upper Midwest, 1937-1946* (Madison: University of Wiscosin Press, 2015).

14. Karl Hagstrom Miller, *Segregating Sound: Inventing Folk and Pop Music in the Age of Jim Crow* (Durham, N.C.: Duke University Press, 2010); Elijah Wald, *How the Beatles Destroyed Rock 'n' Roll: An Alternative History of American Popular Music* (New York: Oxford University Press, 2009), chap. 7; *White Country Blues (1926-1938): A Lighter Shade of Blue*, Columbia 47466, 1993; *Minstrels and Tunesmiths: The Commercial Roots of Early Country Music Illustrated with Early Recordings from 1902-1923*, John Edwards Memorial Foundation JEMF-109, 1981. On work songs from both white and African American roots, see Ronald D. Cohen, *Work and Sing: A History of Occupational and Labor Union Songs in the United States* (Crockett, CA: Carquinez, 2010).

15. Patrick Huber, *Linthead Stomp: The Creation of Country Music in the Piedmont South* (Chapel Hill: University of North Carolina Press, 2008); Tony Russell, *Country Music Originals: The Legends and the Lost* (New York: Oxford University Press, 2010); Tony Russell, *Country Music Records: A Discography, 1921-1942* (New York: Oxford University Press, 2008); Barry Mazor, *Ralph Peer and the Making of Popular Roots Music* (Chicago: Chicago Review Press, 2014).

16. Ronald D. Cohen, *A History of Folk Music Festivals in the United States* (Lanham, Md.: Scarecrow, 2008); Bill Malone and Jocelyn R. Neal, *Country Music, U.S.A.*, 3rd rev. ed. (Austin: University of Texas Press, 2010).

17. Chad Berry, ed., *The Hayloft Gang: The Story of the National Barn Dance* (Urbana: University of Illinois Press, 2008); Paul L. Tyler, "Hillbilly Music Re-imagined: Folk and Country Music in the Midwest," *Journal of American Folklore* 127, no. 504 (2014): 159-90; Charles Wolfe, "The Triumph of the Hills: Country Radio 1920-50," in *Country: The Music and the Musicians*, ed. Paul Kingsbury and Alex Axelrod (New York: Abbeville, 1994), 41-63.

18. Patrick Huber, "The New York Sound: Citybilly Recording Artists and the Creation of Hillbilly Music, 1924-1932," *Journal of American Folklore* 127, no. 504 (2014): 140-58; Jack Palmer, *Vernon Dalhart: First Star of Country Music* (Denver: Mainspring, 2005); Chuck Mancuso, *Popular Music and the Underground: Foundations of Jazz, Blues, Country, and Rock, 1900-1950* (Dubuque, Iowa: Kendall/Hunt, 1996); Allen Lowe, *American Pop from Minstrel to Mojo: On Record, 1893-1956* (Redwood, N.Y.: Cadence Jazz Books, 1997); Ben Sidran, *There Was a Fire: Jews, Music and the American Dream* (n.p.: Nardis Books, 2012), chap. 4; Anthony Harkins, *Hillbilly: A Cultural History of an American Icon* (New York: Oxford Uni-

versity Press, 2004, particularly chap. 3). Harkins also discusses old-time string bands in Upstate New York, such as Woodhull's Old Tyme Masters and the Hornellsville Hillbillies, who were drawing on "the localized meaning of hillbilly," which had no southern connection (93). See also Simon J. Bronner, *Old-Time Music Makers of New York State* (Syracuse, N.Y.: Syracuse University Press, 1987): "The Woodhulls were not alone in presenting the [hillbilly] image around the area [in the 1920s]. Rivaling the Woodhulls were the Hornellsville Hillbillies out of Hornell, New York, Orr's Woodchoppers (Kouf Family) from Ithaca, the North Country Hillbillies from Oneida, the Rusty Reubens out of Wellsville, Woody Kelly's Old Timers from Perry, the Trail Blazers from Cortland, Old Dan Sherman and his Family from Oneonta, and the Lone Pine Ramblers, the Bennett Family, and the Tune Twisters from Elmira" (66–67). The Woodhulls, the most popular of the groups, did not record for RCA until 1941, a four-record set that was only released in 1948.

19. Charles K. Wolfe and Ted Olson, eds., *The Bristol Sessions: Writings about the Big Bang of Country Music* (Jefferson, N.C.: McFarland, 2005); Nolan Porterfield, *Jimmie Rodgers: The Life and Times of America's Blue Yodler* (Jackson: University Press of Mississippi, 2007); Barry Mazor, *Meeting Jimmie Rodgers: How America's Original Roots Music Hero Changed the Pop Songs of a Century* (New York: Oxford University Press, 2009); Mark Zonitzer with Charles Hirshberg, *Will You Miss Me When I'm Gone? The Carter Family and Their Legacy in American Music* (New York: Simon and Schuster, 2002). For a different take on early hillbilly performers and the Carter Family's music, with an emphasis on their modernist approach, see Edward P. Comentale, *Sweet Air: Modernism, Regionalism, and American Popular Song* (Urbana: University of Illinois Press, 2013), chap. 2. See also Ben Wynne, *In Tune: Charley Patton, Jimmie Rodgers, and the Roots of American Music* (Baton Rouge: Louisiana State University Press, 2014), for an analysis of southern music's racial complexities.

20. Ted Olson, "'Can You Sing or Play Old-Time Music?': The Johnson City Sessions," *Old-Time Herald* 13, no. 6 (2013): 11–17; Malone and Neal, *Country Music, U.S.A.*, chap. 2.

21. Louise Pound, *Folk-Songs of Nebraska and the Central West* (Lincoln: University of Nebraska Press, 1915); Fannie Hardy Eckstorm and Mary Winslow Smyth, *The Minstrelsy of Maine: Folksongs and Ballads of the Woods and Coast* (Boston: Houghton Mifflin Co., 1927); Fannie Hardy Eckstorm, Mary Winslow Smyth, and Phillips Barry, *British Ballads from Maine* (New Haven, Conn.: Yale University Press, 1929); George Korson, *Songs and Ballads of the Anthracite Miner* (New York: Frederick H. Hitchcock, 1927); Roland Palmer Gray, *Songs and Ballads of the Maine Lumberjacks*

with Other Songs from Maine (Cambridge, Mass.: Harvard University Press, 1924), xii; Franz Rickaby, ed., *Ballads and Songs of the Shanty-Boy* (Cambridge, Mass.: Harvard University Press, 1926); Jennifer C. Post, *Music in Rural New England: Family and Community Life, 1870–1940* (Hanover, N.H.: University Press of New England, 2004); Scott B. Spencer, ed., *The Ballad Collectors of North America: How Gathering Folksongs Transformed Academic Thought and American Identity* (Lanham, Md.: Scarecrow, 2012); Cohen, *Work and Sing*, chap. 1.

22. Kip Lornell, *Exploring American Folk Music* (Jackson: University Press of Mississippi, 2012); Henry Young, *Haywire Mac and the Big Rock Candy Mountain* (Temple, Tex.: Stillhouse Hollow, 1981); Cohen, *Work and Sing*.

23. Foreword to *The March of the Workers and Other Songs* (Chicago: Young Workers League of America, ca. 1925), 5.

24. For a most helpful discussion of the economic, social, cultural, and political context in Chicago during the 1920s and 1930s, but with scant discussion of music, see Lizabeth Cohen, *Making a New Deal: Industrial Workers in Chicago, 1919–1939* (New York: Cambridge University Press, 1990).

Chapter 2

1. Shelly Romalis, *Pistol Packin' Mama: Aunt Molly Jackson and the Politics of Folksong* (Urbana: University of Illinois Press, 1999), 40; Brian Dolinar, *The Black Cultural Front: Black Writers and Artists of the Depression Generation* (Jackson: University Press of Mississippi, 2012), 25–27, for the early development of the NCDPP.

2. George G. Korson, *Songs and Ballads of the Anthracite Miner* (New York: Frederick H. Hitchcock, 1927), ix; George G. Korson, *Minstrels of the Mine Patch: Songs and Stories of the Anthracite Industry* (Philadelphia: University of Pennsylvania Press, 1938); George G. Korson, *Coal Dust on the Fiddle: Songs and Stories of the Bituminous Industry* (Philadelphia: University of Pennsylvania Press, 1943), 451; Angus K. Gillespie, *Folklorist of the Coal Fields: George Konson's Life and Work* (University Park: Pennsylvania State University Press, 1980), 173–74.

3. Alan Calmer, "Early American Labor and Literature," *International Literature*, April 1934, 119.

4. John W. Hevener, *Which Side Are You On? The Harlan County Coal Miners, 1931–39* (Urbana: University of Illinois Press, 1978).

5. Julia S. Ardery, *Welcome the Traveler Home: Jim Garland's Story of the Kentucky Mountains* (Lexington: University Press of Kentucky, 1983),

149–50. For Jackson's recording of "Ragged Hungry Blues," Dave Samuelson and Ronald D. Cohen, comps., *Songs for Political Action: Folk Music, Topical Songs and the American Left, 1926-1953*, Bear Family Records, BCD 15720, 1996, disc 1.

6. Allan Sutton, *Recording the 'Thirties: The Evolution of the American Recording Industry, 1930-39* (Denver, Colo.: Mainspring, 2011); Andre Millard, *America on Record: A History of Recorded Sound* (New York: Cambridge University Press, 1995), chap. 8; William Howland Kenney, *Recorded Music in American Life: The Phonograph and Popular Memory, 1890-1945* (New York: Oxford University Press, 1999), chap. 8.

7. *Brookwood Chautauqua Songs* (New York: Brookwood Labor Publications, ca. 1937); Archie Green, *Only a Miner: Studies in Recorded Coal-Mining Songs* (Urbana: University of Illinois Press, 1972), chap. 7; Holly George-Warren, *Public Cowboy No. 1: The Life and Times of Gene Autry* (New York: Oxford University Press, 2007).

8. Patrick Huber, *Linthead Stomp: The Creation of Country Music in the Piedmont South* (Chapel Hill: University of North Carolina Press, 2008), chap. 3; *Gastonia Gallop: Cotton Mill Songs & Hillbilly Blues—Piedmont Textile Workers on Record: Gaston County, North Carolina, 1927-1931*, Old Hat Records, 2009.

9. *Songs of the Class Struggle: In Memory of Ella May Wiggins and Steve Katovis* (n.p.: Workers' International Relief, 1929); Margaret Larlin, "The Story of Ella May," *New Masses* 5 (November 1929): 3-4; Margaret Larkin, "Ella May's Songs," *Nation*, no. 129 (October 9, 1929): 382-83; Margaret Larkin, "We'll Never Let Our Union Die: Sang Ella May Wiggins, Textile Worker and Poet Who Was Killed by Vigilantes Nine Years Ago Today," *Daily Worker*, September 14, 1938; Ronald D. Cohen, *Work and Sing: A History of Occupational and Labor Union Songs in the United States* (Crockett, Calif.: Carquinez, 2010), 71; Huber, *Linthead Stomp*, 196-200; Vincent J. Roscigno and William F. Danaher, *The Voice of Southern Labor: Radio, Music, and Textile Strikes, 1929-1934* (Minneapolis: University of Minnesota Press, 2004), chap. 6; Timothy P. Lynch, *Strike Songs of the Depression* (Jackson: University Press of Mississippi, 2001), chap. 1; Archie Green, *Wobblies, Pile Butts, and Other Heroes: Laborlore Explorations* (Urbana: University of Illinois Press), 276-80.

10. Margaret Larkin, *Singing Cowboy: A Book of Western Songs* (New York: Knopf, 1931), ix, xi.

11. Margaret Larkin, "Revolutionary Music," *New Masses* 8 (February 1933): 27; John Greenway, *American Folk Songs of Protest* (Philadelphia: University of Pennsylvania Press, 1953), 158-68; *Red Song Book* (New York: Workers Library, 1932).

12. *Song Book for Workers* (New York: Red Star Publicity Service, 1932).

13. Richard A. Reuss with JoAnne C. Reuss, *American Folk Music and Left-Wing Politics, 1927-1957* (Lanham, Md.: Scarecrow, 2000), chaps. 3 and 4; Michael Denning, *The Cultural Front: The Laboring of American Culture in the Twentieth Century* (New York: Verso, 1996), 287-89, 293.

14. "The Freiheit Gezangfarein," *Worker Musician* 1, no. 1 (1932): 14; Nathan Nevins, "Reviews," *Worker Musician* 1, no. 1 (1932): 13.

15. *Songs of Struggle* (New York: Workers Bookshop, n.d.).

16. Harold Meyerson and Ernie Harburg, *Who Put the Rainbow in The Wizard of Oz?* (Ann Arbor: University of Michigan Press, 1993), 44-55; *Brother, Can You Spare a Dime? American Song during the Great Depression*, New World Records NW270, 1977.

17. Guido Van Rijn, *Roosevelt's Blues: African-American Blues and Gospel Songs on FDR* (Jackson: University Press of Mississippi, 1997), 16-29.

18. See, in particular, the four-CD compilation *Songs of the Depression: Boom, Bust and the New Deal*, Bear Family Records, BCD16029, 1998.

Chapter 3

1. See the informative, and highly illustrated, Roger G. Kennedy and David Larkin, *When Art Worked* (New York: Rizzoli, 2009). For a helpful list of Depression songs, see http://musicfromthedepression.com.

2. Ira Katznelson, *Fear Itself: The New Deal and the Origins of Our Time* (New York: Liveright, 2013); Michael Denning, *The Cultural Front: The Laboring of American Culture in the Twentieth Century* (New York: Verso, 1996).

3. Harvey Funson, *Ballads of the Kentucky Highlands* (London: The Mitre Press, 1931); John Szwed, *Alan Lomax: The Man Who Recorded the World* (New York: Viking, 2010), 34-51; Nolan Porterfield, *Last Cavalier: The Life and Times of John A. Lomax* (Urbana: University of Illinois Press, 1996), 296-304.

4. Librarian of Congress to Doctor [John] Lomax, September 13, 1933, AFC 1933/001, John A. and Alan Lomax Manuscript Collection, American Folklife Center, Library of Congress, Washington, D.C.; Alan Lomax, "'Sinful' Songs of the Southern Negro," in *Alan Lomax: Selected Writings, 1934-1997*, ed. Ronald D. Cohen (New York: Routledge, 2003), 9-31; John A. Lomax and Alan Lomax, *American Ballads and Folk Songs* (New York: Macmillan, 1934).

5. John A. Lomax, "'Sinful Songs' of the Southern Negro," *Musical Quarterly* 20, no. 2 (1934): 184.

6. Lomax and Lomax, *American Ballads and Folk Songs*, xxvi-xxvii, xxxiv.

7. John's first wife, Bess Brown Lomax, had died in February 1931.

8. Alan Lomax to John Lomax, ca. 1933, 3D222, folder 4, Lomax Family Papers, Center for American History, University of Texas at Austin (hereafter LP); Alan Lomax to John Lomax, October 20, [1933], ibid.

9. Alan Lomax to John Lomax, fall 1934, 3D222, folder 4, LP; John Lomax and Alan Lomax, *Negro Folk Songs as Sung by Lead Belly* (New York: Macmillan, 1936); Charles Wolfe and Kip Lornell, *The Life and Legend of Leadbelly* (New York: HarperCollins, 1992); Jeff Place and Robert Santelli, *Lead Belly: The Smithsonian Folkways Collection*, Smithsonian/Folkways, 2015.

10. Foreword to *Workers Song Book 1934 No. 1* (New York: Workers Music League, 1934), 3.

11. Lan Adomian, "What Songs Should Workers' Choruses Sing," *Daily Worker*, February 7, 1934; Marc Endsley Johnson, "'The Masses Are Singing': Insurgency and Song in New York City, 1929–1941" (PhD diss., City University of New York, 2003), 118, 154–56; Richard A. Reuss with JoAnne C. Reuss, *American Folk Music and Left-Wing Politics, 1927–1957* (Lanham, Md.: Scarecrow, 2000), 64–65.

12. Guido Van Rijn, *Roosevelt's Blues: African-American Blues and Gospel Songs on FDR* (Jackson: University Press of Mississippi, 1997), 43–75.

13. John Jacob Niles, *Impressions of a Negro Camp Meeting* (New York: Carl Fisher, 1925); Niles, *Seven Kentucky Mountain Songs* (New York: G. Schirmer Inc., 1929); Niles, *Seven Negro Exaltations* (New York: G. Schirmer Inc., 1929); Niles, *Songs of the Hill Folk* (New York: G. Schirmer Inc., 1934); Niles, *More Songs of the Hill Folk* (New York: G. Schirmer Inc., 1936); Ron Pen, *I Wonder as I Wander: The Life of John Jacob Niles* (Lexington: University Press of Kentucky, 2010).

14. Pen, *I Wonder as I Wander*, 176.

15. *Log Cabin Songs by Johnny Crockett* (New York: Headman and Goodman, 1931); *Carson J. Robison's World Greatest Collection of Mountain Ballads and Old Time Songs* (Chicago: M.M. Cole Publishing Co., 1930); *Play and Sing: America's Greatest Collection of Old Time Songs and Mountain Ballads* (Chicago: M.M. Cole Publishing Co., 1930).

16. *Kentucky Wonder Bean: Sensational Collection of Mountain Ballads and Old Time Songs* (Chicago: M.M. Cole Publishing Co., 1931); *Elmore Vincent's Lumber Jack Songs* (Chicago: M.M. Cole Publishing Co., 1932); *Frankie and Johnny Marvin's Folio of Down Home Songs* (New York: Southern Music Publishing Co. 1932); *Salty Tunes: A Collection of Sea Chanties and Rollicking Sailor Songs* (New York: De Sylva, Brown and Henderson Inc., 1932); *Bob Miller's Famous Hill-Billy Heart Throbs* (New York: Bob Miller Inc., 1934); *Tiny Texan: World's Greatest Collection*

of *Cowboy and Mountain Ballads* (Chicago: M.M. Cole Publishing Co., 1933).

17. Jean Thomas, *The Sun Shines Bright* (New York: Prentice Hall, 1940), 199, 205–6; Ronald D. Cohen, *The History of Folk Music Festivals in the United States* (Lanham, Md.: Scarecrow, 2008), 5–9.

18. George Pullen Jackson, "Ballad Art Revival at White Top Festival," *Musical America* 54, no. 14 (1934): 8; Annabel Morris Buchanan, "The Function of a Folk Festival," *Southern Folklore Quarterly* 1 (March 1937): 30; Cohen, *History of Folk Music Festivals in the United States*, 10–13.

19. Sarah Gertrude Knott, "Knott Notes: The Mountain Dance and Folk Festival, Asheville, North Carolina, 1927–1973," *Caldwell County Times* (Princeton, Kentucky), undated clipping; Cohen, *History of Folk Music Festivals in the United States*, 13–19; Michael Ann Williams, *Staging Tradition: John Lair and Sarah Gertrude Knott* (Urbana: University of Illinois Press, 2006), 16–38.

20. Sarah Gertrude Knott, "History in 2/4 Time: Or It May Be in Another Tempo but the World's Folk Dances and Songs Have Origins Deep in the Past; Making Folk Festivals Major Cultural Events Rich in Meaning," *Christian Science Monitor*, November 6, 1935, 6; Cohen, *History of Folk Music Festivals in the United States*, 19–21.

Chapter 4

1. Rachel Clare Donaldson, *"I Hear America Singing": Folk Music and National Identity* (Philadelphia, Pa.: Temple University Press, 2014), chap. 1.

2. Alan Lomax to John Lomax, June 18, 1935, 3D222, folder 4, Lomax Family Papers, Center for American History, University of Texas at Austin (hereafter LP); Valerie Boyd, *Wrapped in Rainbows: The Life of Zora Neale Hurston* (New York: Scribner, 2003).

3. Alan Lomax to Family, June 22, 1935, and Alan Lomax to John Lomax, July 15, 1935, LP; Alan Lomax to John Lomax, July 1, 1935, and Alan Lomax to Oliver Strunk, August 3, 1935, in *Alan Lomax, Assistant in Charge: The Library of Congress Letters, 1935–1945*, ed. Ronald D. Cohen (Jackson: University Press of Mississippi, 2011), 3, 11.

4. Alan Lomax to John Lomax, September 4, 1935, LP.

5. Alan Lomax to John Lomax, early September 1935, LP; Susan Quinn, *Furious Improvisation: How the WPA and a Cast of Thousands Made High Arts out of Desperate Times* (New York: Walker, 2008); Roger G. Kennedy and David Larkin, *When Art Worked* (New York: Rizzoli, 2009).

6. Alan Lomax to Francis McFarland, September 12, 1935, and Alan Lomax to Betty Calhoun, September 17, 1935, in Cohen, *Alan Lomax, Assistant in Charge*, 12, 14.

7. Peter Gough, *Sounds of the New Deal: The Federal Music Project in the West* (Urbana: University of Illinois Press, 2015), particularly chap. 7; Kenneth J. Bindas, *All of This Music Belongs to the Nation: The WPA's Federal Music Project and American Society* (Knoxville: University of Tennessee Press, 1995). In 1939, the FMP became the WPA Music Program, under the direction of Earl Moore, which lasted until 1943; under the new designation, local and state governments were required to cover 25 percent of costs. Starting in 1940, all music programs had to focus on national defense.

8. David King Dunaway and Molly Beer, *Singing Out: An Oral History of America's Folk Music Revivals* (New York: Oxford University Press, 2010), 43–44.

9. Pete Seeger, "Becoming a 'Folk Singer' (1935–1947)," in *Pete Seeger in His Own Words*, ed. Rob Rosenthal and Sam Rosenthal (Boulder, Colo.: Paradigm, 2012), 11, 12.

10. Earl Robinson with Eric A. Gordon, *Ballad of an American: The Autobiography of Earl Robinson* (Lanham, Md.: Scarecrow, 1998), 69; Lawrence Gellert, "Negro Songs of Protest in America," *Music Vanguard* 1, no. 1 (1935): 13; Bruce M. Conforth, *African American Folksong and American Cultural Politics: The Lawrence Gellert Story* (Lanham, Md.: Scarecrow, 2013).

11. Anne Livingstone, "Negro Music," *Music Front* 1, no. 2 (1935): 2, 4.

12. Lawrence Gellert, *Negro Songs of Protest* (New York: American Music League, 1936), 7; Lawrence Gellert, *"Me and My Captain"* (New York: Hours, 1939).

13. Foreword to *Workers Song Book No. 2* (New York: Workers Music League, 1935), inside front cover.

14. Samuel H. Friedman, ed., *Rebel Song Book* (New York: Rand School Press, 1935); Review of *Workers Song Book No. 2* and *Rebel Song Book*, *Music Vanguard* 1, no. 2 (1935): 91; Marc E. Johnson, "'The Masses Are Singing': Insurgency and Songs in New York City, 1929–1941" (PhD diss., Graduate Faculty in Music, City University of New York, 2003), 208–16.

15. A.G., "Working Class Song Records," *Daily Worker*, December 19, 1935; Irma and Mordecai Bauman, *From Our Angle of Repose: A Memoir* (New York: privately published, 2006), 22. The three 78 rpm records were packaged together in plain boards, which was somewhat unusual at that time. Fancy albums with multiple records did not become popular until the 1940s.

16. "Musicians on W.P.A. 'Boondoggling,'" *Unison* 1, no. 1 (1936): 2; "Negro Songs of Protest," *Unison* 1, no. 1 (1936): 4; "American Sings," *Unison* 1, no. 3 (1936): 4; "Manhattan Chorus," *Unison* 1, no. 4 (1937): 6; Richard A. Reuss with JoAnne C. Reuss, *American Folk Music and Left-Wing Politics, 1927-1957* (Lanham, Md.: Scarecrow, 2000), 117-21; Elizabeth B. Crist, *Music for the Common Man: Aaron Copland during the Depression and War* (New York: Oxford University Press, 2005), 23-34.

17. Mike Gold, "Change the World," *Daily Worker*, November 22, 1934, 5.

18. Alan Lomax to John Lomax, September 19, 1935, LP.

19. Oliver Strunk to the Haitian minister in Washington, D.C., November 24, 1936, in Cohen, *Alan Lomax, Assistant in Charge*, 15, and see 16-37 for related correspondence; *Alan Lomax in Haiti: Recordings for the Library of Congress, 1936-1937*, Harte Recordings 2009.

20. John A. Lomax and Alan Lomax, *Negro Folk Songs as Sung by Lead Belly* (New York: Macmillan, 1936); Nolan Porterfield, *Last Cavalier: The Life and Times of John A. Lomax* (Urbana: University of Illinois Press, 1996), 364-67; Charles Wolfe and Kip Lornell, *The Life and Legend of Leadbelly* (New York: HarperCollins, 1992), 156-85.

21. Henry Johnson, "Music: New Recordings," *New Masses*, March 31, 1936.

22. John Lomax, *Adventures of a Ballad Hunter* (New York: Macmillan, 1947), 175, 248.

23. Ann M. Pescatello, *Charles Seeger: A Life in American Music* (Pittsburgh: University of Pittsburgh Press, 1992), 136-50; Jannelle Warren-Findley, "Passports to Change: The Resettlement Administration's Folk Song Sheet Program, 1936-1937," *Prospects* 10 (1985): 197-241; Robert B. Cochran, "'All the Songs in the World': The Story of Emma Dusenberry," *Arkansas Historical Quarterly* 44, no. 1 (1985): 3-15.

24. Dunaway and Beer, *Singing Out*, 47; Beth E. Levy, *Frontier Figures: American Music and the Mythology of the American West* (Berkeley: University of California Press, 2012), 185-203; Eric R. Smith, *American Relief Aid and the Spanish Civil War* (Columbia: University of Missouri Press, 2013); and for a fascinating, colorful study, Amanda Vaill, *Hotel Florida: Truth, Love, and Death in the Spanish Civil War* (New York: Farrar, Straus and Giroux, 2014).

25. Elijah Wald, *Josh White: Society Blues* (Amherst: University of Massachusetts Press, 2000).

26. Herbert Halpert, "Federal Theatre and Folksong," *Southern Folklore Quarterly* 2 (1938): 81; Arthur Palmer Hudson, *Folk Tunes from Mississippi* (New York: National Service Bureau, 1937).

27. Harry "Mac" McClintock made the first recording of "Hallelujah, I'm a Bum" in 1928 for Victor; he is usually credited as the composer. Numerous recordings of the song quickly followed, including by Vernon Dalhart and Al Jolson.

Chapter 5

1. For the role of left-wing children's literature and summer camps at this time, see Paul Mishler, *Raising Reds: The Young Pioneers, Radical Summer Camps, and Communist Political Culture in the United States* (New York: Columbia University Press, 1999); and Julia L. Mickenberg, *Learning from the Left: Children's Literature, the Cold War, and Radical Politics in the United States* (New York: Oxford University Press, 2005).

2. Frederick Adams, "Folk Songs of the People," *Daily Worker*, January 30, 1937, 9; *Songs of the People* (New York: Worker Library Publishers, 1937); *March and Sing* (New York: American Music League, 1937).

3. *Brookwood Chautauqua Songs: A Singing Army Is a Winning Army* (New York: Brookwood Labor Publications, ca. 1937).

4. Agnes Cunningham, *Six Labor Songs* (Mena, Ark.: Commonwealth College, n.d.); *Commonwealth Labor Songs: A Collection of Old and New Songs For the Use of Labor Unions* (Mena, Ark.: Commonwealth College, 1938); *Commonwealth Labor Hymnal* (Mena, Ark.: Commonwealth College, 1938); *Songs of the Souther School for Workers* (Asheville, N.C.: Southern School For Workers, 1940); Agnes "Sis" Cunningham and Gordon Friesen, *Red Dust and Broadsides: A Joint Autobiography*, ed. Ronald D. Cohen (Amherst: University of Massachusetts Press, 1999); Ronald D. Cohen, "Agnes 'Sis' Cunningham and Labor Songs in the Depression South," in *Radicalism in the South since Reconstruction*, ed. James Smethurst, Rachel Rubin, and Chris Green (New York: Palgrave Macmillan, 2006), 83–96; William H. Cobb, *Radical Education in the Rural South: Commonwealth College, 1922–1940* (Detroit, Mich.: Wayne State University Press, 2000).

5. *The School for Workers Song Book* (Madison: The University of Wisconsin School for Workers, n.d.); Caroline Wasserman, *Song Book of the Pacific Coast School for Workers* (Berkeley, Calif.: Pacific Coast School for Workers, 1939); *Hudson Shore Labor School: Lift Every Voice and Sing* (n.p.: Hudson Shore Labor School, 1941).

6. Don West, *Songs for Southern Workers* (Lexington: Kentucky Workers Alliance, 1937); James J. Lorence, *A Hard Journey: The Life of Don West* (Urbana: University of Illinois Press, 2007).

7. *Worker Songs* (Monteagle, Tenn.: Highlander Folk School, 1935); *Let's Sing* (Monteagle, Tenn.: Highlander Folk School, 1937); *Songs of*

the Southern Summer School (Monteagle, Tenn.: Highlander Folk School, 1938); *Songs for Workers* (Monteagle, Tenn.: Highlander Folk School, 1938); *Songs for Workers* (Monteagle, Tenn.: Highlander Folk School, 1939); *Songs of Field and Factory* (Monteagle, Tenn.: Highlander Folk School 1940); Zilphia Horton, ed., *Labor Songs* (New York: Textile Workers Union of America, 1939), 2, 4; Alicia R. Massie-Legg, "Zilphia Horton, a Voice for Change" (PhD diss., University of Kentucky, 2014).

8. Timothy P. Lynch, *Strike Songs of the Depression* (Jackson: University Press of Mississippi, 2001), chap. 3.

9. *Let's Sing* (New York: Educational Department, International Ladies' Garment Workers' Union, n.d.), 1; *Songs* (New York: Textile Workers Organizing Committee of the CIO, n.d.); *Sing, Almagated* (New York: Amalgamated Clothing Workers of America, 1940); *CIO Songs* (Birmingham, Ala.: Birmingham Industrial Union Council, n.d.), back cover; Ronald D. Cohen, *Work and Sing: A History of Occupational and Labor Union Songs in the United States* (Crockett, Calif.: Carquinez, 2010).

10. Lee Hays, "From 'The "Post-humous" Memoirs,'" in *"Sing Out, Warning! Sing Out, Love!": The Writings of Lee Hays*, ed. Robert S. Koppelman (Amherst: University of Massachusetts Press, 2003), 56; Lee Hays, "Untitled Column on Emma Dusenberry," ibid., 71; Alan Lomax, "Preface: Our Singing Country," in *Alan Lomax: Selected Writings 1934–1997*, ed. Ronald D. Cohen (New York: Routledge, 2003), 61; Erik S. Gellman and Jarod Roll, *The Gospel of the Working Class: Labor's Southern Prophets in New Deal America* (Urbana: University of Illinois Press, 2011); Charles Joyner, "A Southern Radical and His Songs," in *Dixie Redux: Essays in Honor of Sheldon Hackney*, ed. Raymond Arsenault and Orville Vernon Burton (Montgomery, Ala.: NewSouth Books, 2013), 212–41.

11. Cunningham and Friesen, *Red Dust and Broadsides*, 158; Michael K. Honey, *Sharecropper's Troubadour: John L. Handcox, the Southern Tenant Farmers' Union, and the African American Song Tradition* (New York: Palgrave Macmillan, 2013), 166. Handcox soon moved to San Diego, California, where he lived in relative obscurity until he was discovered in 1985; he performed at labor conferences until his death in 1992.

12. Laura Hillenbrand, *Seabiscuit: An America Legend* (New York: Ballantine Books, 2002); John F. Kasson, *The Little Girl Who Fought the Great Depression: Shirley Temple and 1930s America* (New York: Norton, 2014).

13. Nolan Porterfield, *Last Cavalier: The Life and Times of John A. Lomax, 1867–1948* (Urbana: University of Illinois Press, 1996), 387–95, 402–6.

14. Robert W. Gordon, *Folk-Songs of America* (New York: National Service Bureau, 1938); Phillips Barry, *Folk Music in America* (New York: Na-

tional Service Bureau, 1939); John H. Cox, *Traditional Ballads: Mainly from West Virginia* (New York: National Service Bureau, 1939); Arthur Palmer Hudson, *Folk Tunes from Mississippi* (New York: National Service Bureau, 1937); Arthur Palmer Hudson, *Folksongs of Mississippi and Their Background* (Chapel Hill: University of North Carolina Press, 1936).

15. Alan Lomax to John Lomax, July 23, 1937, and Alan Lomax to John Lomax, August 31, 1937, 3D222, folder 4, Lomax Family Papers, Center for American History, University of Texas at Austin (hereafter LP); John Szwed, *Alan Lomax: The Man Who Recorded the World* (New York: Viking, 2010), 104–11.

16. Alan Lomax to Harold Spivacke, August 14, 1937, in *Alan Lomax, Assistant in Charge: The Library of Congress Letters, 1935–1945*, ed. Ronald D. Cohen (Jackson: University Press of Mississippi, 2010), 41; quote from his official report, "Archive of American Folk Song: A History, 1938–1939," Library of Congress Project, Works Projects Administration, 1940, ibid., 48.

17. Alan Lomax to Harold Spivacke, ca. September 17, 1937; Lomax to Spivacke, ca. September 23, 1937; Lomax to Spivacke, September 28, 1937; Lomax to Spivacke, October 6, 1937, all ibid., 50, 52, 54; Alan Lomax to John Lomax, October 26, 1937, LP; Szwed, *Alan Lomax*, 111–13.

18. Lomax, "Archive of American Folk Song," quoted in Cohen, *Alan Lomax, Assistant in Charge*, 48–49.

19. Alan Lomax, review of *Folk Songs of Mississippi and Their Background*, by Arthur Palmer Hudson, *Journal of American Folklore* 51, no. 200 (1938): 212–13.

20. Quoted in Judah L. Graubart and Alice V. Graubart, *Decade of Destiny* (Chicago: Contemporary Books, 1978), 317.

21. Woody Guthrie, *Bound for Glory* (New York: Dutton, 1943), 233; Dayton Duncan, *The Dust Bowl: An Illustrated History* (San Francisco: Chronicle Books, 2012).

22. Ronald D. Cohen, *Woody Guthrie: Writing America's Songs* (New York: Routledge, 2012); Joe Klein, *Woody Guthrie: A Life* (New York: Knopf, 1980); Ed Cray, *Ramblin' Man: The Life and Times of Woody Guthrie* (New York: Norton, 2004).

23. Erin Royston Battat, *Ain't Got No Home: America's Great Migrations and the Making of an Interracial Left* (Chapel Hill: University of North Carolina Press, 2014), 42–44.

24. Ed Robbin, *Woody Guthrie and Me: An Intimate Reminiscence* (Berkeley, CA: Lancaster Miller, 1979), 26, 41; Will Kaufman, *Woody Guthrie: American Radical* (Urbana: University of Illinois Press, 2011); Peter

La Chapelle, *Proud to Be an Okie: Cultural Politics, Country Music, and Migration to Southern California* (Berkeley: University of California Press, 2007), chap. 2.

25. Paul Taylor and Dorothea Lange, *An American Exodus* (New York: Reynal and Hitchcock, 1939); Jan Goggans, *California on the Breadlines: Dorothea Lange, Paul Taylor, and the Making of a New Deal Narrative* (Berkeley: University of California Press, 2010); Battat, *Ain't Got No Home*, chap. 2; and for the pre-1930s migrant-worker background, Mark Wyman, *Hoboes: Bindlestiffs, Fruit Tramps, and the Harvesting of the West* (New York: Hill and Wang, 2010).

26. Gerald W. Haslam, *Workin' Man Blues: Country Music in California* (Berkeley: University of California Press, 1999).

27. Steven J. Ross, *Hollywood Left and Right: How Movie Stars Shaped American Politics* (New York: Oxford University Press, 2011), 95–106; Paul Buhle and Dave Wagner, *Radical Hollywood: The Untold Story Behind America's Favorite Movies* (New York: The New Press, 2002); Ben Urwand, *The Collaboration: Hollywood's Pact with Hitler* (Cambridge, Mass.: Belknap Press of Harvard University Press, 2013); Thomas Doherty, *Hollywood and Hitler, 1933–1939* (New York: Columbia University Press, 2013); Mark Harris, *Five Came Back: A Story of Hollywood and the Second World War* (New York: Penguin, 2014), chap. 1.

28. Julie S. Ardery, *Welcome the Traveler Home: Jim Garland's Story of the Kentucky Mountains* (Lexington: University Press of Kentucky, 1983), 183; "Hill-Billy Songs," *Daily Worker*, March 17, 1937, 7.

29. Charles Wolfe and Kip Lornell, *The Life and Legend of Leadbelly* (New York: HarperCollins, 1992), 204–12; Stephen Petrus and Ronald D. Cohen, *Folk City: New York and the America Folk Music Revival* (New York: Oxford University Press, 2015).

30. Earl Robinson with Eric A. Gordon, *Ballad of an American: The Autobiography of Earl Robinson* (Lanham, Md.: Scarecrow, 1998), 52; Graubart and Graubart, *Decade of Destiny*, 317. Alfred Hayes (1911–85) later became a novelist and famed screenwriter, including for the 1957 film *Island in the Sun*, which starred Harry Belafonte.

31. Robinson with Gordon, *Ballad of an American*, 51; Lewis Allan, "Abraham Lincoln Lives Again" (New York: Bob Miller, 1938); Lomax quoted in Graubart and Graubart, *Decade of Destiny*, 319; Nancy Kovaleff Baker, "Abel Meeropol (a.k.a. Lewis Allan): Political Commentator and Social Conscience," *American Music* 20, no. 1 (2002): 25–79; Barney Josephson with Terry Trilling-Josephson, *Cafe Society: The Wrong Place for the Right People* (Urbana: University of Illinois Press, 2009), 46–53.

Chapter 6

1. Herbert Halpert, "American Folk Songs," *American Music Lover*, March 1938, 414, 415.
2. Charles Seeger, "Music in America," *Magazine of Art*, July 1938, 411, 436.
3. "'Bosses and Judges, Lis'n to Me': Song for Scottsboro Boys," *Daily Worker*, July 8, 1938.
4. Roger D. Kinkle, *The Complete Encyclopedia of Popular Music and Jazz, 1900–1950*, vol. 1 (New Rochelle, N.Y.: Arlington House, 1974); Elijah Wald, *How the Beatles Destroyed Rock 'n' Roll: An Alternative History of American Popular Music* (New York: Oxford University Press, 2009), chap. 9; David Ewen, *All the Years of American Popular Music: A Comprehensive History* (Englewood Cliffs, N.J.: Prentice Hall, 1977), chaps. 20–24; David W. Stowe, *Swing Changes: Big-Band Jazz in New Deal America* (Cambridge, Mass.: Harvard University Press, 1994); Lewis A. Erenberg, *Swingin' the Dream: Big Band Jazz and the Rebirth of American Culture* (Chicago: University of Chicago Press, 1998); Stanley Green, *Ring Bells! Sing Songs! Broadway Musicals of the 1930's* (New Rochelle, N.Y.: Arlington House, 1971).
5. Carol J. Oja, *Bernstein Meets Broadway: Collaborative Art in a Time of War* (New York: Oxford University Press, 2014), chap. 2.
6. Alan Lomax to John Harrington Cox, March 12, 1938, in *Alan Lomax, Assistant in Charge: The Library of Congress Letters, 1935–1945*, ed. Ronald D. Cohen (Jackson: University Press of Mississippi, 2010), 65.
7. Alan Lomax to Harold Spivacke, April 1, 1938, ibid., 66; Alan Lomax, "Archive of American Folk Song: A History, 1928–1939," ibid., 67.
8. Consult the wonderful album from the Library of Congress recordings, including the Lomaxes' interviews, *Folk Music of Ohio 1938 through 1940*, Ohio Historical Society, 1978.
9. Alan Lomax to John Lomax, May 26, 1938, in Cohen, *Alan Lomax, Assistant in Charge*, 75–76.
10. Alan Lomax to Olin Downes, May 19, 1938, ibid., 72; Lomax to Downes, May 26, 1938, ibid., 76–77. For more of Lomax's world's fair planning, which included a folk music symposium including Charles Seeger and Robert Gordon, as well as a jazz symposium with John Hammond, Louis Armstrong, and Duke Ellington, see Lomax to Downes, June 18, 1938, ibid., 80–82.
11. Howard Reich and William Gaines, *Jelly's Blues: The Life, Music, and Redemption of Jelly Roll Morton* (Cambridge, Mass.: Da Capo, 2003).
12. Lomax quoted in John Szwed, *Alan Lomax: The Man Who Recorded the World* (New York: Viking, 2010), 122–23; Alan Lomax to Melvin

Oathout, June 28, 1938, in Cohen, *Alan Lomax, Assistant in Charge*, 83; Alan Lomax, *Mister Jelly Roll: The Fortunes of Jelly Roll Morton, New Orleans Creole and "Inventor of Jazz"* (Berkeley: University of California Press, 2001), xviii; *Jelly Roll Morton: The Complete Library of Congress Recordings by Alan Lomax*, Rounder Records 11661-1888-2, 2005, with liner notes by John Szwed.

13. Alan Lomax to Harold Spivacke, June 8, 1938, in Cohen, *Alan Lomax, Assistant in Charge*, 79. Theodore Blegen, *Norwegian Emigrant Songs and Ballads* (Minneapolis: University of Minnesota Press, 1936); Earl C. Beck, *Songs of the Michigan Lumberjacks* (Ann Arbor: University of Michigan Press, 1941). The record companies had earlier done much ethnic recording but mostly before World War I.

14. Lomax, "Archive of American Folk Song," 108; James P. Leary, *Folksongs of Another America: Field Recordings from the Upper Midwest, 1937–1946* (Madison: University of Wisconsin Press, 2015).

15. Alan Lomax to Harold Spivacke, ca. fall 1938, 3D222, folder 4, Lomax Family Papers, Center for American History, University of Texas at Austin (hereafter LP); Dunstan Prial, *The Producer: John Hammond and the Soul of American Music* (New York: Farrar, Straus and Giroux, 2006), 109–22; *From Spirituals to Swing: The Legendary 1938 & 1939 Concerts Produced by John Hammond*, Vanguard Records 169/71-2, 1999.

16. Robert Cohen, *When the Old Left Was Young: Student Radicals and America's First Mass Student Movement, 1929–1941* (New York: Oxford University Press, 1993).

17. American Student Union, *Patters for Peace* (New York: American Student Union, ca. 1937), 30; Earl Robinson with Eric A. Gordon, *Ballad of an American: The Autobiography of Earl Robinson* (Lanham, Md.: Scarecrow, 1998), 118–19; Lynne Olson, *Those Angry Days: Roosevelt, Lindbergh, and America's Fight over World War II, 1939–1941* (New York: Random House, 2013). Olson has no discussion of the left-wing antiwar movement. See also Ronald D. Cohen and Will Kaufman, *Singing for Peace: Antiwar Songs in American History* (Boulder, Colo.: Paradigm Publishers, 2015).

18. *It Shall Not Come to Pass*, sheet music published by TAC Radio Division, with no date; on TAC, see Michael Denning, *The Cultural Front: The Laboring of American Culture in the Twentieth Century* (London: Verso, 1996), 326–27. For original recordings of "Spring Song," "Old Paint," and other radical songs from the period, see Dave Samuelson and Ronald D. Cohen, comps., *Songs for Political Action: Folkmusic, Topical Songs, and the American Left, 1926–1953*, Bear Family Records, BCD 15720, 1996.

19. "Concert and Opera," *New York Times*, February 3, 1939.

20. Alan Lomax to Harold Spivacke, n.d. (early 1939), in Cohen, *Alan Lomax, Assistant in Charge*, 123; Lomax to Spivacke, April 8, 1939, ibid., 130; Spivacke to Lomax, April 14, 1939, ibid., 131; "List of American Folk Songs on Commercial Records," *Report of the Committee of the Conference on Inter-American Relations in the Field of Music* (Washington, D.C.: Department of State, September 3, 1940), 126–46. Lomax's two albums for Decca, *Mountain Frolic* and *Listen to Our Story*, reissues of older mainly white and some black recordings—Bradley Kincaid, Uncle Dave Macon, Bascom Lamar Lunsford, Furry Lewis—did not appear until 1947, although his father's compilation of hillbilly songs, *Smoky Mountain Ballads* on the Victor label— Carter Family and Bill and Charlie Monroe—had been released in 1941.

21. Alan Lomax to Harold Spivacke, April 8, 1939, in Cohen, *Alan Lomax, Assistant in Charge*, 130; James Mauro, *Twilight at the World of Tomorrow: Genius, Madness, Murder, and the 1939 World's Fair and the Brink of War* (New York: Ballantine Books, 2010).

22. Judah L. Graubart and Alice V. Graubart, *Decade of Destiny* (Chicago: Contemporary Books, 1978), 317-18; Harold Spivacke to Alan Lomax, May 13, 1939, in Cohen, *Alan Lomax, Assistant in Charge*, 133.

23. Lomax, "Archive of American Folk Song," 135; Alan Lomax, "Folk Music in the Roosevelt Era," in *Alan Lomax: Selected Writings, 1934-1997*, ed. Ronald D. Cohen (New York: Routledge 2003), 95; "Ballad of Old Chisholm Trail Drowns New York's Subway Roar as Texas Singer Practices for White House Date with King," *Dallas News*, June 4, 1939. The Jackson recordings were finally issued as *Aunt Molly Jackson: Library of Congress Recordings*, Rounder Records, 1002.

24. Alan Lomax to Harold Spivacke, n.d., in Cohen, *Alan Lomax, Assistant in Charge*, 135-36; Alan Lomax to Davidson Taylor, June 16, 1939, ibid., 136.

25. David Goodman, *Radio's Civic Ambition: American Broadcasting and Democracy in the 1930s* (New York: Oxford University Press, 2011).

26. John William Rogers, "Alan Lomax to Give Series of Radio Programs," *Dallas Times Herald*, October 8, 1939; Rachel Clare Donaldson, *"I Hear America Singings": Folk Music and National Identity* (Philadelphia, Pa.: Temple University Press, 2014).

27. James Agee and Walker Evans, *Cotton Tenants: Three Families* (Brooklyn, N.Y.: Baffler/Melville House, 2013), 36; Dale Mahridge and Michael Williamson, *And Their Children after Them: The Legacy of Let Us Now Praise Famous Men, James Agee and Walker Evans, and the Rise and Fall of Cotton in the South* (New York: Pantheon Books, 1989).

28. Robinson with Gordon, *Ballad of an American*, 77; Mason B. Williams, *City of Ambition: FDR, La Guardia, and the Making of Modern New York* (New York: Norton, 2013), chap. 7.

29. Marc E. Johnson, "'The Masses Are Singing': Insurgency and Songs in New York City, 1929–1941" (PhD diss., City University of New York, 2003); Susan Quinn, *Furious Improvisation: How the WPA and a Cast of Thousands Made High Art out of Desperate Times* (New York: Walker, 2008), 239–84.

30. Benjamin A. Botkin to Gertrude Botkin, August 6, 1938, quoted in Jerrold Hirsch, "'Cultural Strategy': The Seegers and B. A. Botkin as Friends and Allies," in *Ruth Crawford Seeger's Worlds: Innovation and Tradition in Twentieth-Century American Music*, ed. Ray Allen and Ellie M. Hisama (Rochester, N.Y.: University of Rochester Press, 2007), 206; Jerrold Hirsch, *Portrait of America: A Cultural History of the Federal Writers' Project* (Chapel Hill: University of North Carolina Press, 2003), 231–33; Ann M. Pescatello, *Charles Seeger: A Life In American Music* (Pittsburgh: University of Pittsburgh Press, 1992), 155–56.

31. Helen Hartness Flanders, *Vermont Folk-Songs & Ballads* (Brattleboro, VT: Stephen Daye Press, 1932); Helen Hartness Flanders, *Country Songs of Vermont* (New York: G. Shirmer Inc., 1937).

32. Clifford R. Murphy, *Yankee Twang: Country and Western Music in New England* (Urbana: University of Illinois Press, 2014), 46–55.

33. Nancy-Jean Ballard Seigel, "Ballad Collectors in the Northeast," in *The Ballad Collectors of North America: How Gathering Folksongs Transformed Academic Thought and American Identity*, ed. Scott B. Spencer (Lanham, Md.: Scarecrow, 2012), 107–14; Margaret Anne Bulger, "Stetson Kennedy: Applied Folklore and Cultural Advocacy" (PhD diss., University of Pennsylvania, 1992). Kennedy later became close friends with Woody Guthrie.

34. Woody Guthrie, *Pastures of Plenty: A Self-Portrait, Woody Guthrie*, ed. Dave Marsh and Harold Leventhal (New York: HarperCollins, 1990), 7; Sidney Robertson, *The Gold Rush Song Book* (San Francisco, Calif.: Colt Press, 1940).

Chapter 7

1. Richard Randall, "Fighting Songs of the Unemployed," *Daily Worker*, September 2, 1939, 2. See Guido Van Rijn, *Roosevelt's Blues: African-American Blues and Gospel Songs on FDR* (Jackson: University Press of Mississippi, 1997), particularly the discography, 260–65.

2. Paul Rosenfeld, "Folksong and Culture-Politics," *Modern Music* 17 (1939): 21–22, 23–24.

3. Alan Lomax to Davidson Taylor, August 17, 1939, in *Alan Lomax, Assistant in Charge: The Library of Congress Letters, 1935–1945*, ed. Ronald D. Cohen (Jackson: University Press of Mississippi, 2010), 138.

4. Alan Lomax to John Lomax, September 28, 1939, 3D222, folder 4, Lomax Family Papers, Center for American History, University of Texas at Austin (hereafter LP).

5. Alan Lomax to Harold Spivacke, October 2, 1939, in Cohen, *Alan Lomax, Assistant in Charge*, 145; Alan Lomax to Earl Beck, October 4, 1939, ibid., 146.

6. Alan Lomax to Harold Spivacke, November 29, 1939, ibid., 152; Simon Bronner, *Old-Time Music Makers of New York State* (Syracuse, N.Y.: Syracuse University Press, 1978); Norman Cazden, Herbert Haufrecht, and Norman Studer, *Folk Songs of the Catskills* (Albany: State University of New York Press, 1982).

7. Alan Lomax to Alec Saron, December 16, 1939, in Cohen, *Alan Lomax, Assistant in Charge*, 156.

8. Robert Santelli, *This Land Is Your Land: Woody Guthrie and the Journey of an American Folksong* (Philadelphia: Running, 2012); John Shaw, *This Land That I Love: Irving Berlin, Woody Guthrie, and the Story of Two American Anthems* (New York: Public Affairs, 2013).

9. Lomax quoted in Roger G. Kennedy and David Larkin, *When Art Worked* (New York: Rizzoli, 2009), 208.

10. On Ford's film *The Grapes of Wrath*, see Joseph McBride, *Searching for John Ford: A Life* (New York: St. Martin's, 2001), 308–16.

11. Pete Seeger, "This Young Fella, Pete, 1999," in *Pete Seeger: In His Own Words*, ed. Rob Rosenthal and Sam Rosenthal (Boulder, Colo.: Paradigm, 2012), 13–14. See also *The Golden Gate Quartet: Traveling Shoes*, Bluebird 66063-2, 1992.

12. Pete Seeger to his grandmother, February 18, 1940, in Rosenthal and Rosenthal, *Pete Seeger*, 14–15. Browder was the general secretary of the Communist Party, 1929–45.

13. Pete Seeger, "Pete and His Banjo Meet Some Fine Mountain Folks" (1940), in *The Pete Seeger Reader*, ed. Ronald D. Cohen and James Capaldi (New York: Oxford University Press, 2014), 62–64. For Seeger's memories of Guthrie, see *Pete Seeger: Pete Remembers Woody*, Appleseed Recordings APR CD1131, 2012, disc 1.

14. Helen Hartness Flanders to Alan Lomax, December 20, 1939, Nancy Jean Ballard Collection, Bethesda, Maryland; Flanders to Lomax, February 12, 1940, ibid.; Blanche Lemmon, "American Folk Songs," *Etude* 58 (April 1940): 220, 274.

15. *Columbia's American School of the Air: Teacher's Manual and Classroom Guide* ([New York]: Columbia Broadcasting System, Department of Education, [October 10, 1939]), 16. See also *Freedom: The Golden Gate Quartet and Josh White at the Library of Congress (1940)*, Bridge 9114,

2002, recordings made at the "Festival of Music" at the Library of Congress, December 18, 19, 20, 21, 1940.

16. *The American School of the Air: Teacher's Manual 1940–41* ([New York]: Department of Education, the Columbia Broadcasting System, [1940]), 29; Andrea Lynn Woody, "*American School of the Air*: An Experiment in Music Education and Radio Broadcasting" (master's thesis, University of Texas at Austin, May 2003); Rachel Clare Donaldson, *"I Hear America Singing": Folk Music and National Identity* (Philadelphia, Pa.: Temple University Press, 2014).

17. R. P. Wetherald to Alan Lomax, April 29, 1940, in Cohen, *Alan Lomax, Assistant in Charge*, 164; Howard Taubman, "Records: The Dust Bowl," *New York Times*, August 4, 1940, 108; Bill Nowlin, *Woody Guthrie: American Radical Patriot* (Cambridge, Mass.: Rounder Records, 2013).

18. *Time* quoted in Allan Sutton, *Recording the 'Thirties: The Evolution of the American Recording Industry, 1930–39* (Denver: Mainspring, 2011), 167; Earl Robinson with Eric A. Gordon, *Ballad of an American: The Autobiography of Earl Robinson* (Lanham, Md.: Scarecrow, 1998), 97.

19. Robinson with Gordon, *Ballad of an American*, 102.

20. Howard Taubman, "Records: Chain Gang," *New York Times*, August 18, 1940, 110; Elijah Wald, *Josh White: Society Blues* (Amherst: University of Massachusetts Press, 2000), 62–65.

21. John A. Lomax and Alan Lomax, *Our Singing Country: A Second Volume of American Ballads and Folk Songs* (New York: Macmillan, 1941), ix, xii. Alan had earlier assisted his father in publishing a revised and enlarged edition of *Cowboy Songs and Other Frontier Ballads* (New York: Macmillan, 1938), which included many songs from published sources.

22. Alan Lomax, Woody Guthrie, and Pete Seeger, *Hard Hitting Songs for Hard-Hit People* (New York: Oak, 1967), 8, 15.

23. Pete Seeger to Millard Lampell, October 1, 1987, in Rosenthal and Rosenthal, *Pete Seeger*, 16–17; [Lee Hays], "Prospectus of the American Workers Song Book for Publication Spring 1939," copy in possession of the author.

24. Davidson Taylor to Alan Lomax, July 17, 1940, AFC 1939/002, Alan Lomax CBS Radio Series Collection, American Folklife Center, Library of Congress; Alan Lomax to John Lomax, July 26, 1940, in Cohen, *Alan Lomax, Assistant in Charge*, 175.

25. Lomax quoted in Bernard Eisenschitz, *Nicholas Ray: An American Journey* (London: Faber and Faber, 1993), 44–45.

26. Alan Lomax to John Lomax, n.d. [early August 1940], in Cohen, *Alan Lomax, Assistant in Charge*, 180–81; Alan Lomax to Clifton Fadiman, n.d. [September 1940], ibid., 186. Early the next year, Lomax brought

Mainer to perform at an "Evening of American Folklore" for the first family at the White House. Dick Spottswood, *Banjo on the Mountain: Wade Mainer's First Hundred Years* (Jackson: University Press of Mississippi, 2010), 9–14.

27. Burl Ives, *Wayfaring Stranger* (New York: Whittlesey House, 1948), 206–7; Corey Murray, email to the author, September 26, 2014.

28. Ives, *Wayfaring Stranger*, 246; Lomax quoted in Sally Osborne Norton, "A Historical Study of Actor Will Geer, His Life and Work in the Context of Twentieth-Century American Social, Political, and Theatrical History" (PhD diss., University of Southern California, 1980), 330.

29. Alan Lomax to John Lomax, October 12, 1940, in Cohen, *Alan Lomax, Assistant in Charge*, 186; Alan Lomax to Harold Spivacke, memo, n.d. [ca. August 1940], ibid., 176–77; Lomax to Spivacke, memo, n.d., ibid., 178.

30. Bess Lomax Hawes, *Sing It Pretty: A Memoir* (Urbana: University of Illinois Press, 2008), 39; Alan Lomax to Davidson Taylor, December 31, 1940, in Cohen, *Alan Lomax, Assistant in Charge*, 197–98.

31. Alan Lomax to R. P. Wetherald, September 16, 1940, in Cohen, *Alan Lomax, Assistant in Charge*, 184; Alan Lomax to William Fineschriber, February 10, 1941, ibid., 208. Ives has no mention of Lomax in his autobiography, *Wayfaring Stranger*.

32. Alan Lomax to Woody Guthrie, November 1, 1940, in Cohen, *Alan Lomax, Assistant in Charge*, 189; Lomax to Guthrie, February 4, 1941, ibid., 205.

33. Henrietta Yurchenco, *Around the World in 80 Years: A Memoir* (Port Richmond, Calif.: MRI, 2002), 37–38; "Adventures in Music: Kentucky," July 13, 1940, script held by WNYC Archive Collection and used with permission.

34. Woody Guthrie to Henrietta Yurchenco, October 3, 1940, quoted in Henrietta Yurchenco assisted by Marjorie Guthrie, *A Mighty Hard Road: The Woody Guthrie Story* (New York: McGraw-Hill, 1970), 103–4; Yurchenco, *Around the World in 80 Years*, 48.

35. Joe Klein, *Woody Guthrie: A Life* (New York: Knopf, 1980), 166–72.

36. Sidney Snook, "Hill Billy and 'River' Songs at Their Source," *Etude* 58 (August 1940): 513, 555.

37. Charles Todd to Alan Lomax, January 23, 1940, in Cohen, *Alan Lomax, Assistant in Charge*, 162; Lomax to Todd, February 7, 1940, ibid., 162.

38. Alan Lomax to Charles Todd and Robert Sonkin, July 20, 1940, ibid., 173; Charles Todd and Robert Sonkin, "Ballads of the Okies," *New York Times*, November 17, 1940; Robin Fanslow, "Voices from the Dust Bowl:

The Charles L. Todd and Robert Sonkin Collection," *Folklife Center News* 20, no. 2 (1998): 3–9.

39. Jannelle Warren-Findley, "Journal of a Field Representative: Charles Seeger and Margaret Valiant," *Ethnomusicology* 24, no. 2 (1980): 169–210; Ann M. Pescatello, *Charles Seeger: A Life in American Music* (Pittsburgh: University of Pittsburgh Press, 1992), 142–46.

40. John H. Cowley, "Don't Leave Me Here: Non-commercial Blues: The Field Trips, 1924–60," in *Nothing but the Blues: The Music and the Musicians*, ed. Lawrence Cohn (New York: Abbeville, 1993), 279–84. Some of these recordings can be found in Alan Lomax, comp., *Anglo-American Shanties, Lyric Songs, Dance Tunes and Spirituals*, Library of Congress Music Division Recording Laboratory, AFS L2, 1942, as well as in the other four records issued in this series and later reissued by the Library of Congress as LPs; *The Ballad Hunter: John A. Lomax, Parts I and II*, Library of Congress Music Division Recording Laboratory, AAFS L49.

41. Quoted in David Dunaway and Molly Beer, *Singing Out: An Oral History of America's Folk Music Revivals* (New York: Oxford University Press, 2010), 47.

42. Ellen Schrecker, *Many Are the Crimes: McCarthyism in America* (Boston: Little, Brown, 1998), 89–105; Jennifer Luff, *Commonsense Anticommunism: Labor and Civil Liberties between the Wars* (Chapel Hill: University of North Carolina Press, 2012); Robert Justin Goldstein, ed., *Little "Red" Scare: Anti-Communism and Political Repression in the United States, 1921-1946* (Burlington, Vt.: Ashgate, 2014), in particular, Athan Theoharis, "The FBI and the Politics of Anti-Communism, 1920–1945" (23–44), and Timothy Cain, "Little Red Schoolhouses: Anti-Communism and Education in an 'Age of Conflict'" (105–33).

43. Larry Ceplair and Steven Englund, *The Inquisition in Hollywood: Politics in the Film Community, 1930-60* (Urbana: University of Illinois Press, 2003), 154–65.

44. Moe Foner, *Not for Bread Alone: A Memoir* (Ithaca, N.Y.: Cornell University Press, 2002), 17–18.

45. Eli Jaffe, *Oklahoma Odyssey: A Memoir* (Hyde Park, N.Y.: privately printed, 1993); Shirley A. Wiegand and Wayne A. Wiegand, *Books on Trial: Red Scare in the Heartland* (Norman: University of Oklahoma Press, 2007).

46. Agnes "Sis" Cunningham and Gordon Friesen, *Red Dust and Broadsides: A Joint Autobiography*, ed. Ronald D. Cohen (Amherst: University of Massachusetts Press, 1999), 182, 193.

47. *Oklahoma Witch Hunt* (October 1941) can be found ibid., 307–23.

48. John Lomax to Alan Lomax, June 30, 1941, LP.

49. Roy Harris, "Folksong—American Big Business," *Modern Music* 18 (November–December 1940): 9–11; *Time* 37, no. 1 (1941): 36; liner notes to *Roy Harris: Folksong Symphony 1940*, Vanguard Everyman SRV 347 SD, 1975.

50. Alan Lomax, "Music in Your Own Back Yard," in *Alan Lomax: Selected Writings, 1934–1997*, ed. Ronald D. Cohen (New York: Routledge, 2003), 47, 55.

51. Gregory d'Alessio, *Old Troubadour: Carl Sandburg with His Guitar Friends* (New York: Walker, 1987), 44.

Epilogue

1. Michael Denning, *The Cultural Front: The Laboring of American Culture in the Twentieth Century* (London: Verso, 1996), chaps. 9–11.

2. Lou Cooper, "Folk Music," *New Masses*, January 7, 1941, 23, 26; Olin Downes and Elie Siegmeister, *A Treasury of American Song* (New York: Howell, Soskin & Co., 1940); Rachel Clare Donaldson, *"I Hear America Singing": Folk Music and National Identity* (Philadelphia: Temple University Press, 2014), chap. 3.

3. Alan Lomax, "Folk Music in the Roosevelt Era," in *Alan Lomax: Selected Writings, 1934–1997*, ed. Ronald D. Cohen (New York: Routledge, 2003), 95–96; Eleanor Roosevelt, "My Day," *Washington Daily*, February 19, 1941, 22; John Szwed, *Alan Lomax: The Man Who Recorded the World* (New York: Viking, 2010), 196–200. For the story of MacLeish's fascinating life and cultural milieu, see Amanda Vaill, *Everybody Was So Young: Gerald and Sara Murphy, a Lost Generation Love Story* (New York: Houghton Mifflin, 1999). MacLeish had definite left-wing credentials, having worked with Ernest Hemingway and the filmmaker Joris Ivens on the pro-Loyalist film *The Spanish Earth* (1937) about the Spanish Civil War.

4. For Guthrie's creative work in May 1941 see, for example, Greg Vandy, *26 Songs in 30 Days: Woody Guthrie's Columbia River Songs & the Planned Promised Land In the Pacific Northwest* (New York: Sasquatch Books, 2016).

5. Chester Kallman, "I Hear American Singing," *Harper's Bazaar*, June 1941, 71; "Thar's Gold in Them Thar Hillbilly and Other American Folk Tunes," *Billboard Band Year Book*, September 26, 1942, 86; "Hillbilly Disks Hit New Midwest High, Say Dealers," *Billboard*, July 31, 1943, 16. For Pete Seeger's extensive FBI file see, http://m.motherjones.com/politics/2015/12/pete-seeger-fbi-file.

6. Annegret Fauser, *Sounds of War: Music in the United States during World War II* (New York: Oxford University Press, 2013), chap. 3.

7. Judith E. Smith, *Visions of Belonging: Family Stories, Popular Culture, and Postwar Democracy, 1940–1960* (New York: Columbia University Press, 2004); Carol J. Oja, *Bernstein Meets Broadway: Collaborative Art in a Time of War* (New York: Oxford University Press, 2014), chap. 5.

8. Ian Buruma, *Year Zero: A History of 1945* (London: Atlantic Books, 2013); Richard Lingeman, *Noir Forties: The American People from Victory to Cold War* (New York: Nation Books, 2102).

9. Pete Seeger, "A Shoestring Operation," 1961, in *Pete Seeger in His Own Words*, ed. Rob Rosenthal and Sam Rosenthal (Boulder, Colo.: Paradigm, 2012), 39; Ronald D. Cohen, *Rainbow Quest: The Folk Music Revival and American Society, 1940–1970* (Amherst: University of Massachusetts Press, 2002), chap. 2.

10. "Tables for Two," *New Yorker*, December 21, 1946, 48–49. Oscar Brand's radio show was still on the air in 2015.

11. Judith E. Smith, *Becoming Belafonte: Black Artist, Public Radical* (Austin: University of Texas Press, 2014); Ronald D. Cohen and Rachel C. Donaldson, *Roots of the Revival: American and British Folk Music in the 1950s* (Urbana: University of Illinois Press, 2014).

12. See, for example, Stephen Petrus and Ronald D. Cohen, *Folk City: New York and the American Folk Music Revival* (New York: Oxford University Press, 2015).

Index

"Abraham Lincoln Lives Again" (song), 94
Adams, Frederick, 75–76
Adomian, Lan, 33, 48, 64; heads Workers Music League, 63; at the Yorkville Casino festival, 66, 67
Adventures in Music, 139
African American blues, 22; records, 69–70
African American folk singers, 10
African American folk songs, 11
African American music, 35
African American phonograph records, 13–15
African American protest songs, 11, 62–63, 64
African American songs, 13, 42
The Aladdin Playparty, 17
Allen Brothers, 15, 40
Almanac Singers, 134, 153–54
Americana (musical), 36
American Ballads and Folk Songs, 42, 43–44
American Ballads and Songs, 7
An American Exodus, 91
American Federation of Labor, 79
American Federation of Musicians, 155
American Folklife Center, 158
American Folk Song Festival, Ashland, Kentucky, 50, 52–53, 60
American League for Peace and Democracy, 105
American Music League, 63; *March and Sing!* (songbook), 76; *Unison*, 66–67; Yorkville Casino festival, 66, 67

American Musicological Society, 119
American Peace Mobilization, 106
American Record Company (ARC), 26
American School of the Air, 111, 112, 120–21
The American Songbag, 7, 8, 149
American Student Union: *Patters for Peace* (songbook), 105
"An Evening of American Music in Conjunction with the Exhibition of Rural Arts," 144
Appalachian music, 12–13
Archive of American Folk Song, 10, 158; during the Depression, 83; interface with jazz, 102–3
Archive of Folk Culture, 158
Asch, Moses, 155, 157
Ashley, Clarence, 19
As Thousands Cheer, 156
Autry, Gene: biography of, 27–28; "Death of Jimmie Rodgers," 27; "The Death of Mother Jones," 27–28
Auville, Ray and Lida: *Songs of the American Worker*, 67

Back Where I Come From (radio show), 135–36, 137–38
Bad-man ballads, 42
Baez, Joan, 157
Bailey, Bud and His Downeasters, 116
Bailey, Deford, 17, 27
Baker, James "Iron Head," 41, 42
Ballad for Americans (album), 131

The Ballad Hunter (broadcasts), 144
Ballads and Songs of the Shanty-Boy, 20
Ballads of the Maine Lumberjack, 20
Barn-dance shows, 16–17
Barnicle, Mary Elizabeth, 56–58, 84, 85; in New York City, 1930s, 92
Barrel-house ditties, 42
Barry, Phillips: *British Ballads from Maine*, 19; *Folk Music in America* (book), 83
Bauman, Mordecai, 65, 66
Bechet, Sidney: on *Back Where I Come From* (radio show), 136
Beck, Earl C., 103, 121
Belafonte, Harry, 157
Bentley Boys, 19
Berg's String Entertainers, 16
Bernay, Erik, 153
Bernstein, Leonard, 155
Billboard Band Year Book, 154–55
Blake, Blind, 14
Blegen, Theodore, 103
Blitzstein, Marc, 33; *The Cradle Will Rock* (labor musical), 98; heads Workers Music League, 63; pianist for Mordecai Bauman, 65
Bloch, Ray, 141
Blue Angel (club), 157
Bluebird label, 26–27
Blues: African American southern, 22; before 1920s, 13; female singers, 14; in New Deal programs, 48; regarding hard times, 37; rural, 14
Bob Miller's Famous Hill-Billy Heart Throbs, 51

Bogan, Lucille, 48
Boogie-woogie pianists, 104
Boone County Jamboree (radio show), 50
Botkin, Benjamin A.: biography of, 114; heads Writers' Program Unit, Library of Congress, 115
Botkin, Gertrude, 115
"The Bourgeois Blues" (song), 93, 109
Bradford, Roark, 114
Brand, Oscar, 156
Breau, Harold. *See* Hal Lone Pine and Betty Cody
Brewster, Paul, 100
British ballads, 12, 13, 19
Brockway, Howard: *Lonesome Tunes: Folk Songs from the Kentucky Mountains*, 12
Brookwood Chatauqua Songs, 28, 77
Brookwood Labor College, 28, 76–77
Broonzy, Big Bill, 14, 27; "Working on the Project," 118–19
Brown, Milton, 40
Brunswick, 14, 19
Buchanan, Annabel Morris starts White Top Festival, 53–54
Burl Ives Show (radio), 137

Cabin in the Sky (musical), 125, 156
Café Society (interracial nightclub), 95, 107, 140, 155
Cajun music, 20
Calhoun, Betty, 59
California Folk Music Project, 60, 117
California political tone, 1930s, 90–92
Calmer, Alan, 23–24
Campbell, John C., 12

Campbell, Olive Dame, 12; *English Folk-songs of the Southern Appalachians*, 12–13
Camp Kinderland, 94
Camp Unity, 93–94
Camp Woodland, 122
Caney, Josephine, 100
Cannon's Jug Stompers, 14
Carlisle, Cliff, 15
Carmen Jones, 156
Carolinians, 131–32
Carson, Fiddlin' John, 15, 16
Carson J. Robinson's World's Greatest Collection of Mountain Ballads and Old Time Songs, 51
Carter family, 18, 19, 21, 27, 52; "When the World's on Fire," 123–24
Cazden, Norman, 60, 144
Center for Folklife and Cultural Heritage, 158
Chain Gang (album), 131–32
Chaplin, Charlie, 74
Chaplin, Ralph, 20
Child, Francis James: *The English and Scottish Popular Ballads*, 11, 12, 70
CIO Songs (booklet), 80
Clauch, W. E., 144
Cleveland Orchestra, 149
Columbia Concert Orchestra, 129
Columbia Records, 14, 17, 19, 25
Comden, Betty, 155
Committee on Un-American Activities, 114
Commonwealth College, 77
Commonwealth Labor Songs (songbook), 77
"Commonwealth Labor Songs—A Collection of Old and New Songs," 134

Communications Act of 1934, 112
Communist Party, 21, 32–36, 46–48; camps, 93, 94; convention, 1940, 131; International Music Buro, 48; and New Deal arts programs, 56; recordings, 65; scrutiny of/backlash against, 146; turn toward folk music, 75
"Company Union" (song), 77
Composers' Collective, 33; *Music Vanguard* (journal), 62
Congress of Industrial Organizations uses music as an organizing tool, 79
Cooke, Alistair, 102
Coon Creek Girls, 99; on *Back Where I Come From* (radio show), 136
Coon songs, 13
Cooper, Lou, 152
Copland, Aaron, 33–34, 47, 120; "Into the Streets May First," 64; at the Yorkville Casino festival, 66, 67
Corley, Odell, 30
Corn songs, 42
Corwin, Norman, 131
"Cotton Mill Colic," 128
Country music: radio programs, 16–18; upsurge, 1930s, 91; urban interest in, 139
Cowboy bands, 59
Cowboy songs, 28, 30–31, 116
Cowboy Songs and Other Frontier Ballads, 11, 149
Cowell, Henry, 33, 67
Cowell, Sidney Robertson, 60
Cox, Bill, 40
Cox, John Harrington, *Traditional Ballads Mainly from West Virginia* (book), 84

The Cradle Will Rock, 156
Crazy Barn Dance (radio show), 50
Crissman, Maxine, 899
Crockett Kentucky Mountaineers, 51
Crosby, Bing: "Brother, Can You Spare a Dime?," 36; *Earl Robinson–John L Touche: Ballad for Americans* (album), 132
Cunningham, Agnes "Sis," 82, 147, 148; in Almanac Singers, 153; edits songbooks, 77; during World War II, 154

Daily Worker Chorus, 48
Dalhart, Vernon, 17, 18, 51
Davis, Stuart, 40
Day, Robert, 100
Dear Mr. President (album), 154
Decca Records, 27, 118–19
Degeyter Music Club: *Music Front* (journal), 62–63
Denver Annual Folk Festival, 59–60
Dick, Sheldon, 122
Dies, Martin, 114
Dixon Brothers, 16
Dorsey, Georgia Tom, 14
Downes, Olin, 101, 108; *A Treasury of American Song*, 152
Down Homers, 116
Dusenberry, Emma, 70–71, 81; "The Dodger" (song), 71; *Our Singing Country*, 133
Dust Bowl, 87–92
Dust Bowl Ballads, 130
"Dusty Old Dust (So Long, It's Been Good to Know Yuh)," 89
Dyer-Bennet, Richard: "'Grapes of Wrath' Evening," 125
Dylan, Bob, 157

Earl Robinson–John L Touche: Ballad for Americans (album), 132
Eckstrom, Fannie Hardy, 19
Edwards, Teddy "Big Boy": "The WPA Blues," 118
Eisler, Hanns, 34, 48; compositions, 65; pianist for Mordecai Bauman, 65
Elmore Vincent's Lumber Jack Songs, 51
Engel, Carl, 10, 42
Engel, Lehman, 67
The English and Scottish Popular Ballads, 11, 12
Ethnic records, 15, 60
"Evening of Negro Music" (stage show), 108
Event songs, 31
Exploring the Arts and Sciences (radio show), 97

Fadiman, Clifton, 134, 135
Falcon, Joseph, 20
Farm Security Administration, 72; camps, 142; photography unit, 91
Federal Communications Commission, 112
Federal Music Program, 60
Federal One program, 56, 58
Federal Theatre Project, 73, 97; abolished, 114; music research unit, 73; plays with a folk component, 73
Federal Writers' Project, 115
Fiddle contests, 16. *See also* individual contests
Field recording methods, 143
Fields, Don and His Pony Boys, 116
Fineschriber, William, 138
Finger, Charles: *Sailor Chanteys and Cowboy Songs*, 11

Flanders, Helen Hartness, 115, 122; on Alan Lomax's radio shows, 127; *Country Songs of Vermont*, 116; *Vermont Folk-Songs & Ballads*, 116

Flannigan, Hallie, 73

Florida Writers' Project, 116

Folk festivals, 52. *See also individual festivals*

Folklife Festival (Smithsonian), 158

Folk music: commercial, 109, 124; growing popularity, late 1930s, 97; importance of, 152; link with radical politics, 97; mid-1950s, 157; popular interest in, 118; progressive v. traditional, 144–45, 151; to promote the war effort, 153

Folk Music of America (CBS programs), 120–21; becomes *Wellsprings of Music*, 129; guest spots, 128–29; *Teachers Manual and Classroom Guide*, 127–28

Folk revival, 1950s, 157

Folk Song Festival (radio show), 156

Folk-Songs of America (book), 83

Folkways Records, 158

Foner brothers, 146–47

Friends of the Workers School, 65

Friesen, Gordon, 148, 154

"From Spirituals to Swing" concerts, 104–5

Fuson, Harvey, 41

Garland, Jim, 31, 109; biography of, 92; "Give Me Back My Job Again," 78; on *Kentucky* (radio show), 139; radio program, 92

Garland, Mary Magdalene. *See* Jackson, Aunt Molly

Geer, Herta, 123

Geer, Will, 98, 117, 122; biography of, 90; moves to New York, 123; *Tall Tales* (film), 137

Gellert, Hugo, 62, 63

Gellert, Lawrence, 9, 35, 41, 131; biography of, 10–11; "Ku Kluck Klan" (song), 67; "Me and My Captain," 63–64; "Negro Songs of Protest" (article), 62; *Negro Songs of Protest* (book), 63, 66–67

Gennett label, 14

Geographically focused songs, 19–20

Georgia Old-Time Fiddler's Convention, 16

Gilbert, Ronniie, 157

Gilliland, Henry, 15

"Give Me Back My Job Again" (song), 78

Glazer, Tom, 156

Gold, Michael, 67; "The Strange Funeral at Braddock," 66

Gold Diggers of 1933 (musical), 36

Golden Gate Quartet: on *Back Where I Come From* (radio show), 135; on *Folk Music of America*, 129; "'Grapes of Wrath' Evening," 125; records for RCA Victor, 130; at the White House, 152

The Gold Rush Song Book, 117

"Goodnight Irene," 46, 140

Gordon, Robert, 41, 53; biography of, 9–10; *Folk-Songs of America* (book), 83

Gordon, Taylor, 35

Gorney, Jay, 36

Grand Ole Opry (radio show), 17, 50

The Grapes of Wrath: film, 91, 125; novel, 90, 91

"'Grapes of Wrath' Evening," 125, 136
Gray, Roland Palmer, 20
Green, Adolph, 155
Green, Johnny, 104
Greenwich Village folk community, 1930s, 92–95
Grofé, Ferde, 120
Gummere, F. B., 9
Guthrie, Jack, 89
Guthrie, Woody, 123–27, 139–41; in Almanac Singers, 153; on *Back Where I Come From* (radio show), 135, 136; "The Ballad of Pretty Boy Floyd," 125; biography of, 88–92; *Bound for Glory* (autobiographical novel), 88; boxed record sets of recordings, 158; *Dust Bowl Ballads*, 130; emerges as popular artist, 118; on *Folk Music of America*, 128–29; "'Grapes of Wrath' Evening," 125; *Hard Hitting Songs for Hard Hit People*, 133; on *Kentucky* (radio show), 139; on Lead Belly, 140; on Lomax's radio show, 130; moves back to Texas, 123; moves to California, 141; moves to New York, 117, 123–24; newspaper correspondent, 90; "On a Slow Train through California" (songbook), 124; *Our Singing Country*, 133; radio shows, 89, 123; records songs and stories at Library of Congress, 129; road trip with Pete Seeger, 126, 134, 147; temperament, 138–39; "This Land Is Your Land," 123–24; "Tom Joad," 130; "Union Maid" (song), 147; "Woody Sez"

column, 117, 124, 141; during World War II, 154

"Hallelujah I'm a Bum" (song), 74
Hal Lone Pine and Betty Cody, 116
Halpert, Herbert, 58, 115, 144; defines folk songs, 96; field recordings, 73
Hammond, John, 104; produces *Chain Gang* album, 131–32
Handcox, John: biography of, 81; "There Are Mean Things Happening in This Land" (song), 122; "There Is Mean Things Happening in This Land" (song), 82
Handy, W. C., 103
Harburg, E. Y. "Yip," 36
Harper, Roy, 19
Harris, R. H. and the Soul Stirrers, 68
Harris, Roy, 120; on Alan Lomax, 149; on Cecil Sharp, 149; "Folksong—American Big Business," 148–49; *Folksong Symphony*, 148, 149; on John Lomax, 149
Haufrecht, Herbert, 71
Hawaiian musical combos, 59
Hawes, Butch, 153
Hawes, Pete, 13
Hayes, Alfred, 93
Hays, Lee, 133–34, 157; in Almanac Singers, 153; biography of, 80–81; "Commonwealth Labor Songs," 134; during World War II, 154
Held, John, Jr., 12
Hellerman, Fred, 157
Henry, Mellinger, 53
Herrmann, Bernard, 129
Highlander Folk School, 78, 126, 141

Hill, Joe, 20; "Casey Jones," 64
Hillbilly music, 15, 51; cross-racial influences, 15
Hillbilly records, 17, 27; difference from popular records, 18
Hispanic music, 59
Hold on to Your Hats (musical), 125
Holiday, Billie, 95
Hoosier Folk Lore Society, 100
Hornellsville Hillbillies, 122
Horton, Myles, 78
House Un-American Activities Committee, 145–46
Houston, Cisco, 141, 154
Howard, Pappy and his Connecticut Kernels, 116
Hudson, Arthur P., 53; *Folk Songs of Mississippi and Their Background*, 84, 86; *Folk Tunes from Mississippi*, 74, 84
Hudson Shore Labor School, 77
Hunt, John M. "Sailor Dad," 53, 152
Hurston, Zora Neale, 56–57, 69, 116; collecting in the black communities, 57
Hurt, Mississippi John, 14

I Hear America Singing (radio show), 102
"I'm a Stranger Here Myself" (radio program), 134
Industrial Workers of the World (IWW), 20; "Hallelujah I'm a Bum," 74; songbooks, 76
"The Internationale," 65
Interracial shows, 155–56
Iowa Barn Dance Frolic (radio show), 50
Isolationism, 105–6
"It Shall Not Come to Pass" (song), 107

Ives, Burl, 118; on *Back Where I Come From* (radio show), 135, 136; biography of, 136–37; *Burl Ives Show* (radio), 137; at "'Grapes of Wrath' Evening," 125, 136; *Okeh Presents the Wayfaring Stranger* (album), 137; *Tall Tales* (film), 137; tours with Will Geer, 136; on *Wellsprings of Music* (radio show), 129; at the White House, 152; during World War II, 154

Jackson, Aunt Molly, 119; biography of, 24–25; on *Folk Music of America*, 128; "'Grapes of Wrath' Evening," 125; "Hungry Ragged Blues," 22, 25; musical autobiography of, 58; in New York City, 1930s, 92; *Our Singing Country*, 133; repertoire, 110; during World War II, 154
Jackson, George Pullen, 53
Jackson, Papa Charlie, 14
Jaffe, Eli, 147, 148
Jazz, 101–5
Jefferson, Blind Lemon, 14
Jennings, Mary, 88
Jerome, V. J., 65
Jerry and Sky, 116
Jewish musicians, 60–61
Jim Garland and His Kentucky Mountain Folk Singers (radio program), 92
Jimmy Dwyer's Sawdust Trail, 141
John Henry (musical), 114
Johnson, Guy, 11; *The Negro and His Songs*, 13; *Negro Workaday Songs*, 13
Johnson, Henry, 69–70

Johnson, Lonnie, 14
Johnson, Malcolm, 141
Johnson, Zilphia Mae: biography of, 78–79; edits songbooks, 78
John Steinbeck Committee to Aid Farm Workers, 117, 125
Joint Committee on Folk Arts, WPA, 115
Joint Legislative Committee to Investigate the Educational System of the State of New York, 146
Jones, Mary Harris "Mother," 28
Jordan, Charlie, 37
Josephson, Barney, 95
Jukebox industry, 27

Kallman, Chester, 154
Kapp, Jack, 27
Karnot, S., 76
Karpeles, Maude, 12, 13; *English Folk-Songs of the Southern Appalachians*, 13
Kazan, Elia, 134
Keene, Hank and His Connecticut Hillbillies, 116
Ken Mackenzie Tent Show, 116
Kennedy, Stetson, 116–17
Kent, Rockwell, 40
Kentucky (radio show), 139
Kentucky Workers Alliance, 78
Kerby, Marion, 53
Kerr, Walter, 155
Kester, Frank, 9
Keynote Records, 153
Kienzle, Raymond Nicholas. *See* Ray, Nicholas
Kincaid, Bradley, 116
Kingston Trio, 157
Kittredge, George Lyman, 9, 12, 46

Knott, Sarah Gertrude, 99, 100, 109; begins National Folk Festival, 54–55
Korson, George, 19–20; *Coal Dust on the Fiddle: Songs and Stories of the Bituminous Industry*, 23; *Minstrels of the Mine Patch: Songs and Stories of the Anthracite Industry*, 23; organizes Pennsylvania Folk Festival, 55; *Songs and Ballads of the Anthracite Miner*, 19–20, 23, 24
Kraber, Tony, 139

Labor protests, 76
Labor schools, 76
Labor songbooks, 78–80
Labor songs, 20–21, 27–32; miners, 22–25
Labor Songs (songbook), 78–79
Labor unions, 40
Lair, John, 99
Lamothe, Ferdinand Joseph. *See* Morton, Jelly Roll
Lampell, Millard, 153, 154
Lange, Dorothea, iconic "Migrant Mother" photograph, 91
Larkin, Margaret, 25; promotes Ella May Wiggins, 30; on the *Red Song Book*, 32, 34; *Singing Cowboy: A Book of Western Songs*, 30
La Touche, John, 114, 131
Ledbetter, Huddie "Lead Belly," 41, 42–43, 44; arrested, 109; *Back Where I Come From* (radio show), 137; "Becky Deem, She Was a Gamblin' Gal," 70; becomes politicized, 93; biography of, 45–46; "Bourgeois Blues" (song), 93; boxed record sets

of recordings, 158; emerges as popular artist, 118; in "Evening of Negro Music" (stage show), 109; on *Folk Music of America*, 128; *Folk Songs of America* (radio show), 140; "Goodnight, Irene," 46; "Goodnight Irene," 140; "'Grapes of Wrath' Evening," 125; *Negro Folk Songs as Sung by Lead Belly*, 46; *Negro Sinful Tunes* (album), 109; "Pick a Bale of Cotton," 46; "Pigment Papa," 70; radio show, 140; recording for ARC, 69; recording for John Lomax, 69; recording for Library of Congress, 93; records for RCA Victor, 130; "The Bourgeois Blues" (song), 109; "The Scottsboro Boys Shall Not Die," 93; theme song, 140; during World War II, 154
Lemmon, Blanche, 127
Let's Sing (songbook), 78, 80
Lewis, Elaine Lambert: *Songs of the Seven Million* (program), 140
Lewis, John L., 79
Lewis, Ted, 27
Library of Congress: collection of field recordings, 58; collects hillbilly records, 108; collects race records, 108; music collecting, 42; Radio Research Project, 144; sponsors collecting trips, 56–58; Writers' Program unit, 115
Light (newspaper), 90
Livingstone, Anne, 62–63
Log Cabin Songs by Johnny Crockett (sheet music), 51
Lomax, Alan, 48, 82–87, 119; associated with Zora Neale Hurston, 69; *Back Where I Come From* (radio show), 135–36, 137–38; biography of, 44–45, 68; book projects, 132–34; on Burl Ives, 138; CBS programs, 118; on Clifton Fadiman, 135–36; collecting difficulties, 85–86; collecting trip to Indiana, 100; collecting trip to Vermont, 115, 122; collecting trip with Mary Elizabeth Barnicle, 56–58, 84, 85; collects for Library of Congress, 56–58, 68–69; collects hillbilly records, 107, 108; collects race records, 107–8; criticism of A. P. Hudson's work, 86–887; on the disappearance of folk culture, 84–85; on the discovery of Lead Belly, 150; on Emma Dusenberry, 81; enrolls at NYU and Columbia, 104; FBI file, 110; on field collecting, 149–50; friendship with Nicholas Ray, 135; on the function of folk music, 87; "'Grapes of Wrath' Evening," 125; Great Lakes collecting trip, 100, 103–4; *Hard Hitting Songs for Hard Hit People*, 133; hires Pete Seeger, 126; on the importance of folk songs, 59; on Jelly Roll Morton, 102; on John Lomax, 68; and the Left, 120–23; "List of American Folk Songs on Commercial Records," 108; marries Elizabeth Harold Goodman, 69; on meeting Aunt Molly Jackson, 150; national radio program, 111; in New York, 107–12; at the Office of War Information, 153, 154; on

the Ohio Valley Fold Festival, 99–100; organizes Washington concert, 99; *Our Singing Country: A Second Volume of American Ballads and Folk Songs*, 132–33; on patriotic songbooks, 137; posts bond for Lead Belly, 109; quits Columbia, 109; radio programs, 134–36; radio shows, 127–28; reaction to National Folk Festival, 100; recording trip to Galax, Virginia, 126; recording trips, 41–43; records boogie-woogie pianists, 104; regarding Cabaret TAC, 123; "'Sinful' Songs of the Southern Negro," 42; sings at the White House, 110; speaks at American Writers' Congress, 110; summarizes state of vernacular music late 1930s, 86, 87; teaches at Federal Workers School, 99; on traditional classical music, 129; visits Ohio Valley Folk Festival, 1938, 99; at the White House, 152–53; on Will Geer, 136–37; work at Library of Congress, 98–99; works with Joint Committee on Folk Arts, 115

Lomax, Bess, 108, 137–38, 148; in Almanac Singers, 153; "'Grapes of Wrath' Evening," 125; at Office of War Information, 154

Lomax, John, 148; *Adventures of a Ballad Hunter*, 70; *American Ballads and Folk Songs*, 43–44; biography of, 42; collecting trips, 45, 70, 83; collecting trip through the South, 144; *Cowboy Songs and Other Frontier Ballads*, 8, 11; Lead Belly recordings, 69; marries Ruby Terrill, 44; National Advisor of Folklore and Folkways, WPA, 70, 83; recording trips, 41–43; records Emma Dusenberry, 70–71; "'Sinful Songs' of the Southern Negro," 42

Lonesome Tunes: Folk Songs from the Kentucky Mountains, 12

Lorentz, Pare, 72

Loyalty oaths for government workers, 114

Lumber jack culture, 103

Lunsford, Bascom Lamar, 9, 16, 54; Mountain Dance and Folk Festival, Asheville, NC, 16, 52; stages Ohio Valley Folk Festival, 99

Luther, Frank, 17, 18, 51

Mackenzie, Ken, 116

MacLeish, Archibald, 152

Macon, Uncle Dave, 17

Maddox Brothers and Rose, 91

"Made-up" songs, 42, 43

Mainer, Wade: on *Back Where I Come From* (radio show), 136; at the White House, 152

Maitland, Captain Dick, 110; *Our Singing Country*, 133

Manhattan Chorus, 67

March and Sing! (songbook), 76

Martin Brothers, 31

Marvin, Frank, 17; *Folio of Down Home Songs*, 51

Marvin, Johnny, 51

McCarn, Dave, 16; "Cotton Mill Colic," 28–29, 128

McClintock, Harry "Haywire Mac," 20–21

McFarland, Francis, 59
McGee, Kirk, 17
McGee, Sam, 17
McGhee, John, 31
McGill, Josephine: *Folk-Songs of the Kentucky Mountains*, 12
McTell, Blind Willie, 14
McWilliams, Elsie, 19
Meeropol, Abel: "Abraham Lincoln Lives Again" (song), 94; political compositions, 94
Memphis Jug Band, 14, 27
Men and Dust (film), 122
Mexican American music, 20
Middleton, Ray, 131
Miller, Bob, 17
Miners songs, 23–25, 31–32
Modern Times (film), 74
Morton, Jelly Roll and His Red Hot Peppers, 27, 101–2
Mountain Dance and Folk Festival, Asheville, North Carolina, 16, 115
Mountaineer tunes, 15
Music Front (journal), 62–63
Music industry during the Depression, 26–27
Music Vanguard (journal), 62, 65
My Pious Friends and Drunken Companions, 11–12

Nashville Old Harp Singers, 119
National Barn Dance, 17
National Folk Festival, 54–55
National Service Bureau, 83
National Youth Administration, 144
National Youth Orchestra, 144
Negro Folk Songs as Sung by Lead Belly (book), 69
Negro Sinful Tunes (album), 109
Negro Workaday Songs, 11, 13

New Deal arts programs, 37, 40, 56, 75, 115
New Deal Resettlement Administration, 71–72; films, 72
New Deal songs, 40
Newell, William Wells, 11
New Music Quarterly Recordings, 65–66
New York World's Fair, 1939, 108
Niles, John Jacob: approach to vernacular songs, 50; biography of, 49–50; collecting trips, 49–50; concert career, 49; writing career, 49
Nye, Captain Pearl R., 86

Occupational songs, 19–20, 96
Odum, Howard, 41; *The Negro and His Songs*, 13; *Negro Workaday Songs*, 11, 13
Of Thee I Sing (musical), 36
Ogan, Sarah, 109; on *Kentucky* (radio show), 139
O'Hare, Kate Richards, 77
Ohio Valley Folk Festival, 1938, 99
Okeh Presents the Wayfaring Stranger (album), 137
OKeh Records, 9, 14, 17, 19
The Oklahoma and Woody Show (radio show), 89
Oklahoma Witch Hunt (pamphlet), 148
Old Dan Sherman and His Family, 122
Old Fiddlers' Hour, 17
"Old Paint (The Horse with the Union Label)," 106–7
On the Town, 155
Orozco, Jose, 40
Orquestas tipicas, 59
Ott's Woodchoppers, 122

Index 195

Our Singing Country: A Second Volume of American Ballads & Folk Songs, 84

Pacific Coast School for Workers, 77
Palm Gardens, 140
Paramount, 14
Parsons, Albert, 24
Patriotic songs, 123
Patton, Charlie, 14
Peace songs, 105, 153
Peer, Ralph, 16, 18, 19, 29
Pennsylvania Folk Festival, 55
People's Songs, 156, 157
People's World (newspaper), 90
Perrow, E. C.: "Songs and Rhymes from the South," 12
Peter, Paul and Mary, 157
Peterson, Walter, 51
Pettit, Katherine: "Ballads and Rhymes from Kentucky," 12
Phillips, Washington, 37
Phonograph records, 14
Pierre Degeyter Club, 33
Pinewood Tom. *See* White, Josh
Pins and Needles (musical), 105, 114
Pipe Smoking Time (program), 141
Platt, Mose "Clear Rock," 41, 42
Play and Sing: America's Greatest Collection of Old Time Songs and Mountain Ballads, 51
The Plow That Broke the Plains (film), 72
Poole, Charlie and the North Carolina Ramblers, 16
Popular Front, 75
Popular music: 1938–40, 124; late 1930s, 98
Popular records, difference from hillbilly records, 18
Popular songs, 36–38
Potamkin, Harry Alan: "The Ballad of Harry Simms," 64
Pound, Louise: *American Ballads and Songs*, 7–8; *Folksongs of Nebraska and the Central West*, 19
Prisons, 41, 44, 45, 70
Production Code of 1930, 125
"A Program of American Songs for American Soldiers," 152
Progressive Book Store, 147–48
Protest songs, 73
Pro-war songs, 105
Pruner, Samuel, 109
Pullum, Joe: "CWA Blues," 48
The Pursuit of Happiness (radio show), 131
Putnam, Herbert, 10, 42

Race records, 14, 17, 27, 69–70; female singers, 14
Racial integration, 155
Radio programs, 16–18. *See also individual programs*
Radio shows: featuring country music, 50. *See also individual shows*
Radio stations, song folios from, 51
Rainey, Ma, 14
Randall, Richard, 118
Rand School Press, 64
Rapp-Coudert committee, 146
Rawley, Al and His Wild Azaleas, 116
Ray, Nicholas, 101, 111, 154; *Back Where I Come From* (radio show), 135–36, 137–38; biography of, 134–35
RCA Victor, 26
Rebel Song Book, 64, 65

Record industry during the Depression, 26
Records: popular Northern artists, 17–18
Red Song Book, 32, 34, 47
Reece, Florence, 25
Reed, Blind Alfred, 18
Reeves, Goebel, 20
Resettlement Administration Special Skills Division, 135
Resettlement Folk Singers, 143–44
Richards, J. C. *See* Riegger, Wallingford
Rickaby, Franz: *Ballads and Songs of the Shanty-Boy*, 20
Riegger, Wallingford, 64
Rinzler, Ralph, 158
The River (film), 72
Robbin, Ed, 90
Robbins, Jerome, 155
Robertson, A. C. "Eck," 15
Robertson, Sidney, 71, 115; *The Gold Rush Song Book*, 117; works with Joint Committee on Folk Arts, 115
Robeson, Paul: "Ballad for Americans," 131; "Ballad of Uncle Sam," 131; biography of, 130–31
Robinson, Earl, 62, 106; *Back Where I Come From* (radio show), 137; "Ballad of Uncle Sam," 114, 131; biography of, 93–94; collecting for the Library of Congress, 94; founds American People's Chorus, 94; "Frisco Strike Saga" (song), 76; "Joe Hill" (song), 94; work for Federal Theatre Project, 94; work for New Theatre League, 94; *The Young Go First* (play), 134–35

Robison, Carson J., 17, 18, 51
Rodgers, Jimmie, 18–19, 21, 27, 52
Rogers, Roy, 91
Roland, Walter, 48
Roosevelt, Eleanor, 152–53
Rosenfeld, Paul, 119–20
Run, Little Children, 155
Rusty Reubens, 122

Sailor Chanteys and Cowboy Songs, 11
Salty Tunes: A Collection of Sea Chanties and Rollicking Sailor Songs, 51
Sandburg, Carl: *The American Songbag*, 7, 8, 149; biography of, 7; election song for Roosevelt, 150
Sands, Carl. *See* Seeger, Charles
Scarborough, Dorothy, 13
Schachter, Harold, 106
Schaefer, Jacob, 48
Scott, Sonny, 48
"The Scottsboro Boys Shall Not Die" (song), 93
Seacrist, Walter, 28
Seeger, Charles, 33, 34, 64, 114, 143; "An Evening of American Music in Conjunction with ... Rural Arts," 144; appointed deputy director of Federal Music Program, 60; in Composers' Collective, 61; defines American musical genres, 97; deputy director, Federal Music Project, 115; "Mount the Barricades," 47; Resettlement Administration Special Skills Division, 135; works for Resettlement Administration, 71–72; writings, 47–48

Seeger, Pete, 108, 115; *Back Where I Come From* (radio show), 137; biography of, 61–62, 126–27; forms Almanac Singers, 153; on the Grapes of Wrath concert, 125–26; *Hard Hitting Songs for Hard Hit People*, 133; hired at Library of Congress, 126; influence of Pete Steele on, 100; joins Young Communist League, 126; and Left-Wing music, 61–68; performs at Progressive Education Association conference, 126; plays for American Square Dance Group program, 126; post World War II, 156–57; road trip with Woody Guthrie, 126, 134, 147; on *Wellsprings of Music* (radio show), 129; during World War II, 154

Seeger, Ruth Crawford, 115, 120, 132, 144; work with the Lomaxes, 84

Sensational Collection of Mountain Ballads and Old Time Songs, 51

Sharp, Cecil, 12–13

Shaw, Alan, 148

Shay, Frank: *My Pious Friends and Drunken Companions*, 11–12

Sheet music, 50–51

Shields, Art, 124

Shirkey, Earl, 19

Short, J. D., 37

Siegmeister, Elie, 33, 47, 64, 67; heads Workers Music League, 63; *Sing Out, Sweet Land* (musical), 155; "The Scottsboro Boys Shall Not Die," 47; *A Treasury of American Song*, 152; writes "The Strange Funeral at Braddock," 66; at the Yorkville Casino festival, 66

Simms, Harry (aka Harry Hirsch), 31

"'Sinful' Songs of the Southern Negro," 42

"The Sinful Songs of the Southern Negro" (album), 109

Sing Amalgamated (songbook), 80

Sing for Your Supper (theatrical revue), 114

Singing cowboys, 89, 91

Sing Out, Sweet Land: A Salute in American Folk and Popular Music (musical), 155

Siquerios, David, 40

Six Labor Songs (booklet), 77

Smith, Bessie, 14

Smith, Mamie, 14

Smith Act, 145–46

Smithsonian Folkways label, 158

Smithsonian Institution, 158

Smyth, Mary Winslow, 19

Snook, Sidney, 12

Socialist songbooks, 20–21

Social protest songs, 29

Sokoloff, Nikolai, 59–60

"So Long, It's Been Good to Know You," 141

Song Book (Hudson Shore Labor School), 77

Song Book for Workers, 32–33

Songbooks, 30, 64; Communist, 47; government publications, 83–84; left-wing, 75–76; Socialist, 21; for workers, 30, 32, 34–35, 67, 78. *See also individual songbooks*

Songs (Textile Workers), 80

Songs and Ballads of the Anthracite Miner, 19–20, 23, 24

Songs for John Doe (album), 153
Songs for Southern Workers (songbook), 78
Songs for Workers (songbook), 20, 78
Songs of Field and Factory (songbook), 78
Songs of Struggle, 34–35
Songs of the American Worker, 67
Songs of the Class Struggle: In Memory of Ella May Wiggins and Steve Katovis (songbook), 30
Songs of the People (songbook), 75–76
Songs of the Seven Million (program), 140
Songs of the Southern Summer School (songbook), 78
Sonkin, Robert, 142–43
Sons of the Pioneers, 91
"Soup Song," 35
Southern Summer School for Women Workers, 77
Southern Tenant Farmers Union, 81
Southern vernacular songs, 49
Spand, Charlie, 37
Spanish Civil War, 1936–39, 105, 124
Spanish Earth (documentary), 72
Spivey, Victoria, 27
"Spring Song" (song), 106
Steele, Pete, 100
Steinbeck, John, 133
Stinson Records, 157
Stokowski, Leopold, 144
Stone, May, 12
Stoneman, Ernest V. "Pop," 18
"The Strange Funeral at Braddock," 66

Straw Hat Review, 125
Strike songs, 23; miners, 31–32
String bands, 122
Strunk, W. Oliver, 44, 57, 68
Sugar, Maurice, 35; "Bosses and Judges, Lis'n to Me: Song for Scottsboro Boys," 97; "Sit Down," 80; "The Soup Song," 65
Suspended Swing (band), 146–47
Swift, L. E. *See* Siegmeister, Elie

Tampa Red (Hudson Woodbridge), 14, 37
Tartt, Ruby Pickens, 144
Taubman, Howard, 130, 132
Taylor, Davidson, 120, 138
Taylor, Paul, 91
T-bone Slim: "I'm Too Old to Be a Scab," 80
Tenney, Jack, 146
Textile workers, 28–30, 31
Theatre Arts Committee, 106–7; cabaret performances, 1939, 107; "'Grapes of Wrath' Evening," 125
Theatre of Action, 134
"This Land Is Your Land," 123–24
Thomas, Jean Bell, 50; American Folk Song Festival, 52–53, 60
Thompson, Stith, 100
Thomson, Virgil, 72
Thorp, N. Howard "Jack," 11
Timely Records, 65
Tiny Texas: World's Greatest Collection of Cowboy and Mountain Ballads (song folio), 51
Tippett, Tom, 28
Todd, Charles, 142–43
Tom Glazer's Ballad Box, 156
"Tom Joad," 130, 140
Topical songs, 15–16, 18, 35

Traditional Ballads Mainly from West Virginia (book), 84
A Treasury of American Song, 152

Ulmann, Doris, 49–50
Umble, John, 100
"Union Maid" (song), 147
Unison, 66–67
University of Wisconsin School for Workers songbook, 77

Valiant, Margaret, 142, 143–44
Victor, 14, 17
Village Vanguard, 155, 157
Vinson, Walter, 48

Wade Ward and the Bogtrotters, 128
Wagner Act, 79
"Wake Up Boys" (song), 63
Walker, Frank, 19
Walker, George, 13
Walsman, Leo, 65
Walton, I. H., 103
Ward, Wade, 128
Wasserman, Caroline, 77
Weavers, 157
Weber, Rex, 36
Welling, Frank, 31
Wellsprings of Music (radio show), 129
West, Don, 64, 78
Western Pals (cowboy band), 59
Wetherald, R. P., 138
Wheatstraw, Peetie, 119
Wheeling Jamboree (radio show), 50
"When the World's on Fire," 123–24
White, John: "'Grapes of Wrath' Evening," 125
White, Josh: in Almanac Singers, 153; on *Back Where I Come From* (radio show), 135; biography of, 73; *Chain Gang* (album), 131; emerges as popular artist, 118; *John Henry* (musical), 114; "Silicosis Is Killing Me," 122–23; *Tall Tales* (film), 137; on *Wellsprings of Music* (radio show), 129; at the White House, 152; during World War II, 154
White Top Festival, 53–54; academic conference, 53
Whitter, Henry, 18
Who Fights This Battle? (play), 134–35
Wiggins, Ella May: "The Mill Mother's Song (or Lament)," 29–30
Williams, Bert, 13
Williams, Reverend Claude: "Roll the Union On," 80–81
Willingham, Thaddeus, 144
WLS Barn Dance (radio show), 50
Wood, Bob, 126, 147, 148
Wood, Ina, 126, 147, 148
Woodbridge, Hudson. *See* Tampa Red
Woodhull, Fred, 122
Woodhull's Old Time Masters, 122
Woody and Lefty Lou (radio show), 89
Woody Kelly's Old Timers, 122
"Woody Sez" (column), 124
Workers' choruses, 33, 118
Workers' education. *See* Labor schools
Workers Musicians Club, 33
Workers Music League, 46–47, 48
Workers' Music Olympiad, 47–48
Workers Song Book, 47
Workers Song Book No. 2, 64, 65
Workers Songs (songbook), 78

"Working on the Project," 118–19
Work songs, 42
Works Progress Administration: demise, 1943, 114; investigation by the House of Representatives, 113–14; music projects, 59
"W. P. A. Blues" (record), 70
"The WPA Blues," 118
Wyman, Loraine: *Lonesome Tunes: Folk Songs from the Kentucky Mountains*, 12; *Twenty Kentucky Mountain Songs*, 12

Yellow Jackets (jug band), 29
Yorkville Casino festival, 66, 67
Young People's Records, 157
Yurchenco, Henrietta: *Adventures in Music*, 139; *Kentucky* (radio show), 139

Zeuch, William, 77

www.ingramcontent.com/pod-product-compliance
Lightning Source LLC
Chambersburg PA
CBHW030652230426
43665CB00011B/1057